Moral Fiction in Milton and Spenser

Moral Fiction in Milton and Spenser

John M. Steadman

University of Missouri Press
Columbia and London

Library of Congress Cataloging-in-Publication Data

Steadman, John M.
    Moral fiction in Milton and Spenser / John M. Steadman.
      p.   cm.
    Includes index.
    ISBN 0-8262-1017-1 (alk. paper)
    1. Milton, John, 1608–1674—Ethics.   2. English poetry—Early modern, 1500–
1700—History and criticism.   3. Romances, English—Adaptations—History and criticism.   4. Christian poetry, English—History and criticism.   5. Epic poetry, English—
History and criticism.   6. Spenser, Edmund, 1552?–1599. Faerie queene.   7. Spenser,
Edmund, 1552?–1599—Ethics.   8. Moral conditions in literature.   9. Ethics in literature.   10. Poetics.   I. Title.
PR3592.E8S84   1995
821'.309—dc20   95-12810
                                                  CIP

Text design: Rhonda Miller
Jacket design: Stephanie Foley
Typesetter: BOOKCOMP
Printer and Binder: Thomson-Shore, Inc.
Typeface: Adobe Garamond

For my teachers and mentors—

For Maurice Kelley, who guided me
securely through the underworlds and paradises
of Milton and Dante;

For A. L. Rowse,
most versatile of Elizabethans;

And in memory of Robert R. Cawley
and Thomas H. English
with whom I read Spenser and Milton—

With gratitude and affection.

Contents

Acknowledgments

In writing this book I am grateful for the generosity of the John Simon Guggenheim Foundation and the Henry E. Huntington Library. Chapter 5 was originally published in *The Huntington Library Quarterly* 55, no. 4 (Fall 1992): 535–58. I am indebted to the editors of this journal for permission to reprint this study, with revisions. Formal acknowledgment is also made as follows to publishers for permission to quote from copyrighted material:

Passages from *Complete Poems and Major Prose,* John Milton, edited by Merritt Y. Hughes, are reprinted with the permission of Simon & Schuster, Inc. Copyright © 1957, renewed 1985 by Macmillan College Publishing Company, Inc.

Passages from *World of Odysseus,* by M. I. Finley, preface by Mark van Doren, are reprinted with the permission of Viking Penguin, a division of Penguin Books USA Inc. Copyright © 1954, 1977, renewed 1982 by M. I. Finley.

Passages from *Literary Criticism: Plato to Dryden,* by Allan H. Gilbert, are reprinted with the permission of Wayne State University Press.

Abbreviations

For convenience, the following abbreviations are used in the text to identify sources of material often cited:

CP   John Milton, *Complete Poems and Major Prose*. Edited by Merritt Y. Hughes. New York: Odyssey Press (Simon and Schuster), 1957.

CW   *The Complete Works of Joshuah Sylvester*. 2 volumes. Edited by Alexander B. Grosart. 1880. Reprint, AMS Press, 1967.

FQ   Edmund Spenser, *The Faerie Queene.*

PL   John Milton, *Paradise Lost.*

PR   John Milton, *Paradise Regained.*

PW   *The Poetical Works of Edmund Spenser*. Edited by J. C. Smith and E. de Selincourt. 1912. New York: Oxford University Press, 1942.

Moral Fiction in Milton and Spenser

ἴδμεν ψεύδεα πολλὰ λέγειν
ἐτύμοισιν ὁμοῖα,
ἴδμεν δ᾽, εὖτ᾽ ἐθέλωμεν,
ἀληθέα γηρύσασθαι.

(We know how to speak many false things as though they were true; but we know, when we will to utter true things.)

—Hesiod, *Theogony* (Loeb)

Introduction

This study centers on the Renaissance poet's (and critic's) changing attitudes toward the boundaries of truth and fiction—his sense of the variable relationship between poetic invention and historical fact or moral and theological doctrine. These boundaries are not fixed or determinate, even in the works of a single poet, or indeed within a single poem. On the contrary, they are often mutable, shifting, and indefinite. In certain contexts the poet may attempt to bring them into sharper, clearly defined focus; in other instances these distinctions may be blurred for the sake of a more unified poetic texture.

These boundaries, whether clearly marked or indefinite, are especially significant in the poetry of Milton and Spenser. Both poets use the resources of poetic fiction in the interests of what they regard as moral and historical "truth" and reality; but both differ radically in their poetic and epistemological strategies and techniques. In Spenser's ambiguous image of a romantic never-never land (which is simultaneously Elizabethan England), one may find both a parallel and an antithesis to Milton's fictive image of a prelapsarian world, an image that he must have regarded as an imaginative reconstruction of historical and theological fact.[1]

In their attitudes toward mythical fable and romance the two poets are sometimes analogous, but they also provide on occasion striking contrasts. With Spenser's imaginary symbols of a secular (though sometimes ecclesiastical) English Elysium one may compare Milton's image of a primeval Paradise authenticated by Scripture. Similarly, Spenser's fictive argument, despite its sometimes inconsistent foundation in moral and historical allegory, provides a striking contrast to Milton's biblical argument, based as he believed on historical fact but elaborated through the poet's own imaginary fictions. Again, though both poets make extensive use of the epic "marvellous," they develop it in very different ways in their respective poems, Spenser's epic romance and Milton's neoclassical epic.

Behind the similarities and differences between the heroic poems of both writers, moreover, lies a significant contrast between their views on myth and reality and between their attitudes toward the romance. In his letter to Sir

Walter Raleigh, Spenser explicitly associates his *Faerie Queene* with a generic tradition that embraces not only the classical epics of Homer and Virgil but also Ariosto's romance and Tasso's compromise between epic and romance. Milton, on the other hand, is often critical of the romance tradition, scornful of its feigned battles and imaginary characters, and disdainful of its artistic techniques. Similarly, though he frequently resorts to mythical allusions and to unabashed mythmaking,[2] he often dismisses the classical myths as Gentile fables, untrustworthy in comparison with biblical truth.

Nevertheless, there are inconsistencies in Milton's attitudes toward myth and romance in different poems and indeed within *Paradise Lost* itself. In *Comus,* the Attendant Spirit emphasizes the fundamental truth underlying the myths and fables of ancient poets:

> . . . 'tis not vain or fabulous, . . .
> What the sage Poets taught by th' heav'nly Muse
> Storied of old in high immortal verse
> Of dire *Chimeras* and enchanted Isles,
> And rifted Rocks whose entrance leads to hell.
> (*Comus,* lines 513–518)

Similarly, in *Il Penseroso,* the "pensive man" affirms the validity of the allegorical content of the romances of "great Bards" (lines 116–120).

With these affirmations of the truth underlying the fictions of myth and romance one should, however, contrast the dismissal of myth and romance in *Paradise Lost* and the slighting references to Gentile fables in *Samson Agonistes* (lines 149–150, 496–501). And in *Paradise Regained* (4.295) the divine protagonist dismisses Plato for his "fabling . . . and smooth conceits."

Among the trees in Milton's garden of Eden are some

> . . . whose fruit burnisht with Golden Rind
> Hung amiable, *Hesperian* Fables true,
> If true, here only. (*PL* 4.249–51)

In contrast to Milton's muse Urania, the Calliope of classical myth is merely "an empty dream" (*PL* 7.39). The classical myth recounting the expulsion of Mulciber (that is, Hephaestus or Vulcan) from heaven is a fabulous perversion of the truth:

> . . . and in *Ausonian* land
> Men call'd him *Mulciber,* and how he fell

> From Heav'n, they fabl'd, thrown by angry *Jove*
> Sheer o'er the Crystal Battlements: . . .
>   . . . thus they relate,
> Erring; for he with this rebellious rout
> Fell long before. (*PL* 1.739–748)

The characters and subject matter of the chivalric romances, in turn, are often fabulous, concerned with the adventures of "fabl'd Knights / In Battles feign'd" (*PL* 9.30–31).

All the same, the fabulous element in myth and romance does not prevent Milton from drawing on their material for analogies and comparisons— comparisons that usually affirm the superiority of the true, biblical materials he is presenting (*PL* 1.573–87; *PL* 4.275–79; *PR* 3.335–43; *PR* 4.563–75).

The values and techniques of poetic illusion in the work of Spenser and Milton constitute the principal theme of this book. I shall not, however, be primarily concerned with a detailed comparison of *Paradise Lost* and *The Faerie Queene,* nor with Milton's significant indebtedness to his great Elizabethan precursor. Instead I shall focus on their very different revaluations of epic tradition; on their contrasting relationships to Renaissance literary theories of epic and romance; and, above all, on their diverse approaches to the exploitation of poetic invention and illusion as vehicles of ethical and historical truth.

In the first section of this study I have placed primary emphasis on Milton's treatment of the metaphor of the poet's divine inspiration;[3] in the second section I have concentrated largely on Spenser's exploitation of the conventions of romance epic as vehicles for celebrating Elizabethan achievements and the exploits of his fellow countrymen. In both sections I have to a considerable extent treated these poets as foils to each other: masters of poetic fiction whose essential values emerge in clearer and bolder relief through juxtaposition and contrast.

Both Milton and Spenser assume the stance of the prophetic or visionary poet, but they often differ significantly in their treatment of this venerable poetic topos.[4] In their exploitation of the metaphor of divine illumination and inspiration they are, for instance, in many respects poles apart. Spenser's illusory invocation of the muse of history under the pretense that the events he is recounting are not simply his own imaginative inventions but long-neglected facts stands in striking contrast to Milton's invocations addressed to the muse of biblical poetry and the Spirit of the Judeo-Christian God, and to his own imaginative reenactment of biblical history.

Not infrequently, critics have tended to accept literally the Renaissance poet's claim to divine inspiration and to underestimate the extent to which this is both a conscious literary fiction and a traditional poetic convention. In re-examining this topos I shall place primary emphasis on the poet's mixture of truth and fiction and on the degree to which he deliberately affects a visionary stance. The first section ranges accordingly from the ironically uninspired (and often pedantic) pretense of divine inspiration by such lesser poets as DuBartas to the more skillful exploitation of this poetic convention by Spenser and Milton.

In the case of Milton in particular, scholars have sometimes taken his visionary and prophetic claims at face value. During the course of this century Miltonists have, for instance, debated in considerable detail the problems of the identity of Milton's heavenly muse, the nature of the Spirit invoked in the opening lines of *Paradise Lost,* the degree to which Milton believed his major epic to have been literally inspired by the Deity, and the extent to which he regarded himself as visionary and prophet. Of major importance have been the views advanced by Maurice Kelley, Joseph Anthony Wittreich Jr., William B. Hunter, Jackson I. Cope, Barbara Kiefer Lewalski, and Mary Ann Radzinowicz.

A substantial number of critics have identified Milton's muse with the Holy Spirit, the third person of the Trinity. These include A. D. Barber, Martin A. Larson, Harris Francis Fletcher, and Hunter. Kelley, however, citing Milton's statement in the *De Doctrina Christiana* that the Holy Spirit cannot be invoked, has argued plausibly that Milton's muse was "not the Third Person but a personification of various attributes of God the Father." James Holly Hanford has subsequently endorsed this view.[5]

Hanford had earlier emphasized the "inspiration of Moses" in *Paradise Lost.* Milton "might, in Platonic terminology, say that he was possessed by him, as Ion was possessed by Homer, save that Ion was but a rhapsode . . . , while Milton is a true successor animated by an identical afflatus from on high. . . . Does it follow," Hanford continued, that Milton

> would have claimed for his elaboration of scripture an authenticity equal to that of the sacred record itself? Certainly he regarded his imaginings as something more than poetic fancy, but equally certainly he did not accept or wish others to accept their detail as literal, historic fact. . . . What he did believe was that both *Paradise Lost* and its biblical original were revelations to human capacity of the truth of God, to be looked on with a deeper reverence than is accorded to the ordinary works of men."[6]

In the opinion of Hunter and Stevie Davies the three invocations of books 1, 3, and 7 of *Paradise Lost* are directed toward different persons of the Trinity.

The first is addressed to the triune Godhead, the second to the Son, and the third to the "Holy Spirit, who may be equated with Urania."[7]

In the opening invocation of Milton's epic, Cope finds the poet "doubly validating his own prophetic role through the warrant of his scriptural prototype." In this invocation, as well as in the invocation to light in book 3, "Milton moves from the inspiration of poetry to the inspiration of prophecy."[8]

Among critics who have interpreted Milton's metaphor of divine inspiration rather too literally have been scholars as diverse as William J. Grace and William Kerrigan. In Grace's opinion, "Milton's calling upon the Spirit to illumine him at the beginning of the *Paradise Lost* is to be taken at its face value. There is no historical reason for assuming that such an invocation is merely conventional." Indeed Milton himself "thought he was writing history under the guidance of the Holy Spirit." Observing that "Milton himself believed that *Paradise Lost* was a work of history rather than of fiction," Grace maintained that "Milton actually believed that he was adding historic details to the Scriptures." Subsequently, in *The Prophetic Milton,* Kerrigan has (in Radzinowicz's summary of his arguments) declared that Milton "seriously and literally thought throughout his life that he was uniquely called by God to be His prophet" and that "Milton literally believed that he was the amanuensis of God, a prophet in the line of descent from Moses and Isaiah."[9]

Radzinowicz has effectively challenged some of the more exaggerated claims that critics have advanced concerning Milton's belief in his divine inspiration. Acknowledging that Milton "used the words *inspiration* and *illumination* to describe the inner germination, source, or nearly subconscious, energy of poetry throughout his life," she comments that some critics "have gone much beyond this to claim that Milton literally believed from first to last that he was the amanuensis of God (Kerrigan), a modern prophet in direct line of descent from Moses and Isaiah (Hanford), that his own particular Muse was either the Logos (Cope; Carey and Fowler); or the Holy Spirit (Hunter) or God Almighty (Naseeb Shaheen)." In Radzinowicz's view "the general case for assigning Milton's poetry to a poetic rapture or heroic fury is weak," and "the argument of some critics that the poet is the literal prophet of God in Milton's poetics may be balanced by the argument in others that the poet is the sage or teacher and his work illuminated by truth or wisdom."[10]

Lewalski, in turn, has stressed "the special needs and purposes of a Miltonic Bard who sees himself as a prophet-poet." In her opinion there is "no contradiction" between the fact that in *Paradise Lost* Milton "gives constant attention to the choice of literary forms and the uses of literary art" and "the fact that he also presents himself in that poem as a prophet-poet, an inspired bard. . . . Indeed, the relationship between conscious art and divine inspiration is a major theme of the Bard's personal proems to Books One, Three, Seven, and Nine."[11]

Like A. W. Verity, Helen Gardner, and several other scholars, Lewalski makes a clear distinction between the Heavenly Muse and the Spirit of God invoked in the opening lines of *Paradise Lost*. In her opinion, moreover, the Spirit invoked in line 17 is "clearly . . . not the Holy Spirit of trinitarian theology."[12]

In the opinion of John N. King, "Spenser self-consciously adopted the mantle of the Protestant visionary poet." In his view "a shared pattern of biblical imagery enabled readers to interpret *Piers Plowman, The Faerie Queene,* and *Paradise Lost* as Protestant apocalypses." Milton's epic "offers a clear example of the survival of Reformation themes and conventions in later literary tradition," and "the apocalyptic vision of *Paradise Lost* corresponds to that of John Bale."[13]

The tension between the Renaissance poet's conscious artistry and his claim to divine inspiration is paralleled by the Renaissance preacher's simultaneous indebtedness to the art of rhetoric and his insistence that his eloquence proceeds from the direct motions of the Holy Spirit. According to Debora K. Shuger, "Augustine, and subsequent Christian rhetoricians . . . insist that true passion and eloquence flow from the interior motions of the Holy Spirit stirring the speaker's heart and inflaming his words. Rhetoric as artistic technique becomes correspondingly superfluous." For Melanchthon, "effective and powerful preaching springs from the personal experience of the Word and Spirit." Citing the opening lines of Nashe's *Christ's Teares over Ierusalem,* Shuger comments: "What matters . . . is that Nashe felt obliged at least to feign inspiration. The decorum of Renaissance preaching forbids the preacher from mentioning his debt to rhetoric."[14]

In regard to the controversy over Milton's muse and his attitudes toward the poetics of inspiration, I remain convinced that the prophetic and visionary stance that he assumes in his major epic is not only a conscious adherence to (and reformulation of) a well-established poetic convention but also an important facet of a deliberately contrived vatic persona. In this signal instance of "Renaissance self-fashioning," Milton is skillfully recasting himself in the highly traditional image of the bard as seer. There is, I believe, no conclusive evidence that (like his proto-Romantic admirer and disciple William Blake) he literally regarded himself as prophetic and visionary.

In reexamining Milton's exploitation of the topoi of the poet's divine inspiration and his role as prophet, one should, moreover, bear in mind the wide range of meanings associated with the terms *prophet* and *prophecy* in the course of the English Reformation. During the sixteenth and seventeenth centuries these terms were frequently "applied to the expounding of Scripture by those who spoke 'as the Spirit gave them utterance' in special meetings, or preaching in public services." Also relevant to this topic are the discussions of "enthusiasm" and "direct inspiration by the divine spirit" within such seventeenth-century sects as the Baptists and the Quakers.[15]

Although considerable emphasis has been placed in recent years on Milton's affinities with the radical sects of mid-seventeenth-century England, these bear a much closer relationship to his prose than to his poetry. Although his major poetry does, to a significant degree, represent a radical reorientation of the epic and tragic genres toward his own conceptions of the nature, scope, and limitations of "Christian heroism," and of the implications of man's fall and redemption for the concept of the hero, this reorientation springs rather from a revaluation of the epic (and tragic) tradition than from the radicalism of such groups as the Levellers and the Muggletonians. Antimonarchical and antitrinitarian convictions (and certain other radical or "heretical" elements) are indeed inherent in Milton's epic; but it is most radical, most revolutionary, in its applied poetics (as distinct from Milton's remarks on poetic theory). His scattered observations on the art of poetry are, in fact, "conservative" in a literary (rather than a social or political) sense; they do not mark a significant—much less a radical—departure from the central concerns of Renaissance theories concerning the "rules" of epic and tragedy.[16]

In the invocation of his muse and in his treatment of the "metaphor of inspiration" (as Professor Shawcross has judiciously termed it) Milton was far less "radical," far less innovative, than he would (in the context of the authorial persona) have liked to appear. In contrasting his heavenly muse Urania, the inspiratrix of the Judeo-Christian tradition, with the muses of ancient paganism, he is (as Lily Bess Campbell recognized,[17] and as many contemporary Miltonists would agree) deliberately exploiting a distinction already well established in late Renaissance poetry. In this instance his "radicalism" is high conventional, a consciously elected pose. As such it is a crucial element in a carefully crafted poetic persona.

Consonant with the distinctions between Virgilian neoclassical epic and Ariostean romance-epic are the different poetic strategies and aesthetic methods that Milton and Spenser employ in attempting to present the realities of moral philosophy and history. In contrast to Spenser's extensive resort to myth and fantasy and the techniques of personification allegory, Milton (with such notable exceptions as the allegory of Sin and Death and the personified abstractions of the Abyss) prefers to represent ethical concepts through the medium of the narrative exemplum, consistently structuring his fable with an eye to apparent probability and verisimilitude.[18]

Part I

"Bardic Voices"?

Moral Vision and the Persona of the Poet
A Revaluation

Chapter 1

Enthousiasmos and the Persona
of the Inspired Poet

DuBartas and Spenser

The poet "speaks more loftily in his own person and discourses with
another tongue, like one who feigns to be rapt out of himself by divine
inspiration."

(. . . parla più altamente il poeta in sua persona e quasi ragiona con
un'altra lingua, siccome colui che finge d'esser rapito da furor divino
sopra se medesimo.")

—Tasso, *Prose*

Tasso's observations are relevant not only to the higher style that Milton
frequently assumed when speaking in propria persona but also to the kind of
persona that he fashioned for himself. Tasso's statement occurs in the context of
an extensive discussion of the style ("elocuzione") appropriate for heroic poetry,
including the manner in which the poet might state the argument of his poem
and implore divine assistance. Though Tasso cites Castelvetro's opinion that
invocations are suitable only for poets, since these alone are "moved by divine
furor," he nevertheless insists that philosophers and orators likewise make use
of the invocation and that poets should invoke divine aid not only in extended
works like the epic but also in brief poems like the lyric. (He tactfully refuses to
discuss the invocation in the Psalms, because these are rather a "consecration of
the hymn to God [Giove].") He rebuts Castelvetro's criticism of invocation as
a sign of pride and presumption, along with the analogous view of Protagoras:

that Homer had called on his muse in an "imperious manner, as though he wished to command her." Some critics, on the other hand, have maintained that an invocation is a sign of modesty. In Tasso's own opinion, however, it is rather an argument of piety and religion, as long as the poet does not invoke a deity whom he regards as false—or at least not with the actual intention of calling on a false god. Thus Dante's invocation to the "good Apollo" can be excused as poetic license and "good intention." He was on safer ground, however, in calling on the muses since these were believed to be intelligences, on genius (*ingegno*), and on memory (*la mente*).[1]

In two of the examples that Tasso cites, the poet's invocation to the muses is specifically a request to confer distinction on his style: "Bembo called upon the Muses in these graceful lines: 'Oh Goddesses, for whom Helicon freely opens and closes, . . . grant lasting life to my poetry, which sprang from my sorrow, after I shall be extinguished and buried.'(Diva, per cui s'apre Elicone e serra, / Date a lo stil, che nacque de' miei danni / Viver quando io sarò spento e sotterra.)"

So, too, Monsignor della Casa invoked the muses in his first sonnet:

> Oh daughters of Jove, if any care for me
> Ever spurs you at the first trumpet blare,
> Lend my poetry wings to fly after that sound."
>
> (Oh se cura di voi, figlie di Giove,
> Pur suol destarmi al primo suon di squilla,
> Date al mio stil costei seguir volando.)[2]

In addition to the initial proposition, Tasso observes, poets customarily introduce others later in the poem, as Homer and Virgil do.

In discussing the style appropriate in the statement of the epic propositions, Tasso cites Horace's condemnation of Antimachus for the bombastic manner in which he had announced his theme: *Fortunam Priami cantabo, et nobile bellum* ("Of Priam's fate and famous war I'll sing.")[3] But Tasso immediately counters this view with Pindar's belief that the beginning of a poem should be "grand, magnificent, and splendid," like the facades of palaces. A lofty beginning is appropriate as long as the poet maintains the same elevated vein. Thus Virgil combined the high style and the illustrious in his proposition, and would have continued at the same height and with the same splendor throughout his epic if he had not voluntarily elected to vary his forms of discourse on occasion.[4]

After this brief allusion to stylistic variation within the *Aeneid*, Tasso temporarily dropped the subject to discuss it later in greater detail. It had long been a critical commonplace that, in fidelity to the principle of decorum, discourse should be accommodated to subject and genre, to character and thought, to the various passions and "affects," and to the intent of the speaker and the nature of his audience. A lofty subject demanded a comparable elevation in style. Yet within the same poem the style might vary appreciably with the poet's matter and his thought. Because of its amplitude, its comprehensiveness, and its variety of materials, the epic could encompass a variety of stylistic modes in addition to the "magnificent" style—though all of these should necessarily be accommodated to the prevailing majesty proper to this genre.

Though strongly influenced by Demetrius's categories of style, Tasso's views were also firmly based on the actual practice of epic poets. With inevitable exceptions, the poets had used a loftier style in passages of invocation or narration or description than in dialogue. The more elaborate epic similes, for instance, and the epic catalogues had usually occurred when the poet was speaking in his own voice, rather than imitating the discourses of his characters. Similarly, as Tasso observed, the tragic poet has usually assigned a more elevated style to the Chorus than to the dramatis personae.

In the passage quoted earlier, Tasso rationalized the higher style, often assumed by the poet speaking in propria persona, in terms of the special decorum appropriate to the persona of the inspired bard. In the same context (book 4) he specifically linked the conventional epic invocation with the need for a lofty style. In regard to style, he declared, the poet was accustomed, in his invocations, to ask divine aid for the gift of elevated discourse, as well as for the memory of things already buried in oblivion: "ne la [elocuzione] si dimanda l'aiuto divino per favellare altamente, non meno che per la memoria de le cose già sepolte ne l'oblivione."[5] These principles were consonant both with the actual practice of classical poets in invoking the muses or their mother, Mnemosyne, and with the usage of Christian poets in seeking assistance from the Deity, the saints, or the *muse chrétienne*. Milton's invocations consistently implore divine inspiration either for knowledge of the hidden and obscure events in which the Spirit itself had been an eyewitness or an active participant, or for the lofty utterance appropriate to his high subject—but we shall return to this point later.

1.

The persona of the inspired poet, as Milton and Spenser present him, is largely dependent on the skill with which both, in varying contexts, have selectively emphasized and combined (or brought into sharp opposition) a few principal images and motifs, drawn out of a wide range of alternative conventions. Not only is there a close correlation between the nature of the muse whom the poet invokes and that of the persona he assumes, but both of these also often vary with the character of the subject he has elected and with the qualities of style that it demands. In different contexts the poet may assimilate diverse kinds and sources of *enthousiasmos*—pagan or Christian, erotic or prophetic or bacchic—or, alternatively, stress the contrasts between them. In these instances also, his treatment of the imagery of inspiration—ecstasis, vision, winged flight—frequently varies with his subject. In both writers, moreover—Spenser as well as Milton—there is interaction (interpenetration as well as opposition) between poetic conventions of invocation and inspired flight and Platonic or Christian concepts. The techniques whereby they construct these images of the poet also vary with subject and context. It may be useful therefore to compare their methods of constructing the authorial persona with those of a lesser poet whose work was familiar to both.

DuBartas's poetry was widely read in the late sixteenth century and in the following century, and it has been argued that his influence on Milton was neither inconsiderable nor insignificant.[6] Since both were concerned with hexaemeral materials, exploitation of the same commonplaces or topoi was virtually inevitable; little can be proved from such material parallels. A few verbal parallels ("Immutable, immortal, infinite") indicate how closely Milton must have read Sylvester's translation. His most important debt, however, was the muse Urania herself and (to some extent) the image of the inspired bard "rapt above the Pole" and guided by his celestial patroness to the very scenes he must describe. Though DuBartas developed these motifs with less skill and imagination than Milton, he used them more frequently and more extensively. Moreover, in his representation of poetic fervor or enthusiasm, he frequently combined Platonic and Christian elements, much as earlier Renaissance poets had done and as Spenser and Milton would do.

In *Urania or the Christian Muse,* the heavenly muse reveals herself to the poet and denounces the habitual neglect of sacred subjects for profane (*CW* 1:1–7). She herself (she declares) possesses the power to transport mortal man above the poles, to teach him to see, behold with his own eyes, touch with his own hands, all that transpires in the court of heaven. She can "quintessence" the soul (Sylvester is fond of this verb), endowing the poet with divine discourse and enabling him to surpass himself and to reveal supernal things to the deafest of men—instilling vision (so to speak) through the ear. Urging DuBartas to elect herself to guide his pen, she exhorts him to "soar up to Heav'n." Poetry is a "meer" heavenly gift and therefore demands a "sacred fire." It cannot be acquired by art. In exploiting the Platonic image of the poet, who sings by divine inspiration but without conscious art, as an argument for choosing a subject based on biblical materials, DuBartas does not qualify this view (as did Milton, E. K., and others) by suggesting that art, exercise, and learning are also necessary.

Man must transcend his own humanity through ecstasy (the muse continues) as though he were actually in a holy trance. To utter immortal poetry, he must place his *"Sensive part"* at Urania's disposal; for divine fury and sacred frenzy alone can make him more than himself and lift him above the heavens.

Verse was first and exclusively invented (Urania asserts) as a vehicle for sacred mysteries; as examples she refers to the poets of the Old Testament: Moses and Deborah and Judith, David and Job and Jeremiah. Subsequently, Satan had appropriated this divine invention for his own purposes, using verse for the oracles of the ancient Gentiles. This mode of delivery had been retained by the early theological poets among them. Apollo and the Sibyls had delivered their messages in verses, as had the oracle at Dodona. Such poets as Orpheus, Linus, and Hesiod, in turn, had treated religious subject matter, albeit pagan. Most of the examples that DuBartas cites, from either pagan or biblical tradition, were prophets; by thus associating poetry with prophecy, and emphasizing the analogy as well as the contrast between the sacred poetry of the Gentiles and that of Israel, he is not only suggesting the latter's superior claim to the title of *vates* but also presenting a model or paradigm for the *poeta Christianus* as divine poet. Like the Platonic topos of poetry as a heavenly gift, these vatic parallels reinforce the argument for preferring biblical materials as subjects for poetry and the true God as a source of inspiration, but they also help to shape the kind of authorial persona that DuBartas would assume in *La Sepmaine* and other poems, and that some of his successors would employ.

Like other poets—including Milton and Spenser—DuBartas was aware of the principle of decorum and the correlation between altitude of theme and style. Though he may not have encountered Longinus's statement that great ideas are themselves a source of the sublime, he was familiar with the rhetorical principle that style (*verba*) must follow the material or the ideas (*res*) and with the view (expressed by Saint Augustine and other authorities on rhetoric) that the speaker or writer must concentrate primarily on what he intends to say rather than on precisely how he will say it. If he attends first to the thought, appropriate discourse ought to follow. (Milton, as we observed, asserts that his own thoughts "voluntary move harmonious numbers" [*PL* 4.37–38].)

DuBartas's "Christian Muse" assures him that he need feel no anxiety on this point. A great theme of itself calls forth grave and stately words and, in a sense, gilds itself.

2.

As DuBartas's image of the inspired poet appears principally in his invocations, let us examine the kind of aid that he asks of his muse and how he represents the topos of inspiration. (The marginal glosses accompanying Sylvester's translation are also relevant.) The First Day of *La Sepmaine* (First Week) begins with two invocations directed to the Deity, for Sylvester has joined DuBartas in prayer:

> The Poet imploreth the gracious assistance of the true God of Heaven, Earth, Aire, and Sea, that he may happily finish the worke hee takes in hand. He calls on the Deity for elevation of soul, for learned art, for sweet discourse, and prays that (discerning God's powers in the beauties of the universe), he himself may learn in endeavoring to teach others:
> Lift up my Soule, my drowsie Spirits refine:
> With learnèd Art enrich this Work of mine.
> O Father, grant I sweetly warble forth
> Unto our seed the WORLD's renownèd BIRTH.

Thereupon, "The Translator knowing and acknowledging his own insufficiency for so excellent a labour, craveth also the aid of the All-sufficient God." May the architect of wonders—"Whose mighty voyce speaks in the midst of Thunders" and teaches "dumb Infants thy dread Praise to speak," inspiring wisdom and knowledge in the ignorant, grant the translator "Judgement, Grace, and Eloquence" corresponding to the excellence of the task he has undertaken:

> That in some measure, I may seem t'inherit
> (*Elisha*-like) my deare *Elias* spirit. (*CW* 1:19)

In the Second Day the poet invokes the Deity, as the "Source of Learning" for sweetness and copiousness of style answerable to his subject:

> . . . make my Pen distill
> Celestiall *Nectar*, and this Volume fill

With th' *Amalthean* Horn: that it may have
Some correspondence to a Theam so grave. (*CW* 1:27)

The introductory verses of the Third Day are chiefly interesting for their exploitation of the motif (also used by Milton) of the flight or descent of the poet (or his muse) in accordance with his subject matter: "From the Heaven and Regions of the Air, the Poet descendeth to the Earth and Sea." In the previous book he had described the creation of the firmament and the elements of air and fire; in this he will relate the formation of the remaining elements. His muse varies her flight accordingly:

My sacred Muse, that lately soarèd high,
Among the glistring Circles of the Sky, . . .
Commanding all the Winds and sulph'ry Storms,
The lightning Flashes, and the hideous Forms
Seen in the Aire: with language meetly brave
Whilom discours'd upon a Theme so grave:
But, *This-Day*, flagging lowly by the *Ground*,
Shee seems constrain'd to keep a lowly sound:
Or if, sometimes, she somewhat raise her voice,
The sound is drown'd with the rough Ocean's noyse.

Again he invokes "the true God," who created and rules both elements, to teach him to sing their nature in "learned numbers," and "with a flowring stile the Flowrs to limn." (*CW* 1:40)

As the Fourth Day concerns the creation of the stars, "our Poet prayeth to be lift up in the Heavens that he may discourse . . . of the stars, fixed and wandring." May the Deity who had carried the prophet Elijah aloft in a chariot of fire be his coachman through the skies. And may his poetry, like a magnet, draw others upward to the heavens:

Pure Spirit that rapt'st above the firmest Sphear,
In fiery Coach, thy faithfull Messenger . . . :
O! take me up; that, far from Earth, I may
From Sphear to Sphear, see th' azure Heav'ns *To-day*.
Be thou my Coach-man, and now Cheek by Joule
With *Phoebus*' Chariot let my Chariot roule;
Drive on my Coach by *Mars* his flaming Coach;
Saturn and *Luna* let my wheels approach;
That, having learn'd of their Fire-breathing Horses,

> Their course, their light, their labor, and their forces;
> My Muse may sing in sacred Eloquence,
> To Vertue's Friends, their vertuous Excellence;
> And, with the Load-stone of my conquering Verse,
> Above the Poles attract the most perverse. (*CW* 1:52)

In this passage, DuBartas's images of rapture and interplanetary flight are specifically correlated with his theme, but he has also linked them with other motifs. If the imagery of magnetism recalls the Platonic metaphor of poetic enthusiasm, the emphasis on the attractive force of eloquence also evokes the motif of Hercules Gallicus, drawing multitudes after him in willing chains. The conceit is that by close-up vision—achieved in a sort of chariot race with the stars—he will learn his subject firsthand; he does not know these things already (he pretends), and must acquire this knowledge by the grace of God. Temporarily concealing his own erudition, the learned poet (the *poeta doctus*) assumes the stance of the inspired poet. In this instance, moreover, his own muse and the Spirit are distinct.

The Fifth Day represents the creation of fish and fowl; accordingly DuBartas invokes the true God, who rules the sea and winds to bring him to the scene of his argument:

> Provide me (Lord) of Steers-man, Star and Boat,
> That through the vast Seas I may safely float:
> Or rather teach me dive, that I may view
> Deep under water all the Scaly crew;
> And dropping wet, when I returne to land
> Laden with spoyls, extoll thy mighty hand. (*CW* 1:61)

The Sixth Day concerns the creation of the beasts of the earth; this subject evokes an oblique allusion to the myth of Orpheus. In his invocation to the Deity, DuBartas does not mention the pagan poet directly, but beseeches the true God for the sweetest honey from the "Muses' mount," so that he may tame the fiercest of beasts—lion, tiger, and bear—with "the sweet charm of my victorious Verse" (*CW* 1:72).

3.

In *The Second Week*, the poet follows much the same procedure as in its precursor. At the beginning of the first day ("Eden"), both the poet and his translator seek divine assistance in their tasks. As before, the type of aid that DuBartas asks of his divine patron is specifically associated with the scene of his narrative and with its subject. In this invocation, however, he employs the usual classical formula (*dic mihi*):

> Walk thou, my Spirit, through all the flowring alleys
> Of that sweet Garden . . . : tell me what mis-deed
> Banisht both *Eden's Adam,* and his seed:
> Tell who (immortall) mortalizing, brought us
> The balm from heav'n which hoped health hath wrought us:
> Grant me the story of thy Church to sing.
>
> (*CW* 1:99)

In the same invocation he alludes to his ambitions to cover the entire sacred history of the world from the first Sabbath to Doomsday. To recount the fall of man ("The Imposture") he calls on the Deity in a later invocation for wisdom and discourse: "Instruct my spirit, and give my tongue smooth scope" (*CW* 1:107).

At the beginning of the Second Week's second day ("The Ark"), the poet speaks in a more dejected mood, but employs certain images and motifs that are not dissimilar to those that Milton employs in the autobiographical passages in his invocations and introductions. His sacred rimes no longer "distill / With Artlesse ease" from his pen. Banished from "the learned Fount," "cast down head-long from the lofty Mount / Where sweet *Urania*" sits, his humbled muse flags in "a lowly flight." But the blame lies with the cruel ingratitude of the times, his household cares, his ill health, and many sorrows (*CW* 1:132).

As "The Colonies" concerns the migrations of Noah's posterity, DuBartas's scene in this episode must be global. Thus compelled to take a world tour himself, in the company of his remote ancestors over lands and seas, he draws on the imagery of travel and exploration: the voyages of maritime discovery and the journey of the Magi:

> While, through the World's unhanted wildernesse
> I, th' old, first Pilot's wandring House address:
> While (*Famous* DRAKE-*like*) coasting every strand
> I do discover many a *New-found-Land:*
> And while, from Sea to Sea, with curious pain
> I plant great *Noah's* plenteous Vine again: . . .

> What fiery Pillar shall by Night direct me
> Toward each People's primer Residence . . . ?

For guidance and illumination he calls on the star of Bethlehem itself:

> . . . drive the darknesse forth
> Which blindeth me: that mine adventurous Rime,
> Circling the World, may search out every clime.

For in this long voyage, his "speciall drift" is to lead his readers to the "dear Babe," the Man-God of Bethlehem himself (*CW* 1:145).

"The Columnes" deals with mathematics, including astronomy; and "our Poet here imploreth especiall assistance in handling so high and difficult a Subject." As in *La muse chrétienne,* he exploits the imagery of sacred rage, ecstasy, and trance ("rapt above the *Pole*"). Specifically, he calls on God to purify his soul and to grant him the altitude of style appropriate for his high subject:

> If ever (Lord) the purest of my Soule
> In *sacred Rage* were rapt above the *Pole:*
> If ever, by thy Spirit my spirit inspir'd,
> Offred thee Layes that learned *France* admir'd,
> Father of light, Fountain of learned Art,
> Now, now (or never) purge my purest part:
> Now quintessence my Soule, and now advance
> My care-free Powrs in some celestiall Transe.

May "thy divine addresse" guide the poet through heaven. There, in the company of Urania and her sisters, ravished by the music of the spheres, he may contemplate the "Starry Arches" of God's temple:

> Unto this end, that as (at first) from thee
> Our Grand-sires learn'd Heav'n's Course & Quality;
> Thou now maist prompt me some more lofty Song,
> As to this lofty Subject doth belong.
>
> (*CW* 1:154)

4.

The third day begins with the vocation of Abraham and concludes with the anointing of Saul. Feeling the amplitude of the field before him, DuBartas feels concern lest his muse, given unwonted liberty and confronted by an *embarras de richesses,* should find it difficult to make "the best choyce in so boundlesse Store." Hence the two of them—poet and muse—will "over-run the *Annals* of all Ages," selecting only the "chiefest Personages / And Prodigies" in Hebrew history, presenting these as offerings to the glory of God. In the first section ("The Vocation") the scene has shifted to the plain, and the poet's invocation to his muse takes cognizance of the altered topography. Hitherto she has been "boundifi'd" and confined within "straight lists": but she now can "behold th' art in the open Plain," and she has begun to feel her oats. She has the whole world to herself, and, like a horse that has burst his halter, she may "corvet, & turn, run, prance, advance, & pride-thee, / As *sacred fury* of thy *Zeal* shall guide-thee" (*CW* 1:164).

There is intentional humor in this spectacle of a sportive (though now seemingly wingless) Pegasus cavorting through the ashes of the Cities of the Plain, among the herds of the patriarchs, and over the pages of history. Yet in specifically Renaissance contexts, the metaphor of the uncontrolled horse was more frequently pejorative than favorable. If it could suggest the license of fancy, this was fancy without the reins of judgment; Plato had associated this image with the lower faculties of the soul, and for DuBartas's near contemporaries it was frequently a symbol for unbridled appetite: it needs the control of reason. DuBartas's use of this image in association with "sacred fury" is the more interesting insofar as it recalls Virgil's application of similar imagery to the frenzies of the Cumaean Sibyl before she submits completely to Apollo's control. It is noteworthy that after maintaining previously that sacred fury was sufficient in itself without the aid of art, DuBartas now suggests that judicious selection of materials is also necessary.

The "sacred Voyce" of the poet (DuBartas asserts in "The Law") out-shrills the clamor of trumpets and clarions, guns and bombards; "my *Stentorian* Song, / With warbled Ecchoes of a silver Tongue," shall be heard from India to Spain and thence to the Arctic. Yet the inspiration and the voice are not his own:

> It is the spirit-inspiring Spirit, which yerst
> On th' eldest Waters mildely movèd first,
> That furnishes and fils, with sacred winde,
> The weak, dull Organs of my *Muse* and minde.

Here the terms of the invocation, as well as of the introductory verses, are conditioned not by the poet's subject matter (as is usually the case) but by the immediate historical context: the civil wars in France, which (as a Huguenot) he must have felt very keenly. Accordingly, "in these tumultuous times," he invokes the Deity to give "Peace to my Soule, soule to my Rimes."

> And while in FRANCE fell MARS doth all devour,
> In lofty stile (Lord) let me sing thy Power. (*CW* 1:184)

In this passage he does not invoke his own muse; and here again she is distinct from the Spirit of God.

"The Captains" begins with Joshua's exhortations to achieve "the Conquest of Canaan" and with the crossing of the Jordan, but it also includes the exploits of the Judges. After beginning (appropriately) with an apostrophe to the river itself, the poet professes to behold with his own eyes the men whose *magnalia* he will now celebrate:

> . . . I see you all,
> Under the conduct of my Generall,
> NUN's valiant *Son:* and under GEDEON's Sway,
> SANGAR, and SAMSON, BARAC, DEBORA.

Proposing to sing the "high Feats" of heroic men, he invokes divine aid to make his poetry worthy of his noble theme:

> O Spirit, which wert their guide, guard, strength, & stay,
> Let not my Verse their Vertue's praise betray. (*CW* 1:198)

This is, again, essentially the same kind of formula that Milton would employ in *Paradise Regained* and in the initial invocation in *Paradise Lost:* simultaneously invoking the Spirit for aid and specifically alluding to his role in the events described.

The fourth day covers the period from Saul's alienation from God to the Chaldean conquest of Jerusalem. "The Tropheis" is devoted to the exploits of David, and in his invocation DuBartas asks for the Psalmist's harp and verse to "worthy-sing" the glory of God and His anointed king: "For, none but *DAVID* can sing *DAVID's* worth" (*CW* 1:213).

In the introductory verses to "The Magnificence," DuBartas explicitly ac-knowledges the uneven character of his poetry, juxtaposing images of drudgery and divine inspiration. Other poets, authors of sonnets and epigrams, write or stint as their own "*Fury* fits"; they do not exhaust their "learned brain" in long and extended labors. DuBartas, on the other hand—fettered to his "hard Task" like a galley slave—is perpetually busy, like a millstone. Hence it is that

> I humme so harsh; and in my Works inchase
> Lame, crawling Lines, according to the Fire,
> Which (more or lesse) the whirling *Poles* inspire:
> And also mingle (Linsie-woolsie-wise)
> This gold-ground Tissue with too-mean supplies.

Temporarily using the metaphor of flight, he compares the other poets, writing as they please in briefer genres, to birds of spring—nightingales, flitting from bush to bush and tune to tune. DuBartas, on the other hand, is like the swallow:

> Not finding where to rest mee, at one flight
> A bound-lesse ground-lesse Sea of Times I passe.

He must sing the year round, summer or winter, spring or fall. Moreover, his course is as uneven as it is endless: now gliding smoothly, now sliding headlong, now climbing or crawling, straying or stumbling—and "sometimes down I fall." To connect his "queint Discourse," sometimes he mixes "loose, limping, and ill-polisht Rimes."

All the same, he is not yet altogether "voyd of sacred heat"; he calls on the Deity to grant "that a few faults may but lustre bring / To my furies where I sweetest sing." The stance of the inspired bard has been difficult to maintain, and the poet feels misgivings at times, lapsing from his high fury (*CW* 1:226–27). In Milton's poetry, on the other hand, the motif of inspired rapture is the more effective for being used more sparingly.

Relating "Isaac's civill Brawls and Broils and *Jacob's* Revolt," "The Schisme" (according to the gloss) portrays the "misery of a State distracted by factions into Civill Wars," and the poet again draws an analogy between his poetic argument and contemporary conditions in his own country:

> Ah! see we not some seek the like in *France?*
> With rage-full swords of civill Variance,
> To share the sacred *Gaulian* Diadem? . . .
> And (as it were) to *Cantonize* the State.

Instead of asking for poetic inspiration, he prays for the preservation of the French monarchy ("let not us / Serve servilely a hundred Kinglings thus") and the reestablishment of peace and justice. Nevertheless, the rapture of Elijah in this section affords the poet an opportunity to develop a favorite theme:

> A sudden whirl-winde, with a whiffing Fire,
> And flaming Chariot rapts him up intire.
> Burns not, but 'fines; and doth (in fashion strange)
> By death-less Death, mortal immortall change.
> A long-tail'd squib, a flaming ridge, for rut
> Seems seen a while, where the bright Coach hath cut.

"This sacred Rape, nigh rapt Elisha too," the poet comments—and proceeds to describe Elijah's ascent to "th' *Emperiall Pole*," where the prophet contemns this world and eventually becomes an angel. "O happy passage!" DuBartas concludes, "O sweet, sacred Flight! / O blessed Rape! thou raptest so my sprite / In this Dispute" that "the more I doe contend, / I more admire, and less I comprehend" (*CW* 1:240, 245–46).

The final section of the fourth day ("The Decay") relates to the extirpation of Ahab's sons by Jehu, the overthrow of Jehu's own line, and the tyranny of Athalia. The initial verses are devoted to a diatribe against ambition, and the address to God Himself is centered on the theme of tyranny and the divine Providence that permits its existence (*CW* 1:251–62).

5.

DuBartas's treatment of the apotheosis of Enoch ("The Handycrafts") is interesting both for its fusion of Platonic and Christian contemplative motifs and for the analogies it suggests with the kind of metamorphosis that the purified soul may experience in *Comus* and in *Paradise Lost*. In Milton's masque, "oft converse with heav'nly inhabitants" begins to "cast a beam on th' outward shape, / The unpolluted temple of the mind, / And turns it by degrees to the soul's essence, / Till all be made immortal."[7] If Adam and Eve remain obedient (Raphael suggests), "Your bodies may at last turn all to spirit, / Improv'd by tract of time, and wing'd ascend / Ethereal, as wee" (*PL* 5.491–504).

This is the actual fate of Enoch ("Henoch"), as DuBartas describes it:

> Lo, how he labours to endure the light
> Which in th' *Arch-essence* shineth glorious-bright:
> Now rapt from sense, and free from fleshly lets,
> Sometimes he climbs the sacred Cabinets

> Of the divine *Ideas* everlasting,
> Having for wings, Faith, fervent Prayer & Fasting.

Sometimes, though still "in earthly clod," he enjoys the fruition of God. At other times, "mounting from form to form, / In form of God he happy doth transform." Thus God "sets the stairs / That lead from hence to Heav'n his chosen heirs."

Progressively climbing the "Supernall stories," Enoch now dwells with God: his mortal body, "chang'd in quality / Of Spirit or Angel, puts-on immortality," and he drinks "deep of the celestiall wine" in a perpetual Sabbath (*CW* 1:128).

Enoch's transformation occurs in the context of a prophetic ecstasis in which Adam reveals to Seth the future course of the world. After the work of six days' labor followed by the first Sabbath, the world will endure for six ages, concluding in an eternal Sabbath. Foretelling the lives of Lamech and Enos and Enoch, the mixture of the houses of Seth and Cain and the brood of giants ("Plagues of the World, and scourges of Mankinde"), Adam concludes with the destruction of the first world by the flood. At this point, "The prophetizing spirit forsook him"—much as his visionary powers would fail him, at virtually the same point, in Michael's prophetic survey of what would "befall his posterity" in *Paradise Lost* (*CW* 1:128–29; see the marginal gloss).

In *La Sepmaine,* Adam prophesies, but apparently sees no visions of the future. Instead, he experiences the vision of God. In describing this scene the poet explicitly contrasts the patriarch's "sacred fury" with the frenzied ravings of "Bedlam *Bacchanalian* froes." This passage (the gloss comments) emphasizes "The power of God's spirit in his Prophets: and the difference between such, and the distracted frantike ministers of Satan." Soaring like an eagle to fix his eye on the sun, Adam mounts on "the burning wings / Of a *Seraphick* love," leaving earthly things and cleaving "the starry Sphears."

> And on God's face his eyes he fixtly bears:
> His brows seem brandisht with a Sun-like fire,
> And his purg'd body seems a cubit higher. (*CW* 1:127–28)

(This last detail is reminiscent of the manner in which the inspired Sibyl appears to Aeneas.)[8]

Milton's fallen Adam experiences no such ecstasy; his visionary experience is of a soberer character, and there is neither rapture nor vision of God. Unlike the Adam of "The Handy-crafts," he has still to face the experience of exile; the eagle he has just glimpsed is not a symbol of divine contemplation but rather an image of his own expulsion.

Elsewhere in the *Divine Weeks,* there are allusions to music's power to ravish the soul and to its affinities with prophecy. "The Columnes" concludes with "the power of Musick towards all things"—toward men; toward "Beasts, Birds, Flies, and Fishes"; and "Towards God himself":

> O! what is it that *Musick* cannot do!
> Sith all-inspiring Spirit it conquers too:
> And makes the same down from th' *Emperiall Pole*
> Descend to Earth into a Prophet's soule:
> With divine accents tuning rarely right
> Unto the rapting Spirit the rapted Spright. (*CW* 1:160–61)

6.

Of the *Sepmaines* completed by DuBartas, we have considered only the two that Milton would have known through Sylvester's translation. In the course of writing them, the poet's commitment to his heavenly muse would appear to have become increasingly an affair of drudgery rather than inspiration. Though he employs the image of enthusiasm more frequently than Milton, he does so methodically and systematically. The variation of invocational conventions in association with a constantly changing subject matter undercuts the very illusion of inspiration that he is endeavoring to foster. As he assumes the role of scuba diver—and invokes the Deity for a fisherman's catch—the artifice becomes increasingly transparent; contradicting the pretense of artless fury, it reduces the invocational formulas themselves to a sequence of predictable conceits.

Although the principle underlying this technique is not at fault, the manner in which DuBartas applies it seems—in comparison with Milton and by the standards of a later generation—deficient in judgment and taste. But this was not entirely a matter of poetic competence. The artificiality of these invocations would have been less obvious and less painful if DuBartas had left the first week of *La Sepmaine* as it stood instead of undertaking a survey of sacred history. In the latter instance his material itself, and the kind of organizational schema he applied to it, placed him at a formidable disadvantage. Though traditional, the extension of the hexaemeral formula to the history of mankind—the six ages of the world—did not provide an adequate pattern or paradigm for structuring an encyclopedic epic extending from the Creation to the Last Judgment. The material itself lacks the unity of theme, the coherence, and the clearly defined schema implicit in the Genesis account of the first week. The subdivision of the days of the Second Week resulted, accordingly, in a loosely connected series of separate poems, each with its separate introduction and (as a rule) with its own distinct invocation. The attempt to adapt the invocational formulas to a subject matter so varied and diverse tended to become more and more forced and contrived; the topos of sacred fury, increasingly pedestrian.

Nevertheless—though a lesser poet than Milton, and Englished by a more pedestrian translator—DuBartas was far more apt to take to the skies whenever occasion offered. He employed the imagery of flight and rapture and sacred fury more frequently; in comparison, Milton's was a soberer and less ecstatic muse.[9]

The image of the divinely inspired poet, as DuBartas developed it, was closely associated with the divine nature of his subject matter. They complemented each other. In theory at least, the lofty subject should inspire a comparable style. Moreover, the invocation of the very Deity who had originally inspired the Scriptures—and who had played the major role in the events themselves—was especially appropriate for the subject matter of a biblical poem. This was a more truly "celestial" inspiration than the "Ethnic" Plato could ever have known or surmised. DuBartas's association of the sacred fury of the poet with the sacred subject—the true God, the biblical subject, the creation itself—his image of the "Christian muse" Urania, and the example of *La Sepmaine,* it has been argued, encouraged later authors to elect biblical arguments themselves or urge others to do so. Such works were "divine poems" because they were devoted to biblical or theological subjects.

The epithet "divine," however, is ambiguous, and it may be helpful to reexamine it briefly. In the first place and for a variety of reasons, writers of the period used this encomiastic term with no less license than vagueness. Applied to a poet or artist (the "divine" but lascivious Aretino, for instance!) it could be rather a eulogy of his originality and imagination, the quasidemonic force of his native genius (*ingenium*), than an indication of the kind of subject matter he was treating. It simply signified that his abilities seemed extraordinary and superhuman, above those of ordinary men. For the same reason, the hero had been called a *seios* (or *theios*) *aner* and a "divinus vir." In the Renaissance tradition, moreover, one habitually transferred the imagery of heroic virtue to men of learning.

The term *divina scientia* or "divine science" had been applied to metaphysics —and subsequently transferred to theology—because of the nature of their subject matter. That the poets themselves should subsequently appropriate this term was almost inevitable.[10] Attacked by clerics for Gentilism or (worse still) for overt paganism, they countered by asserting the divine origins of poetry and its affinities with prophecy and theology. Like theology, poetry was a "divine science," an inspired wisdom communicating the knowledge of celestial things. The precedent of the legendary poets of preclassical and preliterate antiquity—primitive theologians like Orpheus and Linus—along with the poetic books of the Old Testament and the allegorical and symbolic method of the Apocalypse, reinforced the argument that poetry was in fact theology (indeed superior to dogmatic theology) as long as it concerned itself with revealed truth.

The epithet "divine" had, of course, been applied, long after its initial appearance, to Dante's *Commedia;* but this could refer alternatively to its superlative excellence or to its preoccupation with theological doctrine. The poet's guides through hell, purgatory, and heaven were, in fact, representative of natural, dogmatic, and mystical theology. *Sacra theologia* was "divinity"; the priest or theologian was "the divine." For the *poeta theologus,* one did not need to look beyond Dante to Orpheus or Linus or Hesiod. One of the striking features of the *Divina Commedia* was the fact that its literal subject, the state of souls after death, belonged to the level of meaning that theologians themselves would have termed "anagogical"; the hidden or allegorical meaning was the moral or tropological sense: the respective rewards of virtue and vice.

On the title pages of his epics, Milton (or his publisher) merely designated their genre as poetry ("A Poem"); references within the poems themselves, however, indicate that he regarded the argument of the earlier epic as *truly* heroic, and that of the latter as *above* heroic (that is, divine). And indeed Addison, uncertain how to classify *Paradise Lost,* maintained that, if it was not actually a "heroic poem," it was patently a "divine poem." The same term, moreover, was commonly applied to the poetic books of Scripture, divinely inspired or divinely dictated. Moreover, iconographical tradition frequently represented the Evangelists and the Fathers of the Church as seated at a writing desk, with the dove of the Holy Spirit muttering mysteries into their ear. This motif had been associated not only with Saint Gregory of Nyssa but also with Saint Augustine and (parodically) with Mohammed.

Thus a poem might be called "divine" in a wide variety of senses: 1) because it suggested superhuman powers of imagination and expression; 2) because it appeared in the canonical books of the Scriptures; 3) because it was based on an argument derived from the Scriptures; 4) because it dealt with the material of Christian theology (even though, as in Dante's case, the argument itself was the fictive invention of the poet); or 5) because it had been inspired (or represented as inspired) by the Holy Spirit.[11]

The heightened powers, the superhuman flight, the rapture beyond the poles, the analogy between the poet and the prophet—these are traditional; if later readers have found Milton's image of the inspired bard more impressive and more credible than the personae assumed by his contemporaries, this was due not only to the themes he was treating or the manner in which he presented them, to his superior poetic gifts, or to the images of inspiration themselves. It was also attributable in large part to the fact that he had indeed lost his sight. It was this detail that Marvell singled out in comparing him with Tiresias as the blind *vates*. To assert, in an encomiastic poem, that the author has soared aloft "above human flight" was conventional; to compare him with a prophet was not unusual; but it is the biographical fact, the poet's actual blindness, that gives authority and credibility to the praise:

> Just Heav'n thee like *Tiresias* to requite
> Rewards with Prophecy thy loss of sight. (CP, 209)

Though Milton himself had likened his condition to that of the blind poets and prophets of antiquity, he had never claimed to be writing prophecy. As a rule, the prophetic passages in his poetry were ascribed not to the authorial persona, but to some other person in the poem: Saint Peter, Michael the Archangel, or God himself. This was also, in large part, Dante's method. Although the "high vision" was presented as the actual experience of the poet himself, the prophecies, on the other hand (many of them already fulfilled, already past history, when he wrote the poem) were generally assigned to others: usually to the prophetic souls of the dead. For in Dante, as in Lucan and Virgil, the *manes* of the dead, now detached from the body, could foresee and prophesy the future. (The biblical Saul and the Homeric Odysseus, on the other hand, must consult the shades of actual prophets, Samuel and Tiresias, to learn the future.)[12]

In evaluating the "visionary" or "prophetic" aspects of Renaissance poetry, then, one must distinguish between those that are specifically associated with the persona of the poet himself and those that are merely attributed to personae in the epic fable.

7.

Like Milton, Spenser has been (with some justice) styled a "prophetic" or "visionary" poet,[13] frequently airborne and rapt into the heavens, but rather more susceptible to heroic frenzies than the mature Milton. Nevertheless, his furor is rather that of the lover than the prophet, and the wings that bear him so high aloft are as a rule those of Eros. While he retains the conventional notion of the poet's inspired fury, he usually associates it with the inspiration of love; the latter, in turn, is often presented in terms of images and motifs borrowed from the philosophizing eros of the Neoplatonic tradition and transferred to the praise of secular love or Christian *agape.* The most notable example, of course, occurs in the *Fowre Hymnes,* but before examining this work, let us turn briefly to his treatment of poetic inspiration and rapture in other works.

In the October AEglogue of *The Shepheardes Calender,* Cuddie and Pierce hold contrasting views on the ends and origins of poetry, the poet's aims, and his sources of inspiration. When Cuddie laments the lack of material profits and rewards, Pierce responds by stressing its moral and educational value and the Horatian principles of profit and pleasure; it is the poet's glory to restrain the "lust of lawlesse youthe with good advice," or, by enticing his auditors with pleasure, to spur and direct their wills whithersoever the poet chooses. When Cuddie deplores the absence of princely patrons, Pierce stresses the celestial origin of poetry, suggesting that the poet should devote his gifts to heavenly matters. Neglected by high and low estates alike, peerless poesy should make wings of her own "aspyring wit" and fly back to her native heaven. When Cuddie replies that Colin Clout might mount so high, singing "as soote as Swanne," were he not "with love so ill bedight," Pierce replies that love is indeed the source of Colin's poetic inspiration:

> Ah fon, for love does teach him climbe so hie,
> And lyftes him up out of the loathsome myre:
> Such immortall mirrhor, as he doth admire,
> Would rayse ones mynd above the starry skie.
> And cause a caytive corage to aspire,
> For lofty love doth loath a lowly eye.

Cuddie, on the other hand, demurs, ascribing the poetic fury to more material causes. Love is such a tyrant that he expels all other powers, including the muses. The fruit of Bacchus is the friend of wise Apollo, and a better source of poetic inspiration (*PW* 456–59).[14]

In the *Amoretti* (#85), Spenser declares that his lady's high merit, written in the poet's heart, inspires him with "heavenly fury." In another sonnet (#83), her beauty affects him much as the vision of the idea affects the Platonic philosopher; he despises all else on earth as empty shadows:

> Yet are myne eyes so filled with the store
>   of the fayre sight, that nothing else they brooke:
>   but loath the things which they did like before,
>   and can no more endure on them to looke.
> All this worlds glory seemeth vayne to me,
>   and all theyr shewes but shadowes, saving she.

and again (#88):

> Ne ought I see, though in the clearest day,
>   when others gaze upon theyr shadowes vayne:
>   but th'onely image of that heavenly ray,
>   whereof some glance doth in mine eie remayne.
> Of which beholding the Idaea playne,
>   through contemplation of my purest part:
>   with light thereof I doe my selfe sustayne,
>   and thereon feed my love-affamisht hart. (*PW* 576–77)

In his version of *Culex* ("Virgil's Gnat") Spenser imposes an image of inspired rapture upon Virgil's invocation to Pales. While "thou dost tend" the forests and woodlands, Virgil had written, "freely I roam among the glades and caves [antra]."[15]

Not content with speleological exploration, Spenser prefers instead to take to the air:

> Professing thee [Pales] I lifted am aloft
> Betwixt the forrest wide and starrie sky. (*PW* 487)

Though this is a minor detail, possibly based on a misprint or misreading (*astra* for *antra*), it is indicative of Spenser's attitude toward poetic inspiration.

The complaint of Urania in *The Teares of the Muses* assimilates Platonic and Christian motifs in a manner analogous to that of "An Hymne of Heavenly Love." With the Platonic (and Boethian) argument that contemplation of the stars directs man's thoughts from the earthly to the celestial—and thus assists him in his contemplative ascent to heaven—Spenser associates the Psalmist's view that the heavens declare God's glory, and the Pauline doctrine that the attributes of the invisible Creator can be partly known in and through his visible creation. In this context Spenser emphasizes the theme of *contemptus mundi,* exploiting the Boethian topos of the view of the wretchedness of mankind from the vantage point of the heavens.

Spenser associates the muse of astronomy specifically with the knowledge of heavenly things, and—though she falls significantly short of the heavenly muse of DuBartas and Milton so closely associated with the biblical revelation—she nevertheless bears a close resemblance to natural theology. Spenser associates her with "th' heavenlie light of knowledge," which distinguishes men from beasts. By knowledge (she declares) we come to know ourselves and what we owe to God and man. By knowledge we learn to contemplate the Maker's attributes as manifested in the stars:

> From hence wee mount aloft unto the skie
> And looke into the Christall firmament.

There we behold the hierarchy of the heavens: the stars, the celestial spheres, the spirits and intelligences, and the "Angels waighting on th'Almighties chayre." There too we behold God's majesty, His love and truth, His glory and might and mercy. Those who embrace Urania's "heavenlie discipline" can become "heavenly wise, through humbled will."

Nevertheless, like Poetry in the October AEglogue, Urania is despised by mankind and, banished from the earth, takes refuge in heaven. Pleasing herself, she takes delight "In contemplation of things heavenlie wrought" and "loathing earth," flies back again to the skies:

> Thence I behold the miserie of men,
> Which want the blis that wisedom would them breed,
> And like brute beasts doo lie in loathsome den. (*PW* 485)

As Spenser represents her, Urania seems to be more concerned with the moral and theological inferences that can be drawn from the contemplation of the heavens than with astronomical science itself.

In his letter to Raleigh, Spenser associates himself specifically with Homer, Virgil, and Tasso as "Poets historicall" (*PW* 407); it is worthy of note that in book Two of *The Faerie Queene,* Prince Arthur and Sir Guyon do not linger in the chambers of Phantasy and Reason but remain in the chambers of Memory to study the history of Elizabeth's ancestors (*FQ* 2.9.49–60; 2.10.1–77) It is appropriate, accordingly, that in his initial invocation Spenser should invoke the chief of the muses—Clio, the muse of history—instead of Calliope, the traditional muse of epic poetry, and that he should associate her specifically with antiquarian research ("Lay forth out of thine everlasting scryne / The antique rolles" [*FQ* 1.proem.2).[16] The muse is an archivist, and one can almost smell the dust of antiquity upon her records, as in the chamber of Eumnestes.

The assistance that the poet requires of Clio is (first) memory and (second) discourse: "O helpe thou my weake wit, and sharpen my dull tong." After this initial invocation to his muse, he also invokes other divinities—Amor, Venus, and Mars—for, like Ariosto, he intends to celebrate both wars and loves. For actual illumination and inspiration, however, he calls on Queen Elizabeth herself—and in terms that other poets might employ in addressing Apollo, the heavenly muse, or the Deity:

> Shed thy faire beames into my feeble eyne,
> And raise my thoughts too humble and too vile,
> To thinke of that true glorious type of thine,
> The argument of mine afflicted stile.

Spenser's prayer to the Queen to enlighten his mind and elevate his thoughts in proportion to his lofty theme is analogous to Milton's prayer to the Spirit in *Paradise Lost* (*FQ* 1.proem.4).

In book Six the poet professes to be "nigh ravisht" with his own thoughts of Faeryland, and to derive both strength and comfort from them. They are in themselves a source of poetic inspiration. Thereupon he invokes the muses of Parnassus (the guardians of "learnings threasures") to inspire his readers, infusing "goodly fury" into *them*. One might have expected the poet to ask the muses to instill such a furor into himself; but this allusion seems reminiscent of the magnet image in Plato's *Ion*, whereby the divine inspiration passes successively from the divinity through the poet and the rhapsode to the audience. For himself, the poet requests guidance in strange and untrodden ways (a topos exploited by both Milton and Ariosto) that "none can find, but who was taught them by the Muse." After asking them further for knowledge of the source or principle of virtue (including courtesy in particular)—which is hidden from the view of men and the disdain of the world—he promptly converts this theme to the praise of Elizabeth. The Queen is herself the perfect "patterne" of courtesy and the source from which "I doe this vertue bring."[17]

8.

In the *Fowre Hymnes*, the furors of the poet and the lover merge with the contemplative ascent of the Platonic philosopher and the devotional ascent of the Christian. Though the poet deliberately contrasts the earlier hymns with those to heavenly love and beauty, the resemblances between them are in many respects more impressive than the differences. Both categories are preoccupied with the "transcendent." The former are so permeated by Neoplatonic conceptions of heavenly love and beauty that they approximate the latter; the hymns to heavenly love and heavenly beauty, on the other hand, compare Platonic and Christian motifs. The essential difference is that the object of the earlier hymns is a mortal, while that of the latter is God himself; that the later hymns draw more freely on specifically biblical materials; and that the poet seeks inspiration from divine Love itself, the Holy Spirit.

In discussing Spenser's use of the metaphor of the poet's inspiration in these hymns, it will be necessary to analyze in detail his imagery of the celestial inspiration of the true lover and the relationships between secular and divine love and beauty. The hymn of heavenly love recapitulates the life of Christ. The hymn of heavenly beauty introduces Sapience, the wisdom of the Scriptures, instead of the wisdom of Socrates. Yet the analogy between Neoplatonic wisdom as the object of the philosopher's love and the biblical Sapience as object remains; in emphasizing her quintessential beauty Spenser is exploiting, among other things, the Platonic emphasis on the beauty of *phronesis* or *sapientia* if men could only behold her. Both in the "secular" and in the "sacred" hymns, moreover, Spenser exploits the topos of the erotic furor and the contemplative ascent to heaven.[18]

Like fire, *amor* aspires upwards; despite their different subjects, each of the hymns depicts an analogous ascent by love and contemplation toward a higher and more spiritualized "Idea" of beauty. Each moves by degrees from the earthly and material toward progressively purer forms of beauty or love. Three of them depict the origin of the world, emphasizing either the creative powers of love or the paradigmatic concepts of beauty; the fourth stresses analogies between the created universe and its maker. In various contexts the Platonic Idea is presented in its relation to the cosmos, to the lover's mistress, and to the Deity.

Despite their different subjects—the love and beauty of a woman, the love and beauty of God—all four hymns emphatically dissociate the "refined" and purified love celebrated by the poet from lust and "base" earthly desires. The fancies of "baseborne mynds," Spenser declares in the hymn of love, "feele no love, but loose desyre."

> For love is Lord of truth and loialtie,
> Lifting himselfe out of the lowly dust,
> On golden plumes up to the purest skie,
> Above the reach of loathly sinfull lust.

Lust dares not fly to heaven and his "dunghill thoughts" aspire no higher than "dirtie drosse."

> Ne can his feeble earthly eyes endure
> The flaming light of that celestiall fyre,
> Which kindleth love in generous desyre,
> And makes him mount above the native might
> Of heavie earth, up to the heavens hight.
> Such is the powre of that sweet passion,
> That it all sordid basenesse doth expell,
> And the refyned mynd doth newly fashion
> Unto a fairer forme, which now doth dwell
> In his high thought, that would it selfe excell;
> Which he beholding still with constant sight,
> Admires the mirrour of so heavenly light. (*PW* 586–89)[19]

The hymn of beauty, in turn, combines the motif of the demiurge in Plato's *Timaeus* with the idea of absolute beauty in the *Symposium*. The "goodly Paterne" or idea, "to whose perfect mould" the Creator had fashioned the world, is "perfect Beautie, which all men adore," but which surpasses both the knowledge and expression of "mortal sence." The more each earthly thing partakes of this perfect beauty through divine influence, the fairer it becomes,

> And the grosse matter of this earthly myne,
> Which clotheth it, thereafter doth refyne,
> Doing away the drosse which dims the light
> Of that faire beame, which therein is empight.

Since the body derives its form from the soul, a "comely corpse" is a sign of a "beauteous soule" within. At this point the poet exhorts the ladies ("lively images of heavens light") not to darken its brightness by disloyal lust, but to love and manifest the heavenly riches that they bear within. At this point he returns to the topos of the purified, "refined" love that he had discussed in the earlier hymn. With "pure regard and spotlesse true intent," true lovers draw out of the object of their eyes

> A more refyned forme, which they present
> Unto their mind, voide of all blemishment;
> Which it reducing to her first perfection,
> Beholdeth free from fleshes frayle infection.

Conforming this image to the sparks of heavenly light still lingering in his mind, the lover thereupon fashions a "heavenly beautie to his fancies will." Embracing it with his whole mind and admiring the mirror of his own thought, he fixes thereon "all his fantasie" and places therein all his felicity (*PW* 590–93).

The hymn of heavenly love begins with the Holy Trinity, emphasizes the divine love that created the angels, the world, and mankind, and celebrates the incarnation and death of "that great Lord of Love." All that Christ asks in return for so great a love is to love him and our brethren. Exhorting the reader to elevate his mind from the "durty pleasures" of earth to Christ, and to "read through love his mercies manifold," the poet passes to the events of Christ's life and passion. Thus softened and humbled

> Through meditation of his endlesse merit,
> Lift up thy mind to th'author of thy weale; . . .
> Learne him to love, that loved thee so deare,
> And in thy brest his blessed image beare.

Renouncing all other loves, "with which the world doth blind / Weake fancies, and stirre up affections base," the reader will be ravished by love of Christ and delight in no earthly thing except his sight:

> Then shalt thou feele thy spirit so possest,
> And ravisht with devouring great desire
> Of his deare self, that shall thy feeble brest
> Inflame with love, and set thee all on fire
> With burning zeale, through every part entire,
> That in no earthly thing thou shalt delight,
> But in his sweet and amiable sight.

Thenceforth all the glory of earth will seem but dross "in thy pure sighted eye" in comparison with "that celestiall beauties blaze" that dazzles fleshly sense, blinding the eyes and "lumining the spright.

> Then shall thy ravisht soule inspired bee
> With heavenly thoughts, farre above humane skil,
> And thy bright radiant eyes shall plainely see
> Th'Idee of his pure glorie, present still
> Before thy face, that all thy spirits shall fill
> With sweete enragement of celestiall love,
> Kindled through sight of those faire things above. (*PW* 593–96)

Spenser has transferred the Platonic conventions of the refined image that the lover contemplates in his own mind, the Idea of absolute beauty, and the philosopher's contempt of earthly shadows to the incarnate Logos as the perfect image of the Father and divine Love. In the final hymn he passes to the Father himself, associating the Platonic "ladder" of love and contemplation with the motif of knowledge of the Creator through the book of his works. (As we noted earlier, Spenser also develops this motif in the complaint of Urania in *The Tears of the Muses*.) As in *Paradise Lost*, one mounts "aloft by order dew," beginning with the "easie view / Of this base world, subject to fleshly eye" and ascending thence to "contemplation of th'immortall sky" (*PW* 596–99).

In the earlier hymn of beauty each earthly thing was fairer to the degree that it participated in absolute beauty; in this fourth hymn, everything is more beautiful in proportion as it tends upward, the farther from earth and the nearer to heaven growing increasingly "more cleare / And faire . . . , till to his perfect end / Of purest beautie, it at last ascend." The beauty of the visible heavens—defying comparison with all the beauties of earth—cannot compare with that of the invisible heavens beyond them, which grow progressively more beautiful as they approach the Deity. The heaven of blessed souls is less fair than the heaven of the Platonic "*Idees*" and the "pure *Intelligences* from God inspyred." Still fairer are the heavens associated with the angelic hierarchy, each excelling the others in beauty "as to the Highest they approch more neare," and the beauty of the Highest surpasses expression:

> Cease then my tongue, and lend unto my mynd
> Leave to bethinke how great the beautie is,
> Whose utmost parts so beautifull I fynd:
> How much more those essentiall parts of his,

> His truth, his love, his wisedome, and his blis,
> His grace, his doome, his mercy and his might,
> By which he lends us of himselfe a sight.

God reveals himself in the "image of his grace" as if in "a looking glasse"; by this means his creatures, unable to see his face directly, may indirectly behold him. The best means to contemplate his glory is to look upon his works, "Which he hath made in beauty excellent," and therein to read his goodness and beauty, "For all thats good, is beautifull and faire."

> Thence gathering plumes of perfect speculation,
> To impe the wings of thy high flying mynd,
> Mount up aloft through heavenly contemplation,
> From this darke world, whose damps the soule do blynd,
> And like the native brood of Eagles kynd,
> On that bright Sunne of glorie fixe thine eyes,
> Clear'd from grosse mists of fraile infirmities. (*PW* 596–99)

Spenser gives no concrete image, no direct vision, of the Father (one dare not "looke up with corruptible eye / On the dred face of that great Deity"), and instead resorts to personifications to describe the divine majesty. God's throne is built upon Eternity; his scepter is the rod of Righteousness; his seat is Truth, and her brightness hides his throne from the vision of "eyes unsound." Sapience sits in his bosom; and Spenser evokes the inexpressibility topos to describe her excelling beauty. Though angels may behold her face, the poet himself, "with her huge love possest," must be content merely to "admyre so heavenly thing." The men whom God allows to behold the face of "his owne Beloved" are thrice happy, for the vision of her beauty evokes such pleasure and contentment as to bereave

> Their soule of sense, through infinite delight,
> And them transport from flesh into the spright.
>
> In which they see such admirable things
> As carries them into an extasy.
>
> Ne from thenceforth doth any fleshly sense,
> Or idle thought of earthly things remaine.

All other sights seem merely "fayned shadowes"; mortal love seems foul and sinful, earthly pomp and glory base, and riches dross (*PW* 596–99).

So full their eyes are of that glorious sight,
And senses fraught with such satietie,
That in nought else on earth they can delight,
But in th'aspect of that felicitie
Which they have written in their inward ey;
On which they feed, and in their fastened mynd
All happie joy and full contentment fynd.

Spenser concludes this final hymn with an exhortation to his own soul—long beguiled by idle fancies, "false beauties flattring bait," and "vaine deceiptfull shadowes"—to "ceasse to gaze on matter of thy grief" and look instead up to "that soveraine light, / From whose pure beams al perfect beauty springs, / That kindleth love in every godly spright":

Even the love of God, which loathing brings
Of this vile world, and these gay seeming things. (*PW* 596–99)

In this poem, as we noted, Spenser has transferred to the biblical Sapientia the Platonic topoi of the beauty of wisdom as the object of the philosopher's love and of the power of *phronesis* to ravish all beholders if they could only behold her essential beauty. For the philosopher's contempt of the world he has substituted that of the Christian contemplative; for the rapture of the lover and the ecstasis of the Neoplatonist, the mystical transports of the saint. For the "refined" image of beauty in the mind of the Platonic lover, he has substituted the felicity written on the "inward ey" of the lovers of God. The lover's contemplation of his mistress's beauty has been transcended and replaced by meditation and contemplation of the beauty of God.

In the concluding sections of the most "transcendental" of his poems, Spenser does not assume the stance of the visionary; he is content to admire and love the beauty of Sapience from afar, and he leaves the ecstasy, and the vision of her face, to others. Earlier in the same hymn, however, and in a less mystical context, he does exploit the motif of rapture; the furor of the inspired lover and poet is a recurrent theme in the introductory stanzas of all four hymns.

The initial verses of the hymn of love combine motifs introduced by both speakers in the October Æglogue: love as tyrant but also as inspirer of poetry. Invoking the mighty God of love himself to assist in singing his acts and praises, Spenser bids him "Come softly, and my feeble breast inspire / With gentle furie, kindled of thy fire." Thereupon the poet calls on the muses and nymphs, who had felt love's pains (that is, commemorated the lover's sufferings in verse) to prepare themselves to receive Love's triumphal coming. Finally, after calling on the ladies to join in Love's triumphal march, he begins the hymn proper with an apostrophe to the god, asserting his inexpressible power and might (*PW* 586–89).

In the following hymn he represents himself as possessed by the inspired fury of the god and elevated above and beyond his ordinary powers in treating his lofty theme:

> Ah whither, Love, wilt thou now carrie mee?
> What wontlesse fury dost thou now inspire
> Into my feeble breast, too full of thee?
> Whylest seeking to aslake thy raging fyre,
> Thou in me kindlest much more great desyre,
> And up aloft above my strength doest rayse
> The wondrous matter of my fyre to prayse.

Nevertheless, this hymn is devoted not to Love but to Venus as goddess of beauty and mother of love; accordingly, Spenser invokes her both for illumination and adornment: to "beautifie this sacred hymne of thyne." With this invocation he associates a prayer that his lady will relent and grant him some "deaw of grace" after his long sorrow. She herself is also a source of inspiration, "whose faire immortall beame, / Hath darted fyre into my feeble ghost." Moreover, in keeping with the magnet image of the *Ion* and his own practice elsewhere, Spenser involves his audience also in the inspired furor of the lover and the poet:

> And with the brightnesse of her beautie cleare,
> The ravisht harts of gazefull men might reare,
> To admiration of that heavenly light
> From whence proceeds such soule enchaunting might.

In this passage Spenser combines the images of Venus as Hesperus the evening star and as goddess of beauty with the Platonic notion that the sight of the beautiful awakens love, reminds the soul of its largely forgotten vision of absolute beauty, and thus assists it to return to the higher world (*PW* 593–96).

Like the first hymn, the hymn of heavenly love begins with an invocation to Love for inspiration, but on this occasion the praises are directed to the "god of Love, high heavens king." Repenting of the "lewd layes" that he had composed in the "heat of youth" in praise of the "mad fit, which fooles call love," the poet rebukes these past "follies" and emphasizes his change of pitch and tune:

> And turned have the tenor of my string,
> The heavenly prayses of true love to sing.

In this invocation he immediately assumes the role of the inspired lover and visionary, transported to the skies and endowed with superhuman sight by the divine power that possesses him:

> Love, lift me up upon thy golden wings,
> From this base world unto thy heavens hight,
> Where I may see those admirable things,
> Which there thou workest by thy soveraine might,
> Far above feeble reach of earthly sight. (*PW* 593–96)

In the introductory stanza of the hymn of heavenly beauty he again assumes the stance of the inspired contemplative lover, filled with divine furor and ravished by the sight of beauty:

> Rapt with the rage of mine own ravisht thought,
> Through contemplation of those goodly sights,
> And glorious images in heaven wrought,
> Whose wondrous beauty breathing sweet delights,
> Do kindle love in high conceipted sprights:
> I faine to tell the things that I behold,
> But feele my wits to faile, and tongue to fold.

Accordingly, he invokes God himself for inward illumination and inspiration ("Vouchsafe then, O thou most almightie Spright, / From whom all guifts of wit and knowledge flow, / To shed into my breast some sparkling light / Of thine eternall Truth"). As elsewhere, Spenser endeavors to awaken the same divine *enthousiasmos* in his readers. By displaying to "mortall eyes below" some "little beames . . . of that immortall beautie" that he beholds in his own mind, he may (he hopes) kindle similar feelings in others:

> That with the glorie of so goodly sight,
> The hearts of men, . . .
> Transported with celestiall desyre

> Of those faire formes, may lift themselves up hyer,
> And learne to love with zealous humble dewty
> Th' eternall fountaine of that heavenly beauty. (*PW* 596–99)

As in Urania's complaint in *The Teares of the Muses,* Spenser is exploiting the views of Saint Paul and the Psalmist ("*Caeli enarrant*") on the visible works of the Creator as a means of surmising his attributes; it is the beauty of the stars in particular that (in this passage at least) ravishes the poet's thoughts and, by inspiring him with delight and love, directs his mind and affections toward the Father himself. In the hymn itself (as we observed) Spenser combines this approach to the "invisible things" of God through God's works with the Platonic motif (already thoroughly integrated into the Christian meditative tradition) of graduated ascent to the Deity through contemplation and love. In these introductory verses he not only assimilates these motifs to the Platonic commonplace of love and poetry as a celestial *enthousiasmos* but also (like many of his own near contemporaries) replaces the heavenly love and beauty of the Platonic tradition—the celestial Eros and Uranian Aphrodite—with Judeo-Christian correlatives.

In the *Fowre Hymnes,* Spenser's sacred rage is rather that of the lover than the prophet; even as inspired lover he observes the decorum of mortality. Ravished though he is by his contemplation of heavenly things, he nevertheless explicitly dissociates himself from the ecstasy and visionary experience of the mystics. Divine Sapience remains veiled by her own brightness; in extolling her beauty, the poet does not pretend to have glimpsed her face.

One may detect a comparable reticence in Spenser's prayer to the Judeo-Christian God in the final line of his incomplete epic: "O that great Sabbaoth God, graunt me that Sabaoths sight" (*FQ* 8.8.2). In this passage the poet is petitioning for a felicity that can be achieved not in this life nor in this world nor in time, but solely in eternity. He is praying, significantly, not for poetic inspiration but for the saints' eternal rest.

Chapter 2

Enthousiasmos and the Persona of the Inspired Poet

Milton

In Milton's epics, even more than in Tasso's theory, there is an intimate correlation between subject and style, between both of these and the heavenly muse herself, and between the muse and the persona of the inspired poet: transported beyond the normal human condition, beholding invisible things, and relating them "quasi . . . con un'altra lingua," speaking rather with the tongues of angels than of men.[1]

The persona of the poet in *Paradise Lost,* as Jason Rosenblatt and others have recognized, is itself a constructed image, an achievement of poetic artifice;[2] as such it combines a wide variety of diverse though sometimes analogous motifs. By evoking classical conventions concerning the poet and his role—his sacred character and divine inspiration, his prophetic rapture, his intimacy with the gods and his special relationship to his muse, the peculiar holiness of the blind bard and sightless seer—Milton transforms them (and simultaneously transcends them) by assimilating them to Judeo-Christian analogues and to the poet's own life. By fusing autobiographical detail with literary conventions, he can compare his role as theological poet with that of Orpheus, his heavenly muse Urania with the latter's Calliope, his own version of the origin of things and his metaphorical descent into the underworld with that of his predecessor, and the perils that now encompass him with Orpheus's violent death at the hands of the frenzied bacchantes. In much the same way he can exploit parallels with the blind *vates* of pagan antiquity to emphasize the inner vision and spiritual wisdom essential for relating things invisible to mortal sight. By linking yet also distinguishing the two vatic categories—blind singers *and* blind prophets—he redefines his own role as poet-prophet.[3] The analogies with Homer and Thamyris in particular, moreover, also suggest the superiority of his own theme: the latter had allegedly celebrated the war between the gods and the Titans—a myth that Milton regarded as a fabulous corruption of the war of the angels and that he deliberately evoked (along with the parallel myth of the rebellious giants) in describing the war in heaven; the former had sung the wrath of Achilles, which Milton regarded as a less lofty theme than that of man's disobedience.

As Diekhoff recognized, the autobiographical passages in *Paradise Lost* function as "rhetorical aids to proof" (actually as ethical proof—one of the three principal kinds of proof in rhetorical theory).[4] Milton has accommodated them, however, to the decorum of the epic genre and, in particular, to the persona of the inspired poet. In the context of a poem devoted to the obscure beginnings of things and to representations of heaven and hell, chaos and the Earthly Paradise, this persona lends an additional, though largely fictive, authority to his theme. Milton himself had previously acknowledged the different limitations that the media of prose or poetry imposed on an author in speaking of himself:

> For although a poet, soaring in the high region of his fancies with his garland and singing robes about him, might without apology speak more of himself than I mean to do, yet for me sitting here below in the cool element of prose, a mortal thing among many readers of no empyreal conceit, to venture and divulge unusual things of myself, I shall petition to the gentler sort, it may not be envy to me.
>
> (*CP* 667)[5]

After making this distinction, however, he proceeds to discuss his own life and literary ambitions at far greater length than he would do in *Paradise Lost;* and in the *Second Defense* he would emphasize the "almost sacred" character of the blind man, shadowed by the wings of angels and irradiated by an inner light, in a manner that anticipates the image of the blind seer in his epic.

1.

The literary associations of Milton's muse are no less complex than those of the poet's persona, nor can they be adequately considered in isolation from each other, as inspirer and inspired both are inevitably linked in Milton's elaboration of the topos of the poet's sacred rapture. Milton's persona (it has been suggested) incorporates aspects of Moses and David and St. John the Evangelist as poet-prophets; one could extend the analogies further to

Dante and St. Paul, and others rapt to the heavens to behold *invisibilia*. (This motif had, of course, been developed parodically by Chaucer and Ariosto.) Even though the immediate predecessor of Milton's muse was (as Lily Bess Campbell noted) Du Bartas's "Christian Muse" Urania—the muse of divine poetry based on the biblical revelation—DuBartas's muse herself had earlier antecedents besides the classical muse of astronomy.[6] Plato had referred to Aphrodite Urania as the fair and heavenly muse. Urania and Calliope both appear in Fulgentius's *De Continentia Vergiliana*. Dante had invoked Urania in the *Commedia*. The progress from the visible to the invisible heavens, from the contemplation of the stars to the contemplation of God himself might be a major step, but it was nonetheless a logical one. (Both Plato and Boethius had regarded the study of astronomy as an aid to the contemplative ascent to deity through philosophy.) Though DuBartas and Milton alike took pains to dissociate the true Urania from the muse of astronomy, both in fact seem to have exploited certain elements in the mythographical tradition associated with the latter. In explaining her name etymologically, the mythographers usually emphasized her heavenly origin, her knowledge of "heavenly" things, and her ability to "lift up" wise men (and others) to the heavens. These associations, originally applied to the muse of astronomy, could easily be transferred to the Christian Urania. Similarly, the astronomer's metaphorical ascent to the visible heavens to contemplate the stars could be assimilated to the philosopher's metaphorical ascent to the world of Ideas, to the imaginary flight of the poet, and to the visionary ascent to heaven by the prophet or saint. Much of the visionary imagery that DuBartas and Milton employ in relation to the true Urania (both are "rapt above the Pole" [*CW* 1:154; *PL* 7.23], both ascend or descend with their muse to view the particular regions they are writing about) would appear to be a conflation (more judicious on Milton's part) of a variety of motifs: the topos of poetic and prophetic ecstasies, the contemplative flight of the philosopher inspired by love of wisdom and celestial beauty, the exegetical tradition associated with the biblical Sapientia, and the power attributed to the classical Urania of lifting mankind from earth to heaven.

Milton consistently exploits conventions associated with the classical muses to emphasize the superiority of his own celestial guide. His flying steed out-soars Pegasus, the winged horse from whose hoof had sprung the fountain Hippocrene. To the mountains and streams that were the haunts of the ancient muses he opposes those associated with the biblical revelation, the oracle of God: Mount Sinai or Horeb, the brook Siloam. In antiquity and in nobility, in truth and in origin, Urania is superior to all the classical muses: heavenly born, prior to the hills and streams and even to the visible heavens. In associating her so intimately with celestial wisdom, before the creation of the world, moreover, he may have been influenced not only by the text of Proverbs 8:30, but also by the use of the plural form *hokhmoth* in the reference to wisdom in Proverbs 1:20. Thus there could conceivably be more than one wisdom "playing" before the Almighty.[7]

Milton's allusion (*PL* book 7) to the two sisters has sometimes been regarded as a symbolic reference to the second and third persons of the Trinity. This interpretation is feasible, though apparently inconsistent with views expressed in *The Christian Doctrine*.[8] The primary emphasis in this passage falls, however, on the close communion of the two sisters (the Father is essentially a spectator-audience and does not join in their song). One is inclined to interpret this scene not only as an encomium of the divine origin of both sisters but also as a symbolic reference to the ideal union of wisdom and poetry. True poetry is inseparable from divine wisdom; their relationship is analogous to the ideal combination of *sapientia et eloquentia* (or philosophy and rhetoric). In "At a Solemn Music," the union of voice and verse is likewise expressed through the metaphor of heavenly sisters.

2.

Tasso had emphasized two aspects of the poet's invocation for divine aid, verbal and intellectual: lofty style and knowledge or memory of obscure and forgotten things. Moreover, he had explicitly associated the first of these with the fictive image of the poet as "rapt" beyond himself by divine frenzy. Nevertheless, both of these aspects—superhuman knowledge as well as supernormal powers of discourse—had been closely associated with the topos of the poet as *vates,* and both recurred frequently in Renaissance allusions to the poet's divine inspiration. We shall return later, however, to Milton's treatment of the motif of poetic rapture and images of visionary flight. For the moment let us consider the kind of aid that he asks from his muse, and the functions that he attributes to her.

In the first invocation and the lines immediately following, Milton retains the literary convention that the song itself belongs primarily to the muse rather than to the poet; the singer is only the mouthpiece of the divine *inspiratrix.* Combining the proposition and invocation in the Homeric manner instead of separating them, as Virgil had done, he bids her "Sing" the story of man's disobedience and its consequences. Subsequently, however, he takes up a Virgilian formula ("Dic mihi causas"), asking her to "Say first . . . what cause / Mov'd our Grand Parents" to apostatize: "Who first seduc'd them to that foul revolt?" The poet's questions end here, and presumably it is the muse who now assumes the burden of the song along with responsibility for the answer: "Th' infernal Serpent; hee it was." Obliquely, the poet is also asking for knowledge and memory of remote and invisible things; his muse is authoritative since heaven and hell hide "nothing from [her] view." Again obliquely, he is also requesting inspiration (she had inspired Moses, author of Genesis) for an elevated style: his "advent'rous Song intends to soar / Above th' *Aonian* Mount" with no middle flight, pursuing "Things unattempted yet in Prose or Rhyme" (*PL* 1.1–26).

Though the heavenly muse has generally been identified with the "Spirit" invoked in line 17, several critics regard them as distinct; in their view, accordingly there are thus *two* separate invocations: the first addressed to the heavenly muse, the second essentially a prayer to God.[9] Some scholars have emphasized the difference in tone between these passages, but this is hardly conclusive evidence since the difference may have been prompted by the shift in emphasis from external sites associated with the heavenly muse to the pure heart itself, from holy places to a still holier shrine. The ambiguity results partly from Milton's ambiguous syntax: one could alternatively associate "chiefly" with "Thou" or with "th' upright heart." The former interpretation would seem to suggest a distinction between Urania and the Spirit, whereas the latter would encourage the reader to identify them as the same. In this section of the invocation Milton specifically asks for knowledge and memory ("Instruct me, for Thou know'st"), asserting the unimpeachable authority of his divine instructor as an active participant in the work of creation. At this point he converts the motifs of the poet's vision and supernormal altitude of style to a prayer for spiritual illumination and elevation: "What in me is dark / Illumine, what is low raise and support." It is the poet himself who must be made worthy, morally and spiritually, of his lofty theme; he is asking the Spirit to perform (within the microcosm of the poet's own soul) a work of spiritual renovation and creation analogous to the creative act that brought light out of darkness and raised the earth above the waters of the abyss. He does not explicitly, at this point, ask for altitude of style, but rather for the spiritual elevation that will permit him to "assert" to "the highth of this great Argument" the themes of divine providence and justice. As elsewhere in his works, he is exploiting the topos of the poet's character ("himself . . . a true poem" [*CP* 694]) as the necessary precondition for great poetry. As the first essential for his great task, he is asking that he himself be made "upright . . . and pure."

Instead of referring explicitly to his own blindness, as in later invocations, Milton merely suggests it. The prayer "What is dark / Illumine" points forward to the invocation to Light, where the contrast between physical blindness and inner light receives explicit emphasis, and to the autobiographical passages in the invocation to Urania in book 7. The brief and oblique allusion in book 1 is deliberately ambiguous and multivalent: applicable not only to the poet's blindness and need for inner vision but also to the natural limitations of the human intellect and imagination in comparison with the divine wisdom whose ways he is endeavoring to assert and justify. (It is perhaps significant that the only character in the poem who boasts his ability to trace the ways of deity is Satan, disguised as a serpent, and that this boast is a lie [*PL* 9.679–83].)

In employing the metaphor of light, Milton could exploit not only its biblical associations (especially in the Johannine books) but also a variety of classical parallels: its association with prophetic vision and with Apollo (companion of the muses and god of prophecy and light) and with the Platonic imagery of light and darkness and the eye of the soul. Though relevant for vatic vision, the prayer for illumination seems to refer primarily to the spiritual illumination accomplished by the Deity himself in the process of inner regeneration. The true prophet (if the ideas expressed in Milton's *De Doctrina* are applicable here) would appear to be not so much the poet himself as Christ the Logos.

In *Samson Agonistes,* Milton takes the hero's blindness as a point of departure for images of spiritual blindness and inner illumination. In *Paradise Lost,* he converts his own blindness into a source for metaphor; as such it forms a significant part of his complex elaboration throughout the epic of the motif of vision (centering paradoxically on Satan's promise, "your Eyes . . . shall perfetly be then Op'n'd and clear'd, and ye shall be as Gods" [*PL* 9.706–9].) The singular power of Milton's persona as inspired bard (as compared, let us say, with DuBartas and even Spenser) results primarily from the fact that, unlike either of these poets (so unequal in poetic merit), he was indeed blind—and from the skill with which he assimilated autobiography not only to poetic convention but also to a wide range of metaphors from various sources based on blindness and intellectual vision.[10]

Milton's second invocation to his muse addresses her by the name Urania for the first time, thereby associating her with the tradition of "divine poetry" made fashionable by DuBartas in *La muse chrétienne.* He explicitly differentiates her from the classical muse of astronomy by stressing the meaning rather than the name, much as Tasso had emphasized the "intention" behind Dante's invocation of Apollo. Urania belongs to, and is concerned with, the invisible heavens, the empyrean, rather than with the stars, and preoccupation with things truly celestial is emphasized through her sibling relationship with Eternal Wisdom. In this passage she is specifically and primarily associated with the voice or song that conducts the poet beyond the skies to the empyrean and back again to earth. Following her "Voice divine" (*PL* 7.1–5), he has soared above Olympus and the winged horse Pegasus (now significantly a constellation) in the empyrean itself, the dwelling place of the true Deity.

Brief though they are, these classical allusions are in fact polysemous; they can refer simultaneously to the inspiration of classical poetry and to its subject matter. Olympus was one of the several homes of the nine muses, but it was also the home of the gods celebrated by Homer and Hesiod and Virgil. Associated with the muses through the fountain Hippocrene, the winged horse had been traditionally allegorized in terms of the fame bestowed by poets. Yet he had also become a constellation in the highest of the visible heavens, the sphere of the fixed stars. Urania has led the poet to far higher altitudes than those to which her Siren rivals had guided the poets of pagan antiquity, beyond the visible heavens and the ancient gods to the highest heaven, "the Heav'n of Heav'ns," and to the true God. The reference to drawing "Empyreal Air / Thy temp'ring" is likewise equivocal. It can mean (as Merritt Y. Hughes suggests) that she has tempered "the heavenly air to my mortal lungs" (*CP* 346n); but it also evokes specifically musical overtones. Even the allusion to the poet's enemies is presented in terms of music: the "barbarous dissonance / Of *Bacchus* and his Revellers," the "savage clamor" that had drowned the music of Orpheus's harp and voice (*PL* 7.32–39). In this invocation, as the muse of "Celestial Song," Urania's chief function is that of guide and singing mistress, governing the poet's song, leading him back to earth as formerly into the empyrean, and attracting a more sympathetic audience than that of the unfortunate Orpheus. Trees and stones were ravished by his song, but not the drunken Thracians.

The parallel with Orpheus, theological poet and vatic bard, and his intimate relationship to Calliope serves, moreover, not only to underline the superiority of Milton's own muse but also to confirm his own pretensions to the status of vatic poet. He may aspire more truly to this role than his hapless predecessor inasmuch as (with "this additional advantage of being Christian" [*CP* 668]) he possesses a true, and heavenly, source of inspiration, not an empty dream.

These are the only invocations addressed directly to the muse in *Paradise Lost;* nevertheless, both the invocation to light in book 3 and the introductory verses to book 9 allude to her offices. In book 9 she is the nocturnal visitant who dictates the poet's verses "unimplor'd." In book 3 she is described in more elevated terms as the celestial guide who has taught him "to venture down / The dark descent" into the infernal realms and the abyss, and "up to reascend." Figuratively, he has been transported beyond the bounds of nature by her power and, endowed with wings, actually visits and beholds the scenes he is describing. A few lines later, he provides a less figurative account of his poetic inspiration: "Then feed on thoughts, that voluntary move / Harmonious numbers," in song as instinctive as that of the nightingale (*PL* 3.37–40). This is essentially the same office that, in book 9, he attributes to his celestial patroness.

Like the invocation to Urania in book 7, this invocation to light marks a shift in material and in locale; though immediately relevant for the situation in which Milton has left his antihero, on the frontiers of light and darkness, it is primarily significant for the scene that immediately follows. A heightened intellectual vision is essential for beholding and relating the things of heaven; the poet appropriately addresses his prayer rather to "Celestial Light" than to the muse of Celestial Song. For similar reasons he explicitly alludes, for the first time, to his own blindness. The Book of Nature ("the Book of knowledge fair" of nature's works) has been expunged and razed, but not the Book of Scripture, nor the Book of the Soul.[11] With "wisdom at one entrance quite shut out," there is all the greater need for divine illumination:

> So much the rather thou Celestial Light
> Shine inward, and the mind through all her powers
> Irradiate, there plant eyes, all mist from thence
> Purge and disperse, that I may see and tell
> Of things invisible to mortal sight.
> (*PL* 3.51–55)

Milton had written earlier in similar terms concerning his blindness: "Let me be the most feeble creature alive, . . . as long as in that obscurity, in which I am enveloped, the light of the divine presence more clearly shines; then, . . . in proportion as I am blind, I shall more clearly see. O! that I may thus be perfected by feebleness, and irradiated by obscurity!" (*CP* 826).

The prayer for inner illumination in this passage recalls the similar request to the Spirit in book 1, while the intimate correlation between the poet's "thoughts" and his "Harmonious numbers" involves a relationship analogous to that between the muse of Celestial Song and her sister the divine Wisdom in book 7. It is in this passage, moreover, that Milton specifically compares himself with the blind bards and prophets of antiquity, alluding briefly to his desire to be equaled with them in renown.

He does not explicitly reassert his intention to outsoar the ancients, nor compare his own muse with those of pagan antiquity. Nevertheless, the superiority of his own inspiration is implicit. Significantly interwoven with the motif of holy light are analogies between the classical and the Judeo-Christian traditions. He still finds delight in classical literature, but he prefers that of the Bible and, as he appears to suggest, his nocturnal meditations on the Scriptures inspire his verse. He contrasts his own account of Chaos and Eternal Night, under the inspiration of his heavenly muse, with that of the son of Calliope ("With other notes than to the *Orphean* Lyre" [*PL* 3.17]). The logical inference—if one completes the analogy between the blind poets and seers inspired by the muses or by Apollo—is that the blind Milton, illuminated by the true celestial light, may possess a more valid claim to the title of *vates* and divine poet.

Milton had invoked the heavenly muse much earlier in the Nativity Ode, bidding her to outstrip the Magi, presenting her "humble ode" to the newborn Messiah as the first gift at his nativity and joining her voice with those of the angels.[12] The hymn that immediately follows is thus represented as her song. Since "heavenly" was one of numerous conventional epithets for the muses, one cannot assume that he had Urania specifically in mind; on the other hand, he must have been familiar already with DuBartas's image of Urania as the heavenly muse, and to invoke her in a divine poem would underline the sacred nature of his song. In "The Passion" he subsequently referred to his muse as singing a part in the music of the angels on this occasion, but did not mention her by name.[13] The "heav'nly Muse" mentioned in *Comus,* however, who had taught the ancient poets the myths of chimeras and enchanted isles and passages to Hades, could hardly be associated with the *muse chrétienne.*[14]

In *Paradise Regained,* Milton discards the fiction of the muse and invokes the Spirit instead for inspiration. As in the earlier invocation to the Spirit in *Paradise Lost,* the power he is invoking had been an actual participant—and accordingly the most authoritative witness—in the events the poet is attempting to relate:

> Thou Spirit who led'st this glorious Eremite
> Into the Desert, his Victorious Field
> Against the Spiritual Foe, and brought'st him thence
> By proof th'undoubted Son of God. . . .

Moreover, the kind of aid that he seeks from the Spirit is essentially the same assistance that Urania had bestowed on him—inspiration of elevated discourse and memory of things forgotten:

> . . . inspire
> *As thou art wont,* my prompted Song, else mute,
> And bear through height or depth of nature's bounds
> With prosperous wing full summ'd to tell of deeds
> Above Heroic, though in secret done,
> And unrecorded left through many an Age. . . .
>   (*PR* 1.8–17, emphasis added)

The supersession of Urania by the Spirit might be significant if one regarded the muse of *Paradise Lost* as distinct from the Spirit. Her absence from the briefer, and soberer, epic is scarcely surprising, however, in view of the identity of its hero, its Palestinian setting, and the frequent contrasts that the poet develops between Hebrew and pagan traditions: the true God and the false gods, the Bible and Hellenic poetry and philosophy; the spiritual regnum of Israel's true king and the kingdoms of the Gentiles. To invoke in such a poetic context a name so reminiscent of pagan fable would seem to violate decorum; on this occasion Milton preferred, apparently, to discard the name altogether and invoke the reality behind it instead.

In the introductory verses of book 9, Milton restates his theme (as Tasso had suggested a poet might do),[15] emphasizing the tragic change (or *mutatione di stato*) that is about to occur, and again asserting the superiority of his own epic argument to those of classical epic. In emphasizing the shift in subject matter, he does not invoke the muse herself, as he had done in book 7 ("Descend from Heav'n Urania" [*PL* 7.1]), nor does he call on her directly for aid. In keeping with his "Sad task," he assumes a less exalted tone than in his earlier addresses to his *inspiratrix* and a less confident note than in the first. He makes his ambition to outsoar the ancients conditional upon her assistance: "If answerable style I can obtain / Of my Celestial Patroness," "if all be mine, / Not Hers who brings it nightly to my Ear" (*PL* 9.1–47). Bembo and della Casa, as we noted, invoked the muses specifically for "style,"[16] and it is this—a style answerable to the height of his argument—that Milton needs primarily to receive from Urania, and that thus far he has been granted nightly: dictating to him in his sleep or inspiring "Easy my unpremeditated Verse." The notable absence of an invocation in these introductory verses, where the reader might well have expected it, gives additional emphasis to the voluntary grace vouchsafed the poet; his patroness "deigns / Her nightly visitation *unimplor'd*" (*PL* 9.1–47, emphasis added).

3.

The image of the inspired poet is as widely diffused as that of the inspired prophet; in some cultures it has been associated with various forms of possession and diverse modes of the irrational or suprarational. As the shaman, the prophet, the oracle-priest, and the ritual dancer or actor profess to be moved by the gods or the spirits of the dead, the poet might lay claim to an enthusiasm communicated by some power outside and above himself. Such claims have been made by oral poets of central Asia, and they had been advanced on behalf of the English poet Caedmon. In Greece the ideal of the poet-prophet, inspired by Apollo or the muses to sing of things past or passing or to come appears in the earliest recorded poetry. Homer referred to Phemius and Demodocus, and Hesiod to his own inspiration, in these terms.[17] The earliest extended discussion, however, occurs in Plato's dialogues.

The poet, Plato declares in the *Ion,* speaks by the divine inspiration of the muses rather than by conscious art. He is "a light and winged and holy thing, and there is no invention in him until he has been inspired and is out of his senses, and the mind is no longer in him." God "takes away the minds of poets, and uses them as his ministers, as he also uses diviners and holy prophets, in order that we who hear them may know that they speak not of themselves who utter these priceless words in a state of unconsciousness, but that God is the speaker, and that through them he is conversing with us." Thus the God seems to "indicate to us . . . that these beautiful poems are not human, or the work of man, but divine and the word of God; and that the poets are only the interpreters of the Gods by whom they are severally possessed." The inspiration even affects the rhapsode, who recites the poem. "Are you not carried out of yourself," Socrates demands of Ion, "and does not your soul in an ecstasy seem to be among the persons or places of which she is speaking, whether they are in Ithaca or in Troy or whatever may be the scene of the poem?"[18] Along with the *Phaedrus,* this dialogue was perhaps the most significant influence on the topos of poetic furor, but the critics and poets who wrote on this theme tended to develop it with less subtlety and without the ironic stance of Plato's Socrates. Although Plato describes the poet's rapture in the *Ion* as enthusiasm, he frequently treats it elsewhere as madness (mania). Poetry is "no arte," according to *The Shepheardes Calender,* "but a divine gift and heavenly instinct not to bee gotten by laboure and learning, but adorned with both: and poured into the witte by a certaine *enthousiasmos,* and celestiall inspiration." [Spenser, October AEglogue.] It is "a divine instinct and unnatural rage passing the reache of comen reason." Elyot cites both Plato and Cicero on the poet's "celestial instinction," observing that poets were called *vates* or prophets, because they were supposed to possess "science mystical and inspired."[19]

Sidney mentions Landino's views on the poet's "divine fury," and remarks that Plato "attributeth unto poesy more than myself do, namely to be a very inspiring of a divine force, far above man's wit." For Milton's nephew, Edward Phillips, "the height of poetical rapture hath ever been accounted little less than Divine Inspiration."[20]

While using this topos to exalt the art of poetry, critics and poets saw little inconsistency in insisting, almost simultaneously, on the importance of the *art* of poetry, on the need for learning and labor, and on the need for some adherence to the principles of genre. "It is by labor and intent study . . . joined with the strong propensity of nature" that Milton aspired to "leave something so written to aftertimes, as they should not willingly let it die" (*CP* 668).

Milton's ideal of the inspired poet is far from Plato's artless madman. On the other hand, the argument of the divine fury—in the painter or sculptor as well as in the poet—could be invoked to defend apparent violations of classical norms of representation.[21]

An additional problem, which the critics rather than the poets had to reckon with, was Aristotle's reference to the madness of the poet. Noting that the passions are portrayed "most truthfully by one who is feeling them at the moment," Aristotle had added that "poetry demands a man with special gift for it, or else one with a touch of madness in him; the former can easily assume the required mood, and the latter may be actually beside himself with emotion." Castelvetro regarded this text as corrupt: "the words *or of* the madman ought to be written *not of* the madman" ("non da furioso"). He believed, moreover, that Aristotle had intended to censure the opinion that "some attribute to Plato, that poetry is infused into men by divine inspiration."[22]

4.

Though Plato had associated the poetic furor specifically with the muses, leaving the other frenzies—wine, love, and prophecy—to their appropriate divinities,[23] poets frequently ignored such limitations; indeed, there was a constantly shifting relationship not only between the images of poetic and prophetic enthusiasm but also with other sources of inspiration and possession: vinous or erotic, martial or even infernal. The poet might call on higher and more powerful divinities than the muses to assist him, imploring the god of war to instill a martial spirit into his verse, or professing to be inspired by Eros and Aphrodite or by the god of wine. In other contexts he might invoke the furies, the shades of the dead, or (as Lucan had done, albeit ironically), the spirit of a reigning monarch,[24] some potential patron, or his mistress to inspire his song. In sacred poetry he might associate the conventional poetic invocation with the invocation of the Trinity or the saints. Thus, after first addressing his muse, Marino proceeds to call on the Holy Innocents themselves for inspiration:

> E voi reggete voi l'infermo Ingegno
> Nuntii di Christo, e testimoni invitti,
> Che deste fuor de le squarciate gole
> Sangue invece di voce, e di parole:

Or, as Crashaw renders this passage:

> O be a Dore
> Or language to my infant Lipse, yee best
> Of Confessours: whose Throates answering his swords,
> Gave forth your Blood for breath, spoke soules for words.[25]

This tendency to seek inspiration from other sources in addition to, or in place of, the muses was encouraged, moreover, by the rationalization of the mythographical tradition in classical antiquity itself. The muses themselves eventually became little more than symbols—not only for different kinds of poetry, and poetic subjects—but for diverse branches of humane learning. After the triumph of Christianity they survived, like other pagan divinities, only as symbols and poetic conventions. A poet might invoke them in accordance with classical precedent; but if he desired to suggest a valid source of inspiration, he must either invoke directly the God of the saints and angels of his own religion, or allude to the latter obliquely under the veil of pagan fable. Thus Jove could serve as a surrogate for God, Urania as a symbol for the *muse chrétienne;* the doves of Venus could be assimilated to the dove of the Holy Spirit, and the conventions associated with Eros transferred to the love of God.

The association between poetic and prophetic inspiration, as poets of the late Middle Ages and the Renaissance developed it, was encouraged by a variety of factors in addition to the ambiguity of the term *vates*. Closely associated with the nine sisters (sharing the honors of paternity with Jove,[26] and credited with the title of Musagetes, leader of the muses), Apollo was simultaneously the god of prophecy and the patron of poetry. Like the Delphic oracle, which had delivered its messages in hexameter verses, other sibyls had used poetry as a medium for prophecy. Of the numerous prophetic poems that had circulated in ancient Rome under the name of sibylline oracles, some had incorporated motifs from the prophetic and apocalyptic tradition of the Old Testament. A few of these survived into the Middle Ages and the Renaissance; accordingly, the sibyls were incorporated into Christian literary and iconographical tradition as Gentile prophets of Christ. The *Dies Irae* emphasizes the analogy between David and the Sibyl as prophets of the Last Judgment ("Teste David cum Sibylla"), and in the Sistine Chapel the classical sibyls (Delphic, Cumaean, Libyan, etc.) complement the Old Testament prophets.

For similar reasons the poet Virgil was widely regarded as a prophet insofar as his fourth eclogue (the so-called Messianic eclogue) had been interpreted as a prophecy of the birth of Christ ("The great line of the centuries begins anew" [Magnus ab integro saeclorum nascitur ordo]). As author of the Psalms, David was simultaneously poet and prophet. Divinely inspired, the other poetic books of the Old Testament had been interpreted prophetically in terms of the life of Christ and of the last things. Finally, because of its symbolic imagery and its dramatic structure, the Apocalypse was sometimes regarded either as a poem or as virtually identical with poetry in its mode of presentation. Saint John the Divine was thus poet as well as prophet; in Ariosto's epic, Saint John the Evangelist not only elucidates the meaning of the allegory of time, fame, and poetry, but also bitterly denounces the meager rewards that modern writers are receiving for their labors.[27]

If the muses were companions of Apollo, the latter was in a sense landlord as well as brother to Dionysos, sharing his shrine at Delphi with the god of wine and ecstatic revel. In Renaissance tradition, moreover, each of the celestial spheres was sometimes associated both with a specific muse and a specific Bacchus.[28] Love and wine and prophecy were all conventional sources of poetic inspiration; poets were scarcely less free to invoke Apollo or Bacchus, Aphrodite or Eros, than to call on any or all of the nine muses and their mother, Mnemosyne. "For many of the gods patronize the gay elegy," Milton writes to Diodati, "and she calls whom she will to her measures. Liber and Erato, Ceres and Venus are at hand to help her, and beside his rosy mother is the stripling Cupid [Amor]." For such poets, banqueting and wine-bibbing are permissible. But for a poet who would sing of higher themes—heaven and hell and the gods and heroes—abstinence and chastity are essential. He must resemble the holy augur in purity, who enters the presence of the gods clad in sacred vestments and bearing lustral water. Such were the lives of the early poets and prophets—Orpheus and Homer, Tiresias and Linus and Calchas. "For truly the bard [*vates*] is sacred to the gods and is their priest [*sacerdos*]. His hidden heart and his lips alike breathe out Jove" (*CP* 51–52).[29] Later, in *The Reason of Church-Government*, Milton returned to these alternative sources of inspiration, but dropped the classical veneer of his earlier reference to the Deity ("Jove") and instead contrasted the pagan muses with the true God. Great poetry is "not to be raised from the heat of youth, or the vapors of wine, like that which flows at waste from the pen of some vulgar amorist, or the trencher fury of a riming parasite," nor by invoking "Dame Memory and her Siren daughters," but by prayer to the eternal Spirit (*CP* 671).

Milton was no vulgar amorist, but in the most sensual of his elegies he celebrates the rites of spring, inspired by the season itself and the heat of youth. As the spring revives his genius and his powers of song, he assumes the persona of the inspired bard, filled with divine fury and madness, carried in ecstatic flight to the skies, and beholding in spirit heaven and hell. The Castalian spring and the peaks of Parnassus "float before [his] eyes," and he beholds the fountain of Pirene in his dreams. His breast is "aflame with the excitement of [the] mysterious impulse [of spring]," and he is "driven on by the madness [*furor*] and the divine sounds" within him. He beholds Apollo approaching: "Already my mind is being borne up into the sheer liquid heights of the sky and, quit of the body, I go through the wandering clouds. I am carried through shadows and grottoes, the secret haunts of the poets; and the innermost shrines of the gods are open to me. My spirit surveys all that is done on Olympus and the unseen infernal world is not impervious to my eyes." "What is to be the offspring of this madness [*rabies*] and this sacred ecstasy?" (*CP* 38).[30]

In soberer vein, Milton applies to music the imagery of *enthusiasmos* (in the literal sense of possession by some divinity), "Either God, or certainly some third mind from the untenanted skies, is moving mysteriously in your throat," he declares to Leonora Baroni; "in you alone [God] speaks and possesses all His other creatures in silence" (*CP* 38).

5.

In the Fifth Elegy the poet's inspired fury is depicted in terms of ecstasies. He is rapt to the skies in visionary flight, but in the madness of youth he has not yet learned to direct his wings. They carry him everywhere, veering according to the dictates of fancy and spring fever (*CP* 37–41). Ariosto's hero Ruggiero had experienced similar difficulties initially with the hippogriff, but eventually learned to master his winged steed. In *Paradise Lost,* however, the poet's flight is directed by a more reliable divinity than Apollo; it has fixed points of departure and destination. The poet soars or descends to the regions and sites that his story demands; he generally has at least one fixed landmark by which to determine his altitude and his bearings: the Aonian mount that he hopes to outsoar. The images of flight—their direction and their changing altitude—are carefully and specifically coordinated with the poet's mise-en-scène, the localities that he is describing. There is (it would seem) a definite flight plan, and the heavenly muse is a judicious pilot.

It is largely through these images of flight (soaring above Helicon and Olympus, outflying Pegasus, "rapt above the Pole," borne through chaos and hell into the empyrean and back again to earth, carried throughout nature's bounds with "prosperous wing") that Milton simulates the visionary ecstasies of the seer. (The other "visionary" or "prophetic" elements in both epics are for the most part either standard epic conventions or the product of divine or infernal agents.) It may be useful, accordingly, to examine some of Milton's flight images that occur in other poetic contexts, in association with poetic or prophetic ecstasies, with the flight of fancy, and with the apotheosis tradition.[31]

He appears to have had no fear of flying, and indeed to have been obsessed by the idea of flight—though this apparent obsession was strongly conditioned by the nature of his materials and hence by the kind of dramatis personae available to him. Of the principal characters in the epic only Adam and Eve remain earthbound. The majority soar among the spheres, engage in air battles, slide on sunbeams, or fly through outer and middle darkness; the poet himself is among them. It is scarcely surprising that Satan should tempt Eve with flight and that under the intoxication of the forbidden fruit the fallen pair should imagine the wings of divinity sprouting already.

The lines "At a Vacation Exercise" present a flight of fancy in which, rapt above the poles, the poet beholds visibly (and hears with his own ear) the kind of subjects he would like to write about in his native tongue:

> Such where the deep transported mind may soar
> Above the wheeling poles, and at Heav'n's door
> Look in, and see each blissful Deity

> How he before the thunderous throne doth lie,
> Listening to what unshorn *Apollo* sings.

Thereupon he descends through the regions of fire and air to the sea, and to such subjects as the "secret things" that came to pass in nature's infancy, and "last of Kings and Queens and *Heroes* old." Finally, he rebukes his wandering muse for roving from the subject and the academic occasion (*CP* 30–32).[32]

In the incomplete poem "The Passion," Milton employs the convention of ecstatic vision to bring him to the actual scene of Christ's tomb, where he visibly beholds the Holy Sepulcher. He associates his song with Phoebus Apollo, companion of the muses and god of prophecy, and with the wheels of Ezekiel's vision:[33]

> See, see the Chariot and those rushing wheels
> That whirl'd the Prophet up at *Chebar* flood;
> My spirit some transporting *Cherub* feels,
> To bear me where the Towers of *Salem* stood . . . ;
> There doth my soul in holy vision sit,
> In pensive trance, and anguish, and ecstatic fit.

Later in the same poem he suggests that he might be "hurried on viewless wing" from the tomb to the mountains to lament in solitude; but at this point the poem breaks off (*CP* 61–63).

The four winged creatures associated with Ezekiel's visions recur (with slight variations) in the Apocalypse;[34] they were commonly interpreted as symbols of the four evangelists. Milton is apparently suggesting that the prophetic vehicle that bears him to the scene of Christ's passion is the record of these events according to four evangelists, or the divine spirit that inspired them. Alluding specifically to the visions of Ezekiel and Saint John, Dante similarly introduces the four creatures as attendants, rather than wheels, of the triumphal chariot of Beatrice. Representative of the four gospels, they follow the twenty-four elders (a detail borrowed from the Apocalypse and symbolizing the books of the Old Testament) and precede figures representing the remaining books of the New. The two wheels of Beatrice's chariot are reminiscent of Ezekiel's vision, but Dante prefers to follow Saint John rather than the Old Testament prophet in the number of the wings he ascribes to the four creatures (*Purgatorio*, canto 29.)[35] In *Paradise Lost*, Milton bases his description of the "Chariot of Paternal Deity" largely on Ezekiel's vision, but does not include the specific details that would differentiate the four evangelists:

> Flashing thick flames, Wheel within Wheel, undrawn,
> Itself instinct with Spirit, but convoy'd
> By four Cherubic shapes, four Faces each
> Had wondrous, as with Stars thir bodies all
> And Wings were set with Eyes, with Eyes the Wheels
> Of Beryl, and careering Fires between.
>
> (*PL* 6.749–56)

The furor and *enthousiasmos* of the inspired poet had been so frequently compared with that of the inspired prophet that he might easily assume the latter's role. Poetry had sometimes been the medium of prophecy; symbolic and dramatic techniques, several critics believed, were common to both, and in certain cultures the same man might perform the offices of poet, prophet, and priest. The ambiguity of the term *vates* also encouraged the poet to exploit the conventions of prophecy: ecstatic trance, supernatural vision and hearing, and on occasion the motif of flight. In antiquity the author of a lost epic, the *Arimaspeia,* professed to have been bodily transported to the land of the Hyperboreans, where he gathered the materials for his poem.[36] In Plato's vision of Er, the soul of a man supposedly slain in battle ascends to the heavens, where he beholds the spindle of Necessity, the three fates, and the various lots voluntarily elected by different souls. In the *Somnium Scipionis,* the ascent to the heavens occurs in a dream. Dante's visionary journey through hell and purgatory and heaven was sometimes interpreted as a dream vision. Saint Paul alluded to "a man in Christ" who ("whether in the body, or out of the body, I cannot tell") was caught up into the third heaven, into paradise, "and heard unspeakable words, which it is not lawful to a man to utter" (2 Cor. 12:2–4). It was frequently believed that the man was in fact Saint Paul himself; accordingly, this motif also was assimilated to the literature of vision. Dante explicitly contrasts himself with Aeneas and Saint Paul; what the apostle discreetly passed over, the *Visio Sancti Pauli* obligingly invented. The tradition of Mohammed's ascent to the heavens on a winged steed from the site of the temple at Jerusalem inspired a number of visionary journeys, and it has been suggested that some one of these could have been accessible to Dante in Latin translation.[37]

In the apocalyptic and prophetic books of Scripture, the narrator is frequently carried up to heaven in the Spirit and instructed to make his vision manifest to others. (Dante preserves the latter formula in the *Commedia.*) Thus according to Ezekiel, "the Spirit lifted me up between the earth and heaven, and brought me in the visions of God to Jerusalem" (Ezek. 8:3). "Moreover, the Spirit lifted me up, and brought me unto the east gate of the Lord's house" (11:1). "Afterwards the Spirit took me up, and brought me in a vision by the Spirit of God into Chaldea, to them of the captivity" (11:24). (In the two latter instances, however, the emphasis falls not so much on the visions as on the verbal message that the prophet is instructed to deliver.) "The hand of the Lord was upon me, and carried me out in the Spirit of the Lord, and set me down in the midst of the valley which was full of bones" (37:1). "In the visions of God brought he me into the land of Israel, and set me upon a very high mountain, on which was as the frame of a city on the south" (40:1). "So the Spirit took me up and brought me into the inner court, and, behold, the glory of the Lord filled the house" (43:5).

Similarly, the narrator of the Apocalypse is "in the Spirit on the Lord's day" (Apoc. 1:10) when he hears a voice like a trumpet and beholds the vision of the seven golden candlesticks. In a later vision—that of the throne, the twenty elders, and the seven-sealed scroll—he hears a voice bidding him "Come up here, and I will show thee things which must be hereafter. And immediately I was in the Spirit and, behold, a throne was set in heaven, and one sat on the throne" (4:1–2). Subsequently, Saint John is transported by the Spirit into the wilderness, where he beholds the harlot seated upon the beast with seven heads (17:3). Again, "he carried me away in the Spirit to a great and high mountain, and showed me that great city, the holy Jerusalem, descending out of heaven from God" (31:10).

Much of this visionary literature is preteritive: remembered ecstasies or remembered prophecy. The narrator is recounting past experience—his own or another's—and if he requires inspiration at the moment, the divinity he needs to invoke is no longer the spirit of prophecy (that is over), but rather the powers of memory and inspired utterance. The vision itself now belongs to memory. It is past, and he must now endeavor to recall it and express it to others, perhaps with difficulty. For this sort of aid, a poet would normally turn to Mnemosyne and her daughters. Sometimes, like Dante and Chaucer, he will invoke the muses or his own *ingenium* or his memory to awaken remembrance of his vision and to assist him in communicating it to his audience.[38] As a narrator he does not assume a visionary or prophetic stance. In Milton's Fifth Elegy and "The Passion," on the other hand, the poet pretends to be actually transported by divine furor to the scene of his vision; in *Paradise Lost* he professes to actually visit heaven and hell, earth and chaos in the act of describing them (*CP* 37–41, 61–63; *PL* 3.13–21, 7.12–16). By dramatizing the visionary process and transferring it to the present, Milton gives it the immediacy of an action or a meditation that is actually taking place; it becomes more than a record of past experience.

On the other hand, he is primarily a spectator of the scenes and events he is describing, rather than an active participant. (He is, in a sense, imitating his own action—but as singer and seer.) The events themselves are long past, and these he revisits only in imagination. (An exception is the conceit that, present at the Nativity, his own muse may offer his birthday gift to the infant Christ before the arrival of the Magi.)[39] Ezekiel and Saint John the Divine, who are actually present at the scene of their visions, engage to a limited degree in the action (both devour scrolls, for instance, and occasionally exchange words with their divine informants), but—entrusted with the responsibility of revealing the prophecy to others—their primary role is that of seeing and hearing. John's part in the events of the vision is much less prominent than Ezekiel's. Dante, on the other hand, is the protagonist of his visionary journey, engaging actively in conversation with the dead; it is his own experience—his own contemplation of the state of souls after death and the nature of the virtues and vices, his own moral regeneration and ascent by progressive stages (through knowledge and love) to the highest Good, his own progress from the dark wood of this world to the beatific vision—that constitutes the core of the poem.

Like Dante, Chaucer is both narrator and a participant in his dream-visions, professing to actually visit the places he describes and sometimes relating how he got there; on occasion he exploits the motif of the visionary flight. Nevertheless, his primary role is that of spectator. His flight with the eagle in *The House of Fame*—apparently a parodic version of the act of contemplation and visionary ecstasis—serves primarily to bring him to Fame's dwelling and to provide the necessary exposition for the following scene; in comparison with his garrulous mentor, his own remarks are notable chiefly for their comedy and their brevity.

Milton's representation of ecstatic flight in a poem like "The Passion," bringing the poet to the scene of his subject, assimilates the convention of the inspired poet to those of "meditative" and devotional poetry. In addition to the Protestant meditative tradition, Milton was familiar with poetry influenced by that of Roman Catholicism.[40] Moreover, because of the very nature of their arts, poets and painters who had never encountered the "composition of place" as a meditative technique endeavored to give the impression of immediacy: of being actually present, for instance, at the Nativity or the Transfiguration or the Crucifixion. This type of immediacy had been characteristic of much devotional poetry, and it was further encouraged by such rhetorical concepts or devices as ecphrasis and *enargeia* and apostrophe: the former two lending vividness to the scene and bringing it before the reader's eyes, the last often addressing the absent as present. Such immediacy, furthermore, was particularly characteristic of the festival and occasional poetry associated with the ecclesiastical calendar commemorating the acts of saints or the events of Christ's life. On such occasions the clock (or rather time itself) is turned back: on the appropriate days, the church—and the poet—celebrates the Annunciation or the Nativity or the day of the Resurrection as though they were present. In the poem "Upon the Circumcision," for instance, the centuries intervening between the poet and the event itself vanish: he is actually present at the scene and the moment of this rite; the crucifixion still belongs to the future. In contrast to his technique in "The Passion," Milton does not pretend on this occasion to be miraculously ravished to the site in "ecstatic fit." Instead, already present at the scene in devout imagination, he invokes the same angels who had sung at the Nativity to now change their notes to tragic, lamenting with the mourning Church:

> Now mourn; and, if sad share with us to bear
> Your fiery essence can distill no tear,
> Burn in your sighs, and borrow
> Seas wept from our deep sorrow.

Milton employs the plural "our"; the grief is communal, and with the sixteen centuries that divide them temporally annihilated by the act of devotion, the church in England and the angels who had sung nearly two millenia earlier participate simultaneously in the same grief and the same song. The child who "whilere / Enter'd the world . . . *now* bleeds" (emphasis added). After a temporary anachronism—"that Cov'nant . . . satisfied" (a reference to the future from the "timepoint" of the actual circumcision, but to the past from the retrospective viewpoint of the seventeenth century)—Milton returns to the time of circumcision:

> And seals obedience first with wounding smart
> This day; but Oh! ere long
> Huge pangs and strong
> Will pierce more near his heart.

In a perceptive study of time patterns in "baroque lyric poetry," Lowry Nelson has examined in detail the similar, but more elaborate, manipulation of past, present, and future tenses in the Nativity Ode, calling attention to comparable techniques in Continental poetry. Both the Nativity Ode and "Upon the Circumcision" are "liturgical" poetry insofar as they are closely associated with specific days and events commemorated by the church, and with "meditative" poetry insofar as these represent the author's own imaginative reenactment of the scene and his reflections on its implications.[41] The same would appear to be true of Milton's unfinished poem on the Passion; but here, in contrast to these other "liturgical" poems, he presents the meditative and devotional process through the metaphor of ecstasis and visionary flight.

As we have seen, the formula of divine possession—applied to so many varieties of inspiration—enabled the poet and the philosopher alike to appropriate the furors of the lover, the prophet, or the Bacchic initiate. Socrates had his own familiar daimon; the successors of Plato in late antiquity and in the Renaissance aspired to mystical ecstasy. The inspired philosopher was also the inspired lover, and the love of God was assimilated to the "frenzies" of the flesh: the lover's malady of Hereos and the inspiration of wine. Eros, and indeed Dionysos, could not only absorb the roles of Apollo and the muses but also approximate the inspiration of the Spirit itself insofar as they served as symbols for the ecstatic fruition of deity. We have noted the Dionysiac imagery in Milton's representation of the marriage feast of the Lamb in *Epitaphium Damonis,* his exploitation of the myth of Cupid and Psyche in *Comus* to shadow the union of the divine love and the human soul, and his assimilation of the theological virtue of charity to chastity (that is, purity): the purified love of God indwelling in the purified soul. In consonance with the predominant use of classical symbols to shadow concepts belonging to Christian moral philosophy, he has represented Christian ideas of the struggle between flesh and spirit, the purification and cleansing of the soul, and love for the highest Good, in terms of Neoplatonic correlatives, associating the virtues of the *anima Christiana* with those of the Neoplatonic *anima purgata.*

The fact that both of these "frenzies" had been traditionally regarded as sources for poetic inspiration—along with the ambivalence of *amor* in particular, as directed toward earthly or celestial objects—made it easier for poets to draw on the extensive secular literature associated with both and to adapt it, if they chose, to devotional ends. The most obvious instance would be the sacred parody of secular love poetry (or the reverse), and the adaptation of the conventions of earthly love (including the erotic emblem or *devize*) to that of the spirit. Moreover, the fact that both secular and sacred erotic traditions had already absorbed many of the concepts and much of the imagery of Neoplatonism facilitated the interaction between the two. Nevertheless—like the relationship between pagan antiquity and Christianity—the relationship between secular and sacred love could be represented in a variety of ways even by the same poet. On occasion he might depict them as analogous but irreconcilable; one must choose between them, as between pleasure and virtue or between falsehood and truth. On the other hand, the former might serve as a type or symbol of the latter: good and valid in itself, but nonetheless inferior and less "real," a shadow of substance. Or he might portray it as a sort of *preparatio evangelica*,[42] a preliminary but necessary stage in the progress of the soul, the initial steps on the *scala amoris*.

Both the Neoplatonic and Christian traditions emphasized the contrast between earthly and heavenly love and between true love ("refined" or "purified" love) and lust; but in much of the secular love poetry of the late Middle Ages and the Renaissance the poet tended to idealize both his passion and its object by associating them with the higher or heavenly love and emphatically dissociating them from "base lust." The passion itself—the love of a lady—thus becomes a refining fire that purifies the soul, perfects it in virtue, and ultimately leads it heavenwards. Its object, in turn, is also celestial, the incarnate Idea of heavenly beauty and virtue. The poet thus spiritualizes the sensual, exalting a mortal to the skies. The sacred tradition, on the other hand, frequently exploited the sensual to suggest the spiritual, using the imagery of physical love (as the Song of Songs was believed to have done) as symbols for the relationship between Christ and the Church, or between God and the human soul. Writing in specifically devotional contexts, moreover, the poet sometimes employs bolder images than if he were wooing a lady in the idealized Platonic mode. Indeed, the very breach of amatory decorum emphasizes the distortion between the sacred and secular erotic traditions. In a divine poem Donne can employ the metaphor of rape, and Crashaw can, without insult, exhort the Countess of Denbigh to yield "This Fort of your fair selfe" to the siege of love.[43]

6.

Thus far we have said little about the authorial persona of *Il Penseroso*. Like its twin, it has been interpreted in terms of contrasting moods and characters (merry or grave), humors and temperaments (sanguine or melancholy), and modes of life (active or contemplative). Insofar as they juxtapose contraries (the merry man banishes Melancholy and devotes himself to Mirth; the pensive man does the opposite), these companion pieces have been associated with the debate techniques that Milton had applied in his academic exercises at Cambridge. Critics have stressed their affinities with his prolusion "Whether Day or Night is the More Excellent?" as well as with other Renaissance poems in praise of mirth or melancholy. Among the latter were Burton's own verses on the pleasures and terrors of melancholy, and it has been suggested that Milton's poems may have been intended for a new edition of the *Anatomy of Melancholy.*[44] Emphasis has also been placed on the opposition between society and solitude and on the complementary time sequences: the one beginning at dawn with the song of the lark, the other at evening with the fruitless quest of the nightingale. It has also been observed that, as Milton presents them, mirth and melancholy are complementary rather than contrary. It is the more frivolous aspects of mirth, the more terrifying facets of melancholy, that the personae expel.

At the university, Milton had been trained to argue on either side of a given question; and though (like many other humanists) he deplored the pedantries of scholasticism, the experience must have been useful as a preparation for representing the confrontation of opposite views in dramatic debate. The opposition underlying the two poems could have been stated as a question ("Whether mirth or melancholy is the more pleasurable") or as a thesis or paradox ("That melancholy is more pleasant than mirth") to be debated pro and con. But Milton did not choose this alternative, nor did he develop the poems through the conventions of scholastic debate. If there is indeed some reflection of the academic exercises, the closer affinities are with the verses (such as he composed himself) composed on such occasions supporting one or the other view. His own poem on the Platonic Idea, written for another student on the occasion of a disputation, belonged to this category. Though the companion poems use the device of genealogical myth, as the prolusion on night and day had done, it is significant that on that earlier occasion Milton had regarded the subject as better suited to a "poetical performance" than to an "oratorical competition." In *L'Allegro* and *Il Penseroso* he exploits the principle of the juxtaposition of contraries in a manner distinctly different from that of the academic debate, relying instead on poetic conventions like the apotropaic formula and on parallel structure. Both poems use the conventional *veni-*formula in invoking the goddess. Both invite her to bring along with her a host of personified abstractions, her characteristic companions.[45] In both, the description of the typical pleasures of the merry man or the pensive man concludes with a conditional formula of dedication.

The opposition itself (it has been observed) is more apparent than real. The pleasures themselves are not mutually exclusive. It is the terrors rather than the pleasures of melancholy that L'Allegro banishes; in invoking Mirth he specifically dissociates her from the influence of wine and love, deriving her origins instead from the inspiration of spring.[46] The appearance of contrariness is a carefully contrived illusion, and it culminates in formulas of commitment that enhance this illusion. The alternatives *seem* as mutually restrictive as the ways that Virtue and Vice propose to Hercules. The young man—Hercules, L'Allegro, Il Penseroso—is choosing a companion for life.

The hypothesis that Milton is presenting the alternatives of the active and the contemplative lives breaks down,[47] inasmuch as L'Allegro, unaroused by any call to arms or public duty, unexercised in strenuous labors, is scarcely representative of the *vita activa* as classical and Renaissance writers generally depicted it. Accompanied by Liberty the mountain nymph, thoroughly at ease in his pursuit of pleasure, he enjoys the gracious, though sometimes ignoble, *otium* alternately lauded and condemned by poets. Nevertheless, the pleasures that he enjoys, blameless and "unreproved" as they are, are strikingly different from the sensual excesses usually associated with the *vita voluptaria,* the life of pleasure. Il Penseroso's pursuits, on the other hand, are generally characteristic of the contemplative life, the life of retired leisure, but the emphasis falls rather on its pleasures than on its labors. The reading he enjoys—Hermetic and Platonic philosophy, classical and modern tragedy, romance—is notable for its dissimilarity to the curriculum of school-authors. It is vacation reading, the kind of study one undertakes out of sheer intellectual curiosity and for pleasure, not to please a tutor or to prepare oneself to instruct others.

Concerned alternately with the pleasures of mirth and contemplation, society and solitude, these are recreational and (in the better sense) hedonistic poems; they depict the pleasures of imagination and the exercise of fantasy in its lighter and also its more serious aspects. In the earlier poem the fancy is more or less free to roam where and as it will—through fairy tales and comedies, festivals and masques, and a less serious mode of music. There is no real compulsion to look beyond the immediate pleasures of the senses to any graver end, either of action or contemplation. In the later poem this is a more disciplined fantasy, the controlled imagination characteristic of the "fixed mind" and the resolved soul. The poet does not summon Liberty, but rather fasting, retired leisure, and contemplation. He gives little license to fancy; it has graver and more serious operations to perform. As he imps its wings, they become less light but stronger, and it may soar higher. Its freer, less controlled activities he dismisses in terms reminiscent of Spenser's chamber of Phantastes. Those "vain deluding joys" are "the brood of folly"—fatherless, apparently, because conceived by the fantasy alone out of her own resources without the cooperation of the higher intellect. They are mere "toys," the "gaudy shapes" that occupy "fancies fond" and idle brains, like fickle and "hovering dreams" and "gay motes" in a sunbeam. The imagination of the thoughtful man, on the other hand, is subject to rational control or indeed is fixed on spiritual realities that transcend the grasp of reason.

Il Penseroso describes the holy visage of his goddess in language reminiscent of the divine darkness of negative theology. He traces her genesis to the saturnine Golden Age: a mythical analogue of the paradisal state before the Fall when man still conversed freely with angels and with the Deity. Just as her father was a conventional type of the contemplative mind (and, as Hughes suggests, of the "angelic mind"), her mother was closely associated with holy fire: an appropriate symbol for the purified love of God. Though the integrity of this symbol is partly undercut by the imagery of seduction and incest, this too is to be interpreted symbolically; the metaphor of so intimate a union between the *anima purgata* and celestial powers was by no means unconventional. Milton may conceivably have had in mind the ceremonial purity of the vestal virgins, though he transfers this imagery to Melancholy herself: "pensive Nun, devout and pure, / Sober, steadfast, and demure." The iconic description of Melancholy, in turn, transfers to her at least one traditional attribute of Urania, as Linocier and other mythographers had described her: "looks commencing with the skies, / The rapt soul sitting in thine eyes." The goddess herself is inspired with "holy passion," and her companion, the cherub Contemplation, guides the "fiery-wheeled throne" of Ezekiel's vision. This (one recalls) is the same aerial vehicle that had transported the poet-Milton to the Holy Land and the site of the Holy Sepulcher.

Il Penseroso's pleasures are the grave and sober delights of solitude. Unlike his counterpart, who attends the theater for performances of comedy, he reads tragedy ("the gravest, moralest, and most profitable of all other Poems") alone. On the one occasion where he is described in company, the emphasis falls on his inner experience; he looks forward to ending his life in a hermitage. He is obsessed with the supernatural, the occult, and the mysterious; on occasion he approximates the persona of the magus. His reading—largely devoted to mystical philosophy, to dramatic elaborations of Greek myth and legend, and to the covert mysteries of the chivalric romance—is represented metaphorically as an astral communion with the dead, in which he himself plays the part of necromancer. He passes the night with Hermes, unspheres the spirit of Plato, regrets that he cannot summon up the authors of lost or unfinished poems: Musaeus, Orpheus, Chaucer. From Platonic philosophy he is eager to learn the state of souls after death and the nature and powers of the elemental daemons. Tragedy revives the long-dead heroes of Thebes and Troy. In the romances he is interested primarily in the hidden sense underlying the apparatus of the "marvellous." In sleep he desires some "strange mysterious dream," and the music to which he wakes must be supernatural, "Sent by some spirit to mortals good, / Or th'unseen Genius of the Wood." As a hermit he wishes to learn the occult qualities of stars and herbs, and eventually to "attain / To something like Prophetic strain."

Except for his reference to the choral service, there is no explicit reference to Christianity in the poem, and here the emphasis falls on the proverbial power of music to transport the soul and ravish it to heaven:

> As may with sweetness, through mine ear,
> Dissolve me into ecstasies,
> And bring all Heav'n before mine eyes.

As with "our high-rais'd fantasy" in "At a Solemn Music," the imagination of the pensive man is largely directed toward the realm of the spirit; the pleasures of fantasy are essentially those of the soul.

The contrasting inspirations of mirth and melancholy in these companion poems are roughly analogous to the contrasts Milton had drawn elsewhere—in his Sixth Elegy, his Ludlow Mask, *The Reason of Church-Government*—between different kinds of poetic song and their respective sources of inspiration. In each instance, however, the terms of the comparison vary significantly with the immediate context. On an empty stomach ("non pleno ventre") the poet sends his greetings to a friend replete ("ventre . . . distento") with Christmas feasting. "Song loves Bacchus and Bacchus loves songs." "Liber and Erato, Ceres and Venus" and Cupid patronize the elegy; but loftier themes demand that the poet live as sparingly and as soberly as Pythagoras (*CP* 50–53). The songs of Circe and the Sirens, declares Comus, lull the sense with "sweet madness" and in "pleasing slumber"; the song of the Lady, on the other hand, brings a sacred delight and "sober certainty of waking bliss."[48] In the treatise, Milton's brief allusions to diverse sources of poetic inspiration appear in an extended passage of ethical proof, in which he discusses at length his own poetic ambitions. He is endeavoring to counter the charge "that some self-pleasing humor of vainglory hath incited me to contest with men of high estimation" (*CP* 667); he makes his point by arguing that if he had been moved by vainglory, he would not have temporarily shelved these poetic enterprises to write in prose.

The persona of the inspired poet and seer fostered by both Spenser and Milton (and, much less effectively, by DuBartas) is a carefully contrived fiction. Although many critics recognize the significant difference between this fictive persona and the poet's actual or "real" personality, they sometimes overlook this difference—particularly since the writer himself often takes pains to blur this distinction. The visionary narrator is himself a consciously composed illusion and should not, of course, be mistaken for autobiographical "fact."

Part II

Poetic Structure and Moral Vision

Chapter 3

Determinate and Indeterminate Structures

Epic and Romance

The structures and allegorical modes of Spenser's romance-epic are interdependent and, as critics have recognized, cannot be effectively studied in isolation from each other or from the conventions of the Renaissance chivalric romance. Moral categories condition the choice and representation of the personae and the actions depicted, as well as the major quantitative divisions in the poem and (in varying degrees) the structures of the different books. Conversely, exigencies of characterization and narration affect the kind of allegorical references the poet can introduce at a given point in his fable and the manner in which he will present them: the relation between image or icon and idea. Moreover, similar qualities seem at times to characterize plot and allegorical method. Both vary from the indeterminate toward the distinct: the successions of "happenings" flow; the modes of representation shift and change. Multiplicity of incident is paralleled by multiple vision; the "fluidity" of the narrative by the shifting visionary and mimetic focus. Despite the logical framework of moral absolutes, this is in large part the "floating world" of the Buddhists or a Burmese shadow-play.

It is not surprising, accordingly, that interpretations of the poem's structure and allegory have been almost equally varied. The incompleteness of the one and the ambiguity of the other invite diversity of opinion.[1]

1.

Paradoxically, authors of the romances were subject to attack by Renaissance critics not only for basing their arguments on fiction rather than historical fact but also for following the order of the historian rather than the poet. Moreover, the controversy over unity of action involved not only the representation of multiple actions by many heroes, as in the romances of Boiardo and Ariosto, but also the delineation of several actions by a single hero, the kind of biographical epic condemned by Aristotle. Ovid's *Metamorphoses* was also brought into the controversy, inasmuch as it began with the origin of things and continued to the period of the Caesars; passing from one episode to another, it was united only by the underlying motifs of multiplicity and change: the theme of inconstancy.

Like Tasso after him, Minturno insisted on the immutability and universal validity of the classical principles of art, condemning the defenders of romance for attempting "to introduce a new poetic art into the world." And like Tasso, he based his arguments largely on Aristotle's comparison between Homer's narrative method and those of other epic poets. According to its apologists, the romance took "as its object a crowd of knights and ladies and of affairs of war and peace," singling out one knight in particular for glorification above the rest; the poet portrayed as many deeds by this hero and the others as he thought fit, "and he takes for description diverse and contrasted lands and the various things that happened in them during all the time occupied by the fabulous story of the matter he sets out to sing." Though Homer had included the exploits of other Greek heroes besides Achilles, he had nevertheless made all of these events spring from one beginning, and he had directed all of them to one end. Ariosto might have followed Homer's method, but chose not to. Not only did the romances "narrate things of many persons and many years" but also they constantly broke the course of the narration, according to "their own peculiar custom," interrupting a battle or tempest or some other event to relate "some other matter which happened to other persons in other places at the same time, as is the peculiar custom of the romancers without regard to what time demands or the desire of the reader." Furthermore, the romancers showed no regard for the truth, feigning what never was: "neither written history nor fame gives any testimony to the love or the madness of Orlando, yet Boiardo feigned that he was in love and Ariosto that he was mad."[2] If Ariosto had wanted to glorify Ruggiero as well as Orlando, he should have done so in a different poem. Moreover, however skillfully Ovid had managed to knit his diverse fables together, he did not merit the name of poet.

In challenging the so-called rules of Aristotle, Giraldi Cinthio had maintained that an epic poet might legitimately portray the entire life of his hero from beginning to end. If the biographies of great men can delight and instruct us when we read them in prose, they should be equally pleasant and profitable in poetry, when "written in verse in the guise of history as an example to mankind[.]" Suidas must have had such a poem in mind when he declared that epic was history, "for he does not hold it improper to set forth in verse, in the manner of history, the life of a man who fully deserves the name of hero." Ovid's success is a case in point. Emancipating himself from Aristotle's canons, the Roman poet had begun his *Metamorphoses* with the beginning of the world, but had managed to cover a great variety of events in fewer books than Homer.

In the romance, which represents "many and various actions of many and various men," the action begins with the "matter that is of greatest importance and on which all the rest appears to depend," as Ariosto and Boiardo had done. Though the former begins with Orlando and ends with Ruggiero, this is justifiable, for the poet was following the order of events.

The variety of actions in the romance enhances delight. Nevertheless, the digressions should be interconnected, "well joined with a continuous thread . . . to the parts of the subject" that the poet has undertaken to treat, and should carry probability, coordinating the various parts of his poem like the members of a body to produce a symmetrical and well-proportioned whole. For the romances use "another sort of connection than the heroic poetry of the Greeks and Latins." In the latter, the various books had been connected by a continuous narrative with regard to the matter. But the romancers have attempted to do more, "to put in one canto after another, before they come to the continuation of the matter, something to prepare the way for what they intend to say." This technique Giraldi ascribes to the method of the *cantastorie*. Moreover, because they are representing the actions of many persons, the romancers cannot "continue one matter, fully connected, from one canto to another." In order to "bring their work to any end," they must speak now of one character, then of another, "breaking off their first subject to enter upon the deeds of another character," continuing their materials in this manner to the end of the work. Before making the break they deliberately arouse suspense, leading "the reader to such a point before they make the break that they leave in the mind an ardent desire to return to take up the narrative again."[3]

In this context—the spatial and chronological framework, as well as the structure of the plot—Tasso's remarks on the indeterminate are of interest. Arguing in favor of unity of action instead of multiple plots, he maintains that multiplicity leads to the indeterminate and thus to a progression toward infinity. This additive process might continue indefinitely (he declares) unless there were some specific and prefixed end circumscribed by art. In contrast to the one, which is definite, the many participate in infinity. When a poet who has chosen a single action as his subject has brought the action itself to a conclusion, he has reached the logical terminus of his plot and of his poem. If he or anyone else endeavored to continue the work beyond this point, the process might continue indefinitely, for there would then be no "determinata certezza" (determinate certitude) as to where he ought to conclude. A poem depicting many actions is not one poem, but a multitude of poems joined together, "una confusione di molti poemi." Once the poem has reached its end, it is complete and perfect, and to add sequels continuing the action could only introduce imperfection. The reader would be confronted with a tome as massive and forbidding as a legal treatise.[4]

In discussing this point, Tasso did not examine the technique of interlacing plots, characteristic (as Giraldi observed) of the romances, but instead approached the problem of unity versus multiplicity of actions as though it involved a series of consecutive actions instead of parallel and interwoven plots. His strictures might, accordingly, be applicable to *successive* wars depicted by Boiardo and Ariosto—at Albracca, Paris, Biserta, and elsewhere—but not to the technique of *entrelacement* as these poets had employed it.

A work like *Amadis of Gaul* would have been more apposite to Tasso's argument, but (though he mentions it elsewhere in the *Discorsi*) he does not allude to it in this context. The example of DuBartas's *Sepmaine*, the precursor of Tasso's own hexaemeral epic *Il Mondo Creato*, would also have been relevant. The success of the *First Week* encouraged the author to expand the poem through an exhaustive survey of biblical and world history down to the Last Judgment: a task more appropriate (as his critics frequently observed) for the historian than the poet. Essentially, the work became a series of sequels to the original poem, which was already complete in itself. Because of DuBartas's death, the longer poem remained unfinished.

2.

Tasso's remarks on the indeterminate character of the poem representing a sequence of actions—and on its tendency toward an infinite progression, as contrasted with the clearly defined limits of the "well-constructed" plot centered on a single action—foreshadowed the kind of distinction that later aestheticians would make between neoclassical and Gothic approaches to spatial structure, or between "classical" and "romantic" modes. His own aesthetic principles were those which Renaissance humanists had associated with the ancients. Beauty consisted primarily in perfection of form and design, in the unity and coherence of the whole, and in the proportion and symmetry of its parts. Like most of his contemporaries, he also regarded color and variety as elements of the beautiful. Though he recognized the effectiveness of chiaroscuro, he showed no awareness of the aesthetic values of the indefinite and the indeterminate. His observations on the difficulties experienced by the reader in remembering the various events in the complicated romance plots were pertinent, but his objection to continuations of a poem beyond a single action—that the process could be extended indefinitely—was applicable less to the historical subject than to the fictive or imaginary argument. A poet—or series of poets—who endeavored to relate the entire history of the Trojan war, as the cyclic poets had done, must eventually reach an end with the death of Odysseus and Aeneas and other heroes of Troy. The same principle would also apply to the Theban cycle. The final result might be a monster sufficiently vast and misshapen to daunt any reader, but eventually there would be a final, and natural, limit to the actions.

Nevertheless, this is a minor point. More significant for the actual practice of the poet—for the selection and organization of his materials—were the Horatian principle of beginning the action in medias res and the Aristotelian principle of selecting for imitation one complete action with a definite beginning, middle, and end. Insofar as they were applicable to heroic poetry, they served to differentiate Homer's practice from that of the cyclic poets. Instead of beginning ab ovo with the birth of Helen and Clytemnestra from Leda's egg and covering the entire course of the Trojan war and the *nostoi* of the Greek expeditionary forces, Homer had isolated two particular events for epic elaboration: Achilles' wrath and Odysseus's homecoming. Each poem began late in the pattern of events: the tenth year of the siege of Troy, the tenth year of Odysseus's wanderings. Each possessed a definite beginning, which linked the hero's ends, motives, and destiny with the decrees of the gods. The *Iliad* began with the origin of Achilles' wrath, with Thetis's supplications to Zeus on her son's behalf, and with Zeus's oath to vindicate the hero's honor by turning the battle temporarily against the Greeks. The *Odyssey* in turn opened with Athene's intervention on behalf of the homesick hero and with Zeus's command to Calypso to speed Odysseus on his homeward voyage. In each case the "middle" of the poem was complicated by the intervention of hostile or friendly deities as well as by the designs of the human agents themselves. In the course of battle the Greeks were pushed back to their own ships; Patroclus's intervention in Achilles' armor helped to reverse the tide of battle and drive the Trojans back to their citadel; his death at Hector's hand diverted Achilles' wrath from the Atridae to the Trojan champion. Sailing from Ogygia, Odysseus was shipwrecked by Poseidon, cast ashore on the island of Phaeacia, rescued and returned safely home to Ithaca to regain the control of his household from the usurping suitors. Both epics concluded with the slaughter of the hero's enemies and with final reconciliation. Achilles' anger, unappeased by Hector's death, was ultimately pacified by Priam's submission. In the climactic reversal of a "well-constructed" fable, the suitors were ignominiously massacred, the palace ceremoniously purified, the hero reunited with his family, and the schemes of the local families to avenge the death of their relatives frustrated.

Virgil's epic fable similarly began in medias res: the first half was modeled partly on the *Odyssey,* the latter part on the *Iliad.* More important than the personal emotions and desires of the hero—in contrast to the wrath and nostalgia of the Homeric heroes—was Aeneas's submission to divine decree: to the destiny willed by Jove, supported by Venus, resisted by Juno, that impelled him successively onward through country after country to the shores of Latium. The action itself began comparatively late in his wanderings. As he was sailing from Sicily toward Italy, the promised land, a tempest instigated by Juno drove him off course to the coast of Africa. Like his Homeric counterpart, the stranded hero is aided by a woman—though the majestic and tragic queen who breaks her widow's vows for love of the stranger stands in striking contrast to the Phaeacian princess preoccupied with laundering and ball games and thoughts of marriage. The hero's wanderings in search of a continuing city have brought him from the extreme east of the Mediterranean world to the site of Rome's principal rival for control of the western Mediterranean.

From Carthage the Trojans sail successfully to Latium by way of Sicily, concluding an alliance with the aged king Latinus. With the hardships and trials by sea now safely concluded, the tribulations on land commence, as the implacable Juno fills the Latian queen and the Rutulian king Turnus with insane fury against the strangers. (Though described as a second Achilles and closely modeled on this hero, Turnus performs exploits reminiscent of Hector at the enemy camp and ultimately shares the latter's fate; Aeneas avenges the death of Pallas as Achilles had avenged Patroclus.) After the consummation of alliances on both sides and a series of reversals in battle, the epic concludes with the Trojan victory and the death of the Latian queen and the Rutulian king, the only remaining obstacles to the marriage between Aeneas and Lavinia and to the perpetual and indissoluble union of both peoples.

Closely modeled on the *Iliad,* Tasso's epic began at the end of the sixth year of the invasion of Palestine. God himself sets the action in motion, commanding Godfrey to renew the attack on Jerusalem, but this enterprise is obstructed by the powers of hell and their agents the sorcerers Ismeno and Armida, and by the divisions among Godfrey's own followers. Like Achilles, the youthful hero Rinaldo (whom the poet's allegory associates with the "irascible" part of the soul),[5] enraged by a fancied insult from his commander, forsakes the Crusader camp. Tancredi's effectiveness as a warrior has been undermined by his love affair. The Saracen enchantress Armida leads many of the crusaders into captivity and detains Rinaldo himself in voluntary bondage within her bower of bliss. Attempts to construct siege towers and other equipment for the assault on the city are frustrated by demons, who have infested the bewitched wood. Of the various crusaders who endeavor to break the spell, only Rinaldo succeeds. The conquest is further delayed, however, by the valor of the Saracen champions themselves—Argante, Soliman, and the woman-warrior Clorinda—and by Armida's schemes. (Clorinda herself belongs to a long line of *donne guerriere:* Hippolyta in the Theseus legend, Penthesilea in the Trojan cycle, Virgil's Camilla, Ariosto's Bradamante and Marphisa. Argante, in turn, is reminiscent both of Virgil's Turnus and of Ariosto's Rodomonte.) The epic concludes with the death of the Saracen champions and the conquest of the holy city.

Neither Boiardo nor Ariosto began his poem ab ovo. Each centered his romance on a fiction of his own invention; neither attempted to rework earlier or later episodes in Orlando's life, such as his youthful exploits at the battle of Aspromonte, his ultimate betrayal by Ganelon, and his death at Roncevaux. The *Innamorato* opened with the arrival of Angelica and her brother Argalia from Cathay, the latter's challenge to the knights of Charlemagne's entourage, and the rivalry of Christian and pagan alike for Angelica's favors. Subsequently, the action embraced the siege of Albracca by King Agricane of Tartary, the love between the female warrior Bradamante and the pagan knight Ruggiero, and the invasion by Agramante, king of Africa, in alliance with Marsilio, king of Spain. Boiardo may have intended to continue the action through the capture of Biserta by Orlando, but left the romance incomplete. In the final cantos, Rinaldo and Orlando were still rivals for the possession of Angelica. Charlemagne had intervened, reserving the princess as a prize for valor in the next engagement with the Saracens, but in this encounter the Carolinian forces had been defeated, and Angelica herself had fled. Meanwhile the English knight Astolfo had been lured out to sea by the enchantress Alcina.

Ariosto resumed the narrative at this point. Promising to sing of loves and wars, the epic proposition singled out three principal subjects for emphasis: Agramante's expedition from Africa to avenge the death of his father Troiano; Orlando's madness—an argument never attempted in prose or rhyme—and the exploits of Ruggiero, founder of the House of Este. A brief *narratio* brings

Orlando back from the Orient with Angelica to Charlemagne's camp near the Pyrenees, where the king has marshaled the Christian knights of France and Germany against the combined armies of Agramante and Marsilio. Upon the defeat of the Carolinian forces, Angelica makes her escape. The action of the poem begins in the forest where she has taken refuge from her unwelcome suitors; while two of them—Rinaldo and the pagan Ferrau—are dueling for her possession, she continues her flight. In the course of the complicated action, she falls into captivity, is rescued from a sea monster by Ruggiero, makes her escape from that hero, and eventually falls in love with a private soldier in the Saracen army and elopes with him to Cathay. After their unsuccessful siege of Paris the Saracen forces are repulsed, Biserta besieged and captured, and Agramante finally slain. Maddened by the discovery of Angelica's infidelity, Orlando remains a raving lunatic until Astolfo retrieves his lost wits from the moon and restores him to sanity; thereupon he joins the Carolinian forces in capturing Biserta. Held captive first by the enchanter Atlante, afterwards by Alcina, and again by Atlante, Ruggiero is rescued successively by Bradamante, by the benevolent sorceress Melissa, and by Astolfo. After further separations from Bradamante, Ruggiero is eventually reunited with her; the poem concludes with their marriage.

3.

"For the Methode of a Poet historical is not such as of an Historiographer," Spenser declared. "For an Historiographer discourseth of affayres orderly as they were donne, accounting as well the times as the actions, but a Poet thrusteth into the middest, even where it most concerneth him, and there recoursing to the thinges forepaste, and divining of thinges to come, maketh a pleasing Analysis of all" (*PW* 407–8). Although this distinction between natural and artificial order and the methods of historian and poet was a commonplace in critical theory, there are certain similarities in Spenser's treatment of this Horatian topos. The most significant of these was the relegation of the beginning of the action to the very *end* of the poem; this feature, unusual in both epic and romance, would give a circular or cyclical structure to his narrative. In the epics of Virgil and Camoëns—and in the *Odyssey* and *Paradise Lost*—the more extended retrospective episodes are introduced much earlier, often through the device of an after-dinner conversation. In Homeric epic the conventions of archaic hospitality required that a stranger be tactfully left in peace—not pressed to reveal his identity and his background until he had been properly entertained and fed. Thus Odysseus recounts the story of his wanderings to his Phaeacian host shortly after his arrival at the royal palace—after his departure from Ogygia and before his return to Ithaca. In the *Aeneid* these *antecedentia* (as Broadbent has termed them)[6] occur still earlier, in the second and third books of the poem, soon after the hero's reception by the Carthaginian queen. In *Paradise Lost* they occupy the central books in the narrative. In *The Lusiads*, on his outward voyage to India, da Gama recites the past glories of Portugal to a friendly African king.

Predictions of the future are sometimes less extensive, and occur in a variety of contexts. Tiresias's prophecies concerning the future of Odysseus are repeated by the hero himself in his account of his past adventures. Aeneas beholds the shades of his posterity during his visit to the underworld in the sixth book of Virgil's epic. The analogous prophecies concerning Adam's descendants are deferred until the final books of Milton's epic. In addition, further allusions to past or future events (the origin of Odysseus's scar, references to earlier or later generations of heroes, to Aeneas's genealogy or his future death, to the past or future greatness of a nation) are often interspersed throughout the narrative. Dante makes extensive use of both prospective and retrospective allusion through the poet's guides and especially through the shades with whom he converses. In the chivalric romances one encounters frequent allusions to past or future actions: the earlier exploits of Carolinian or Arthurian heroes, the future discovery of the New World, the invention of the cannon. In the dynastic epic or romance particularly, prospective episodes and allusions extolling the deeds of a sovereign or patron and those of his ancestors were common. Ariosto and Tasso had glorified the House of Este through prophecies or visions. Spenser uses the same techniques, as well as the device of the chronicle history, to eulogize Elizabeth's forebears.

Moreover, the personae in his epic often relate their own genealogies and adventures. Paridell recounts the history of the Trojans. Una informs Arthur about the beginning of her quest with the Redcross Knight. Arthur tells of his vision of the Faerie Queene. Fradubio and Amavia describe their disastrous encounters with the sorceresses Duessa and Acrasia. These uses of *antecedentia* and *consequentia* are conventional—though it is interesting that Spenser should refer to the "Analysis" and fragmentation of the story rather than to the synthesis and reintegration of his materials.[7] The real innovation consists in his post-ponement of the "beginning" of the story ("my history") until the final book.

This "history" is, of course, a narrative fable, not an authentic history or even a historical fiction; the term was equivocal (and still remains so in most

European tongues), and it retains this ambiguity in Spenser's own discussion. Concerned with arrangement rather than content, he does not distinguish between the narrative based on fact and the story based on fiction. He is not, in fact, a "poet historicall" in the sense in which Guicciardini, Machiavelli, and Thucydides were historiographers. Nor indeed is he a "historicall" poet in the same sense that Tasso and Camoëns were or that Homer and Virgil were believed to be. In this respect his affinities are with Ariosto and Boiardo; both of these poets had based their arguments not on true history or even on legend but on new inventions, the fictions of their own imaginations.

In a context of pure (or virtually pure) fiction, the beginning in "the middest" of things carried a somewhat different meaning from its significance in history or historical legend. Horace had used this term in relation to the material concerning the Trojan war; later critics had correlated his views with Aristotle's discussion of Homer's epics in comparison with those of the cyclic poets. The material to which Horace refers was to a considerable extent already familiar to the audience. They could be expected to know much about the legends associated with the Theban and Trojan wars, celebrated by epic and tragic poets and subsequently known as the "Trojan Cycle," the "Theban Cycle," or more comprehensively as the *cyclos historicos*.[8] Horace declares that Homer does not begin "The Return of Diomed" with the death of the hero's uncle Meleager—an event that led indirectly to his grandfather's remarriage and thus to the birth of Diomedes' father Tydeus—nor does he commence his account of the Trojan war with Leda's egg, which had hatched out the casus belli Helen of Troy. Instead he "hurries to the crisis and carries the listener into the midst of the story as though it were already known."[9]

4.

A characteristic feature of the controversy over the romance was the attempt by the partisans of the ancients not only to subject it to the "rules" of Aristotle but also to apply to this genre virtually the same critical objections that the latter had directed against the "biographical" and the cyclic or episodic poem. The epic ought to resemble the drama in the construction of its plot—"based on a single action, one that is a complete whole in itself, with a beginning, middle, and end, . . . with all the organic unity of a living creature *[zoion hen holon]*."[10] Epics should not be made like histories *(historiais)*, "in which an account is necessarily given, not of a single action but of a single period of time, i.e. all the events that happened during that time involving a single man or a number of men: each of which events has a merely accidental relation to the rest." Homer's superiority to other poets is evident in the fact that "he did not attempt to compose the War 'whole' either, although it had a beginning and an end." Instead he "picked out one portion of the story and used many of the others as episodes, with which he intersperses his composition." Other poets, on the contrary, composed their work "around one man or one period of time, i.e. one action containing many parts."[11]

In commenting on these passages, Else emphasized Aristotle's contrast between the poet and the historian in their treatments of time: "The poet imitates, or should imitate, a single *action;* the historian makes a report of a single time." Universals themselves are timeless, "and so far as the poet deals with them and not with particulars he is presenting us with events which are not in time, at least in the usual sense." The contrast between "single action" and "single time" is essentially "a contrast between the 'necessary,' the *logical* bond that unites the parts of a true *praxis,* and the arbitrary, merely *chronological* bond that unites actual events." "Concretely, the eschewing of time as a principle of composition must mean that the poet has a sovereign freedom to *put events in the order he feels to be 'necessary,'* regardless of when they happened in history or might happen in real life. In other words the poet is free to play fast and loose with chronology."

The thing for which Aristotle is praising Homer "is not that his *poem* holds to the norm of length, but that its *'story'* or plot does so; and not that a multiplicity of details is excluded, but that they are set apart from the main story as 'episodes.' " By his "invention of the central plot," separating the *mythos* itself from the episodes, Homer achieved "unity-in-diversity and limitation-within-freedom. . . . The main action can be unified . . . ; the poem remains free to cultivate diversity and almost unlimited length. Moreover, this duplex scheme brings the needful epic variety into full play for the first time, for the central action provides a background against which we can properly measure and enjoy the diversity of the episodes . . . Homeric art, like the true art of tragedy, is un- and anti-chronological." It deals with "universals, not with events in time as such."[12]

The kind of retrospective episode characteristic of the *Odyssey* and the *Aeneid* is often associated in practice with the beginning in medias res, but this is not what Horace himself was alluding to, nor is it essential to the latter. The *Iliad* begins in the midst of things, though it lacks any extended *antecedentia,* inasmuch as it opens with the quarrel with Agamemnon and the origin of Achilles' wrath against the Greeks rather than with the origins of the war itself, or with the beginning of the siege, or even with the hero's earlier exploits. The *Aeneid* similarly begins in medias res, not merely because Virgil chose to present the fall of Troy and Aeneas's earlier wanderings through the hero's retrospective discourse but also because he passed over Aeneas's earlier deeds at Troy and the history of the Trojan people. His concern is with the future, with the origins and destinies of the Roman people, not with the past.

5.

Behind the poems of Boiardo and Ariosto—as behind the figure of Spenser's Arthur—there existed a comprehensive body of legend and fiction concerning the paladins of Charlemagne's court and the last kings of Celtic Britain before the Germanic conquests, but none of these poets chose to rework this material. Instead, all three began anew with fresh materials of their own devising. Neither Boiardo nor Ariosto commenced his poem ab ovo, but rather began at the point "where it most concern[ed] him": Boiardo with the origin of Orlando's passion for Angelica; Ariosto where his predecessor had left off. *The Faerie Queene* begins in medias res not simply because its author chose to defer the account of the beginning of each quest until the final book, or because he postponed the commencement of Arthur's quest for Gloriana for a "recoursing to . . . thinges forepaste." To have introduced these would not have significantly altered the action or affected its unity or disunity, though it would have modified the structural design. There were very good reasons for deferring the scene at Gloriana's court until the last book, which would knit up the various threads of the narrative; but to have introduced it at the commencement of the romance would not have meant beginning ab ovo.

In the case of Arthur, as in that of Orlando and the heroes of Thebes and Troy, there was an extensive background of legend "already known" to the reader, but Spenser preferred to allude to his hero's *enfances* only obliquely and retrospectively. The quests, on the other hand, were the poet's own fictions; his readers could not know their origin, and he must explain this to them through the letter to Raleigh as authorial apology and prologue. It is the immediate beginning, not a more remote background, that he has temporarily suppressed; in a significant degree he has blurred the critical distinctions between the beginning and middle of the plot itself (or of the particular action the poet has chosen to imitate) and the larger chronological schemas that both Horace and Aristotle had regarded as inartistic.[13]

The "abrupte" commencement of Spenser's romance—which in his own opinion makes it necessary "to know the occasion of these three knights severall adventures"—may be partly due to the example set by Ariosto. As Tasso had observed, the *Orlando Furioso* wanted a beginning just as the *Orlando Innamorato* lacked an end. The actual beginnings of the actions that Ariosto was describing—the invasion by Agramante and Marsilio, the rivalry of Orlando and Rinaldo and countless other knights and nobles for Angelica, the love of Bradamante and Ruggiero—had been portrayed by Boiardo. Taken alone—as most of its readers approached it, in detachment from Boiardo's epic—the *Furioso* would seem to begin even more abruptly than *The Faerie Queene*. Spenser supplied a beginning for his own poem, but elected to postpone it until the final book.[14]

6.

Since the contrast between the poet and the historian in their treatment of chronological order was traditional, one should not overstress Spenser's allusion to the "pleasing Analysis" of the natural or historical sequence of events. Nevertheless, it is relevant not only to the license that poets usually enjoyed in their treatment of chronology but also to Spenser's own fragmentation of time. He does not merely disintegrate it; he dissolves it, reducing time and space alike to indefinite extension, an indeterminate continuum.

The heroic ages, as later poets conceived them, belonged to eras and societies so remote that they virtually existed outside time. Oral tradition in turn—though generally misunderstood by more literate societies—tended to blur chronological distinctions, aside from other distortions of history. Legendary heroes belonging to entirely different centuries might engage in the same battles. Even apart from the exceptional precocity of Hercules and Krishna, Cuchulain and his son Connla, the exploits of the heroes of epic and romance were such as to astound the pediatrician or the gerontologist. Achilles' son could have been little more than a ten-year-old when he engaged in the sack of Troy. Amadis of Gaul continued his feats of valor long after his son had become a romance-hero in his own right. A poet as sophisticated as Virgil, writing for an educated audience, felt no compunction about making Dido and Aeneas contemporaries. Tasso in turn insisted on the poet's license to alter and rearrange the chronological sequence of historical events to achieve a more coherent plot.

For many critics the principal justification for this restructuring of chronology was the plot itself: the inner tensions developed and resolved through a skillful syntaxis of incidents with a clearly defined beginning, middle, and end. In many of the romances, with their multiple plots and interwoven actions, tensions were created less by the structure of the poem as a whole than (as

Giraldi observed) by breaking off one story at a moment of suspense, leaving the outcome in doubt, taking up another thread of the narrative, and concluding the canto with the action itself still inconclusive and its outcome uncertain. Normally, like a weaver embroidering a tapestry, the poet observed the natural chronological order, synchronizing the different stories in his plot, bringing their different characters together at strategic points in the narrative—a battle, an enchanted castle, and the like—and separating them again. Though he might introduce prophesies at certain points, or retrospective allusions, he rarely included an extended retrospective episode as the epic poets had done. In this respect Spenser's scheme for book 12 was more of a concession to epic tradition than a reflection of romance conventions. The fluid and shifting character of the "world" of the romances, its indeterminate and irresolute qualities, its unpredictability and uncertainty, and its doubtful character were inherent in the technique of this genre and its narrative mode as Boiardo and Ariosto had developed it. The conventions of the species itself encouraged the kind of values, the modes of vision, that Ariosto and Spenser in very diverse ways extracted from or imposed upon it.

One doubts that, even if he had read Aristotle's *Poetics,* Spenser would have linked Aristotle's remarks on chronology with his discussion of the poet's concern with universals, as Else has done. Nevertheless, he was aware (as Sidney had been) of the contrasts between the poet and the historian in their respective concerns with the universal and the particular and with artificial and natural order and method. The indeterminate time-scheme of *The Faerie Queene,* along with its uncertain position in time and space and its variable relationships to contemporary England and to British, classical, and biblical antiquity, is an appropriate vehicle and symbol for the realm of universals, transcending as they do both space and time.[15]

7.

The structural problems presented by the poems of Boiardo and Ariosto, and of Spenser, are not entirely attributable to the method of romance. They are to some extent characteristic of any poem conceived on so vast a scale that the poet cannot bring it to completion, or else alters and revises his designs in the course of composition. In the former case, the reader is confronted with the fragments of a palace—the apse of a royal chapel, a banquet hall, and perhaps a few chambers of state—and must reconstruct the complete design of the structure in his own mind. In the latter case, he is confronted with a building laid out according to one set of blueprints but erected according to others in accordance with the afterthoughts of the architect himself and the tastes and budget of his patron. In still other instances, the poet may not have had a clearly defined pattern in his mind to begin with, but instead merely a clear idea of the next episode or two and a general but tentative conception of the rest. Such a poem would evolve progressively, like the episodes in a soap opera or a film sequence of *The Perils of Pauline,* as new situations suggested new characters and narrative lines and in accordance with the interest shown by the audience. The publication of a part of the incomplete work, moreover, could to some degree tie the poet's hands: he would be less free to restructure the work; the later episodes must be made consistent with what had gone before. This consideration did not deter Spenser, however, from altering the ending of the third book in the second edition of *The Faerie Queene,* thus separating Scudamour once again from Amoretta in order to reunite them in the following book. (Whether they are indeed reunited in book 4, canto 9 remains, however, debatable.) Ariosto later reworked the earlier published versions of his *Orlando,* and Tasso his *Jerusalem Delivered.* In the latter instance, however, the circumstances were largely beyond the author's control, and he himself was hypersensitive to both literary and ecclesiastical criticism.

The hybrid poem—left incomplete by one poet and finished by another—presented further difficulties, confronting the reader as well as the second poet with possible discontinuities not only in plot and character but also in structure, tone, and style. It is hardly surprising that the results should sometimes appear no less marvelous and scarcely less fantastic than the hippogriff.[16]

Not only was Spenser's romance incomplete but also (as several critics have noted) his original conception had apparently undergone significant revisions. As his correspondence with Harvey indicates, he had already completed portions of *The Faerie Queene* by early 1580 (*PW* 612, 618), enough for his Cambridge friend to complain of "*Hobgoblin* runne away with the Garland from *Apollo*" and of its inferiority to Ariosto's *Orlando,* "which notwithstanding, you will needes seeme to emulate, and hope to overgo." Between this time and the letter to Raleigh nearly a decade later, Spenser had ample opportunity to alter his plans. He had read Tasso's epic, assimilating Armida's paradise to that of Ariosto's Alcina as prototypes for Acrasia's bower of bliss. In the meantime, political events on the Continent and in England, and changing conditions at court, could have promoted alterations in earlier plans for historical and personal allegory. (If Arthur indeed shadows Leicester, it had been evident, long before the Earl's remarriage and death, that he would never win the hand of the Faerie Queene, however great the ills he may have suffered, his "undeserved wrong," and his merit. These could earn glory and perhaps royal favor, but that was all. In Raleigh's case, it was judicious to separate the Queen's person from her office.) In the eyes of several critics, moreover, the looser structure of the central books (3 and 4), their more frequent use of the technique of *entrelacement,* their greater exploitation of mimetic modes in proportion to moral allegory, and their more demonstrable indebtedness to Ariosto suggest that much of the poetry in these books represents a reworking of materials composed much earlier. Despite passing allusions to "That noble order hight of Maidenhed" (1.7.46; 3.8.47; 4.4.22, 38, 48), its relation to the narrative action, its nature and composition, its code and its affinities with the Order of the Garter remain elusive. The beginning of book 2, of course, is inconsistent with the schema outlined in the letter to Raleigh.

Critics have also found Spenser's references to the contents of the twelfth book perplexing. According to the letter, it would contain an account of the institution of the twelve quests undertaken during the successive days of the queen's annual feasts. This could be plausibly introduced in the context of the final quest represented by the patron of the twelfth moral virtue, but it would surely include the successful termination of Prince Arthur's quest for the Faerie Queene, and—as a final symbolic triumph of the virtues over the vices— one might expect the twelve champions themselves to make an appearance and receive their due meed of glory in this Elizabethan Elysium.

One cannot know, of course, either when the poet evolved the scheme set forth in his letter or how much he might have altered it afterwards. Between 1590 and 1596 he had revised the ending of book 3, but since much of the material in this and the following book had apparently been restructured, this may have been a special case. There is no real indication that he seriously considered the plan for an epic centered on King Arthur and the political virtues.

Chapter 4

Dissolution and Restructuring

Space and Time in The Faerie Queene

For the greater part of his poem, Spenser follows the chronological order of the historian and the romancer; but I shall consider this subject later in relation to the structure of his epic. For the moment, let us return to the poem's relation to history. Since its argument is based on fiction rather than historical fact or legend, and since its treatment of Arthurian materials is fairly restricted, it bears a different relationship to history than did such "poets historicall" as Homer, Virgil, and Tasso. Moreover, while the views of Horace and Aristotle on Homer's treatment of the history of the war at Troy are significant for *Jerusalem Delivered* and *Paradise Lost,* they are much less so for *The Faerie Queene.* Renaissance critics themselves frequently approached this subject from a variety of angles, assimilating Aristotelian to Horatian concepts. First, unlike the historian, the poet was an imitator and a "maker." If an author attempted to convert Herodotus's histories into verse, Aristotle had declared, the result would still be history, not poetry.[1] Similar objections were raised against Lucan's *Pharsalia* and DuBartas's *Sepmaine.* In urging the epic poet to select a historical subject and then rework and embellish it with his own fictions, Tasso had cautioned against scriptural histories of the highest authority as these would not allow sufficient license to feign and invent.

1.

Intimately associated with the poet's status as imitator were the requirements of the "well-constructed plot" as Aristotle and later critics had conceived it. The structural principles of the dramatic plot, outlined in the *Poetics,* were also normative for epic poetry; Aristotle had praised Homer (as Else observed) for anticipating and observing the principle of unity of action.[2] To achieve a coherent and organic plot, with beginning and middle and end, with *desis* and *lusis* (complication and denouement) and change of fortune, and (in the case of the complex fable) with *peripeteia* (reversal) and recognition, and to connect the various incidents in this principal action logically by verisimilitude and probability, the poet must usually reorganize and modify his historical materials through his own inventions.

The Renaissance moral interpretation of history, which tended to be a repository of ethical and political exempla; the frequent tendency to idealize antiquity; and the preoccupation with the pattern hero as epic protagonist also encouraged the poet to depart from historical fact to fashion a more exemplary hero and a more perfect image of the moral, political, or theological virtues. This had been the conventional method of demonstrative rhetoric, with its sharp division between topoi of praise and blame; it was heightened by the conditions of Renaissance patronage, the glorification of a man's ancestry and of the past history of his family or city or nation. It could be easily assimilated into the context of Aristotle's contrast between the poet and the historian (the one concerned with the universal, the other with the particular), with his statement that Homer had depicted persons "better than we are" (that is, men of the present day), and with Horace's praise of the *Odyssey* for portraying the idea of wisdom in Ulysses.[3] If one is to portray the idea of magnanimity or fortitude or statesmanship in a historical individual, one must omit or minimize his errors (unless they are of exemplary value, representing the temptations of sensuality or wrath).

Finally, in the interests of novelty and variety, for the sake of the marvelous or some allegorical episode, the poet might depart from historical truth. In the case of historical allegory in particular, he might (as in Virgil's case) consciously model his epic hero or other personae on men of his own generation.

With few exceptions, the critics were far more concerned with apparent violations of verisimilitude and probability than of historical fact. Many agreed that the poet ought indeed to depart from truth for the sake of a more convincing appearance of truth; those who preferred a fictive to a historical argument sometimes maintained that the poem should resemble history.[4]

The indeterminate time of Spenser's poem finds its natural correlative in indeterminate space. The lack of a controlling geographical schema, the absence of frontiers and boundaries, the changing and shifting locales, the paths of the various figures crisscrossing seemingly at random in a landscape as fluid as the plot—these stand in significant contrast to the more controlled movement over much vaster areas in the epics of Dante and Milton. Yet the very indefiniteness of Spenser's Faeryland—apparently without fixed coordinates in time or space—enhances the clarity and distinctness of his moral categories, underlining their essentially eidetic character and status as universals.

This imaginary land, set apart from the real world but nonetheless shadowing it and visited anachronistically by ancient Britons and medieval Saracens, possesses obvious affinities with the various worlds of epic and romance but also differs significantly from them. As legends or fables of heroic ages, many of these poems, both epics and romances, are already distanced from the reader by their chronological settings—in preclassical antiquity or in the early Middle Ages. Yet in many instances the sites and locations of the half-fabulous events described were real places, or believed to be such by the poet's audience. The Theban cycle concerned real localities, as did the cycle of Troy. Although Homer and his audience may not have known the site of Pylos or other cities of Mycenaean Greece, or the site of Troy, these were believed to have existed, and travelers of later generations visited the alleged site of the Trojan war.

In the *Aeneid,* geography itself provided a frame of reference and a schema of organization. This was an altogether different kind of ecumenical schema from that of the *Iliad,* where Hellenes from virtually all parts of the eastern Mediterranean were marshaled against barbarian forces from diverse parts of Asia Minor, from Thrace, and (if one should include the cyclic poets) from Ethiopia and the land of the Amazons as well. In Virgil's epic the geographical frame was the *oikoumene* of the future Roman empire. The scenes of the hero's wanderings and sufferings, his searches for a place of settlement, his abortive efforts to found a city, would eventually become the scenes of Roman triumphs. Without realizing this significance, he was exploring the future dominions of his own posterity. At Carthage and at the cave of the Cumaean Sibyl, and on his journey up the river Tiber to the future site of Rome, he was visiting places not only familiar to his readers but intimately associated with the history of their own nation and empire.

Though the spatial schema of *Paradise Lost* is of cosmic dimension—the scene of action narrowing to the earthly paradise—geographical panorama provides the frame of reference for the visions and prophecies that conclude the poem.[5] As in the *Aeneid,* it is a schema that involves both empire and exile, but the values are in a sense reversed. The future empires belong to Adam's adversary, the prince of this world; the geographical frame of reference is the fallen world of his own banishment.

The Lusiads offers yet another variant of the geographical schema. Insofar as it depicts a voyage of exploration, it is presenting regions of land and sea largely unknown to the epic hero, or known only by hearsay. Nevertheless, partly through his own endeavors, they were by now thoroughly familiar to the poet and his audience. However remote these lands and exotic their customs, they were now no longer terra incognita and Camoëns was thus able to combine the strange and marvelous with historical and geographical fact. As in the case of the *Aeneid,* the geographical frame of the epic action is imperial cartography; the chart of the hero's voyages is virtually a map of a future empire.

In Tasso's epic, geography itself is sacralized. The epic action centers on the reconquest of sacred territory: the holy land itself and the holy sepulcher. Like the enchanted forest possessed by demons, holy precincts have been seized by the profane; the attempt to deliver them is resolutely opposed by the powers of hell. In the context of this spiritual war between divine and infernal powers, the land of Palestine itself and the surrounding territories of the Saracens possess something of the typological significance that they had held in medieval exegesis. The Saracen rulers have been assimilated (unfairly) to the Oriental despots of the Old Testament: Pharaoh and the tyrants of Babylon. Even without the poet's allegorical commentary, Middle Eastern geography has been significantly spiritualized if not moralized.

Through the raiding and trading expeditions of the Vikings and their service in the Byzantine imperial guard, motifs from the Near and Middle East had been absorbed by the Norse sagas; medieval romance ranged from Byzantium southward and eastward to Africa and Persia and Cathay. Similarly, in the romance-epics of Boiardo and Ariosto the action moves, with all imaginative license, over three continents and even, in one instance, to the New World. In contrast to the almost worldwide scope of some of these Renaissance epics and romances, Spenser's actions are localized, however indistinctly, in a single imaginary realm.

2.

Against a background of real or legendary localities, the epic poet, like the romancer, introduced the mythical and the fabulous: the marvels of the seaman's yarn, the traveler's hyperboles, the old wives' tale, and whatever *mirabilia* he may have encountered in his reading or dreamed up himself. In a poem often condemned for clinging too closely to history, Lucan exhausted the material of the bestiaries by cataloging the various kinds of serpents encountered by the

Roman soldiers in their march through North Africa. Camoëns concluded his epic of da Gama's voyage by bringing the mariners to an imaginary isle where they reap the delights of the flesh, allegorized as the fruition of fame. Tasso places Armida's imaginary palace on a mountaintop in the Canary Islands, transporting the crusaders there and back in the imaginary bark of Fortune. Boiardo and Ariosto can move freely from real cities and countries to the gardens of fays and the palaces of sorcerers, or introduce the magical and supernatural into actual places: the Pyrenees or the forest of Ardennes.

In contrast to the vague or virtually nonexistent geography of Spenser's faeryland, its topographies are often clearly visualized; in this respect he is indebted to Ovid and Chaucer as well as to Homer and Virgil. In classical and Renaissance heroic poetry, however extensive or comprehensive the background of the action may be, the central events are usually localized, more or less clearly, in time and place. A battle demands a battlefield. Even though the encounter may be largely legendary or entirely fictional—and, if historical, transformed by the poet's inventions—there must be some sort of topographical organization to make the movements of the armies intelligible. However general and imprecise this may be, it must somehow convey the relative positions of the opposing forces and their tactical or strategic objectives so that the audience may visualize the scene. Encampments, hills and streams and other terrain features, the walls and gates of a besieged city—these not only enhance the illusion of reality, conferring verisimilitude on legendary exploits, but also provide a frame of reference for the action. Although the topographical features of the *Iliad* may be largely fictional rather than traditional (scholars are still debating this point), there are nevertheless fixed points of reference: the city itself, standing at some distance from the sea, the defensive works protecting the beached ships of the invaders, and the plain between. It is as essential that the audience be aware of these as that spectators at a stadium know where the goalposts are.

Whether or not the battles were historic or fictional, and whether there was much or little uncertainty as to precisely where they had occurred, the poet possessed considerable freedom in inventing his topography. The essential point was to achieve an appearance of truth without contradicting whatever local knowledge his audience already possessed. A Roman or Alexandrian poet, for instance, could enjoy greater license in describing the site of Marathon than an Athenian; conversely, a Boeotian might feel less free than an Italian writer in depicting the environs of Thebes. In describing the future site of Rome, the hills and river intimately familiar to his readers, as well as other well-known places in Italy, Virgil usually adheres more closely to the facts than in depicting other sites in the Mediterranean world. In his hands, however, this restriction becomes a literary asset. The places themselves, the familiar sites, served to link the legendary past with the present, validating the half-mythical events by associating them with the known world. Indeed Aeneas himself would have meant far less to the average reader than the equally legendary Romulus or Numa Pompilius or the historic Junius Brutus; on the other hand, many of the sites that the half-fabulous Aeneas beholds were not only an integral part of the Roman heritage but part of the reader's everyday experience.

In much the same way the body of classical myth had, in a sense, created a symbolic landscape, through the association of particular sites and localities with specific divinities and legends. Just as the pagan gods themselves acquired a different ontological status, a different kind of reality, once they had lost their claim to belief and veneration, the real localities with which they had been associated tended to become less, yet more, than geographical sites—they became symbols. Mount Olympus and Mount Ida, Paphos and Cythera, Parnassus and Helicon could never have precisely the same meaning for a native of Rome or London or Paris or even Alexandria that they originally had held for a native Greek; the fact that they were indeed real places was largely irrelevant to the use that poets made of them. Few poets have literally climbed Parnassus or tasted the Castalian spring, though many have done so metaphorically. If language is in large part decayed metaphor, the continued metaphors of the poet are in a sense decayed myth: stories of gods who have lost their divinity but survive nevertheless as symbols, as material for narrative fables, and as poetic ornament. Distanced from the "real" world both by a changed structure of belief and by the loss of their original geographical and social contexts, they nevertheless survive as an imaginary world linked to the real one through natural and moral and (to an extent) historical allegory. In this respect they constitute a fictive cosmos, more or less detached from real space and time and in a significant degree analogous to Spenser's land of faerie. If the latter bears a demonstrable resemblance to the "*Orlando* moralized" of Ariosto's sixteenth-century commentators, it also has pronounced affinities with the "moralized" *Metamorphoses* in its construction of a fictional and symbolic world in continuous flux, where the only real constants are moral absolutes.

3.

The "worlds" of classical epic (and, in different degrees, those of Renaissance epic and romance) were in a sense distanced from the real world not only by their mimetic and fictive character—the fact that they were poetic constructions and imitations, not real history or geography or chronology— but also by their material: the exploits of heroic ages. Many of the heroes of preclassical antiquity were themselves demigods or traced their lineage to divinities. They conversed freely with immortals, battled with them, or had love affairs with them. They were set apart from the life and society of the poet's contemporaries not only by their legendary character and their antiquity but also principally by their heroic stature. Some of them were the objects of worship, with their *heroa* or sepulchral shrines; others had been apotheosized and revered as divinities. The gods, on the other hand, were similarly set apart first by their very divinity and later (as the myths themselves were reinterpreted and rationalized) as symbols: metaphors for powers and ideas that were both immanent in the real world and transcendent. In spite of the commonplace that Homer had portrayed his gods like men and his men like gods, there remained one essential distinction between them. However superior to ordinary men, however godlike his achievements, the hero (for all his semidivinity) was subject to death; conversely, however eccentric their morals, however undiscriminating their amours and implacable their vendettas, the gods themselves enjoyed eternal life, a privilege they vouchsafed to few mortals, and then as a rule only after long trials and sufferings.

The heroes of chivalric epic and romance likewise belonged to a remote and essentially legendary antiquity. They exceeded ordinary men in strength and stature and valor; in *The Dream of Rhonabwy,* Arthur remarked scornfully on the diminutive stature of the narrator. They were aided or opposed by enchanters, befriended or harassed by fays, fought by ogres and monsters. In the late Middle Ages the knights of the Arthurian and Carolinian cycles already belonged to heroic ages; in the Renaissance, when the conventions of medieval warfare had become obsolete, the apparatus of chivalry had been reduced largely to conscious archaism and symbol. Like the apparatus of classical mythology, it provided a mode for idealizing the past and eulogizing or deploring the present.

In their treatment of the distinctions between the "real" and the imaginary or fantastic,[6] and between different levels or kinds of reality, Renaissance epic poets exhibited considerable variety. We have already noted some of the problems that confronted the writer who endeavored to imitate the classical poets in his use of epic machinery and some of the ways in which he might solve them. Whether pagan gods or Judeo-Christian angels and devils, such "machining persons" were clearly differentiated from the epic personae by their supernatural character; they might intervene freely in the epic action at strategic moments.

In the case of passage from the "real" world and actual geographical sites to fantastic and supernatural lands, the poet might make the transition gradually or abruptly, blurring or sharply emphasizing the distinction between them. Camoëns's isle of Venus is set apart from the rest of the story by its terminal position in the narrative, its indeterminate cartographic site somewhere in the Indian Ocean, and its patently mythical and symbolic character. The epic commemorating a historic voyage of discovery to the "real" Africa and India concludes not with the heroes' triumphant return to their familiar Portugal but with landfall on an imaginary island off the mariners' charts and outside the real world. Figuratively if not literally, this is the end of the voyage, presenting its ultimate rewards and final cause: the enjoyment of immortal fame.

Through a realistic detail—the necessity of timber for siege machinery—Tasso links the enchanted forest of the romances with the quasihistorical action of his epic. The reader is fully aware that, upon entering the bedeviled wood, he has crossed the frontier between military history and moral allegory and is within the realm of fable. Similarly, the transition between the quasihistorical world of the crusade and the quasimythical paradise of Armida—situated in the Fortunate Isles (the Canaries) on a mountain that is reminiscent not only of Tenerife but also of Circe's isle and the beast-infested mountain allegorically associated with the chimaera—is effected by means of a magical bark. Analogous to the magic boat that returns Odysseus from the legendary island of Scheria to his native Ithaca, the strange bark and its emblematic pilot alert the reader to the fact that he is now leaving history and the real world behind and entering a world of symbol and myth.

In the *Odyssey,* the action is sometimes thrice removed from the "real" world of the poet's contemporaries. Set in a heroic age and in a different society from that of the poet, and presenting a different society and a different breed of men from those of the poet's own age, it also depicts several different levels and modes of reality within the heroic world itself.[7] From the traditional heroic world the voyager journeys to a series of largely imaginary lands—each sharply differentiated from the others—and finally back into the Greece of the heroic age. Throughout he is confronted either by mortal dangers that would cut off his day of return or by allurements that would detain him forever in unknown lands beyond his own world. When Odysseus sails from Troy and raids the city of the Ciconians in Thrace, he is still in familiar territory; he remains within the known world until he is driven past Cape Paleia and the island of Cythera. Among the Lotus-eaters he is still among mankind. The Cyclopes are man-eating ogres but nevertheless mortal creatures. At the island of Aeolus, Odysseus is in the realm of myth and weather-magic. In the land of the Laestrygonians he is once again menaced by giants. On Circe's island he enjoys the favors of a goddess. He journeys to the land of the dead in the great Ocean, and sails past the sirens and between Scylla and Charybdis to the island of the sun god. On the island of Ogygia he is detained by yet another goddess, Calypso; only the direct intervention of the Olympian gods sets him once more on his homeward journey.

This is essentially the world of the märchen and the romance. The ogres and giants, the sundry monsters, the fruit that removes all desire to return to the real world, the spells of the sorceress, the detention by amorous fays—these motifs are standard in folklore and in medieval and Renaissance romance. Even if some of these localities reflect mariners' yarns concerning actual places in the central and western Mediterranean, most of the persons and creatures whom Odysseus encounters belong to the supernatural and the marvelous; with few exceptions, he describes these wonders himself. (Homer, on the other hand, recounts the hero's adventures with Calypso and the Phaeacians in propria persona.)

Among the more significant features of these wanderings are the motif of the voyage within a voyage, the hero's frequent "backtracking," and his progressive isolation. He is twice within sight of Greece, but blown off course; when he finally does reach Ithaca, it is not—paradoxically—through his own nautical skill. Indeed he does not even sight landfall. He is brought back to reality by magic; when he awakens on his own island he does not recognize it. Again, he touches twice at the islands of Aeolus and Circe. After once passing Scylla and Charybdis, he is blown back again upon leaving Thrinacia. He undertakes his voyage to the dead—an entirely different level of reality—not from the real world but from the island of the immortal Circe; he returns to Aiaia before continuing his homeward voyage. His companions perish chiefly through their own folly, but also by the attacks of giants and monsters and (on one occasion) through his own recklessness. Some are slain by the Ciconians, others are killed by the Cyclops. All except one of his vessels are destroyed by the Laestrygonians. Scylla devours several of his crew, and he alone survives the shipwreck that destroys his sacrilegious company after they have slaughtered the cattle of the Sun. On Calypso's island his isolation is complete; in a sense he is at his farthest remove from his own world—a virtual prisoner in fairyland, without hope of return.

At Scheria he is once again among men, not sharing the domestic life of an immortal, but the island itself is unknown and all but isolated from the world. In their earthly paradise the Phaeacians live a blessed life like that of the gods, free from cares; their mariners possess supernatural powers of speed and accuracy. As seamen they are superior to the hero himself. His journey homeward takes place by night and (as in the case of two of his most signal misfortunes) in the midst of heavy sleep. He is still asleep when his hosts deposit him and his belongings near the cave of the nymphs on Ithaca. From now on, he is in familiar territory, in the traditional heroic world; the trials that still confront him are no longer the dangers and marvels of unknown lands and seas but a real domestic crisis.

There are allusions to other half-legendary lands in Homer's epic—the realms of the blameless Ethiopians, divided by the sea, and the blessed islands that await Menelaos and Helen when their days on earth are over. Nevertheless, these do not really enter the story. The gods themselves may visit them, but the hero of the poem does not.[8]

In the medieval and Renaissance romances there are analogous transitions from the known heroic world into the realm of the marvelous. The knight moves freely from a king's court (however fanciful and remote from common reality this may be) to remote castles, each with its own bizarre "customs" and taboos. With the intrusion of the stranger from the outside and the beyond—either as challenger or as suppliant—into the protected and festal milieu of the court, the knight of the quest, isolated from his fellows, is on his own. From the known world and the society of his peers he passes, in virtual solitude, into a fantasy landscape of bewildering forests and magic wells, a realm inhabited by giants and woodwoses, fays and sorcerers, monsters of various shapes and origins, and an occasional divinity of the ancient Gentiles.

We shall return later to the theme of the quest in considering the plot structure of Spenser's epic. For the moment, the significant point is that in Spenser's poem the familiar and traditional world has been left behind, and the reader is plunged from the outset into the unfamiliar realm of the quest; into the midst of *mirabilia* that are, on the whole, more esoteric than exotic. The knights have already left the royal court, where their quests had begun; the contrast between the court setting and the fluid mises-en-scène of the quest have been deferred until the conclusion of the poem. Since Cleopolis is a poetic fiction, there can be no traditional center (as in many other romances) to provide a familiar point of departure for the knight's venture into the unknown, for Cleopolis has no traditional association analogous to those of Arthur's Camelot or Caerleon or Charlemagne's Paris. Nor can there be a movement from the real world—even if this is the romanticized court of Arthur and Charlemagne—

into the realm of fays; Cleopolis itself is the center of Faeryland. In this respect Spenser's poem differs significantly not only from the majority of romances but also from many of the fairy tales of folklore.

As shades of the dead, as nature-spirits, and as decayed divinities, the myth of the fays and their faeryland was widely diffused in European folklore, and its popularity was enhanced by the international diffusion of Arthurian romance. Sometimes identified with swan-maidens and dragon-ladies and even with sirens, the fays also became associated with the fates—partly through verbal analogy and the blessings or curses they traditionally pronounced on marriages and births and at other occasions, but also through Queen Morgain-le-Fay's close links with military success or failure and with destiny. Morgain herself and the Lady of the Lake reappeared in Italian poetry; the romances of Boiardo and Ariosto contained numerous castles and gardens, where knights were held in temporary captivity and seclusion by fays. In addition, the romances introduced a variety of imaginary realms, such as the island of California. Spenser's innovation was to center his action almost entirely in an imaginary Faeryland, to the virtual exclusion of all other realms. The latter he reduced to allegorical fictions (Belge, Fleurdelis, Geryoneo), or else he invested them with the same atmosphere of fable and magic, as with the Britain of Britomart. He shows us little of Britain itself, but what we do see is largely centered on the figure of Merlin. Cleopolis, the city of glory or fame, may shadow London; but in the conventions of Spenser's mythos it belongs not to England but to the land of faerie. Spenser's readers, like his epic protagonists, are located in his imaginary world from the very beginning; they do not, as in the poems of his predecessors, pass from the real world into the enchanted precincts of the fays.

With Lewis Carroll the "real" protagonist enters the imaginary world through a looking glass. In the märchen the standard means of entry were the well or spring, the cave or the barrow. Alternatively, the protagonist might be an inadvertent spectator at a magic hunt and follow the riders to their dwelling; or like Thomas the Rhymer, he might be guided directly to her land by the fay herself. One of its essential features, however—like the land of the dead, which it so closely resembled—was its detachment from the real world, and from actual space and time. A day passes, but it is actually a year; after a seemingly brief visit the mortal may emerge, like Rip van Winkle, a withered old man. Like Odysseus on the island of Calypso (whose name indeed means "hidden"), he has been held outside and beyond the known world, on the further side of reality.

The lack of a determinate background in Spenser's epic brings the clearly realized topographies and the moralized characters and habitations into sharper focus. The ideal is in a sense clearer and more true than the shadowy and indistinct realm in which it appears. This technique is relative (as several critics have observed) to the particular aspects of the world that the poet was endeavoring to emphasize through his fiction. Whereas Tasso had stressed the unity and coherence common to the real world and to the poem, the Renaissance romance often tended to link them through multiplicity and variety, through complexity, and (at times) through deliberate perplexity. The labyrinthine plot, the element of uncertainty and unpredictability, and indeed the allegorical and symbolic nature of the poem could reflect conventional characteristics of the world itself, as the poet's contemporaries conceived it. Though most of Spenser's questing knights have a definite end in view—and frequently a qualified guide—they cannot foresee the numerous accidents that will befall them: the illusions of an enchanter, the challenge of a hostile knight, the theft of a horse, the charms of a strange woman, the need to assist some knight or lady in distress. Like the persons they encounter, the landscapes through which they pass are unpredictable; the travelers are all too apt to lose their way. To a significant degree the "labyrinthine" romance and the unified epic of neo-Aristotelian theory stand in different relationships to the real world. Though one can scarcely maintain that confusion has wrought his masterpiece, there is a sense in which the converse is true: the degree to which a master poet has deliberately sought and achieved the impression of confusion.[9]

Chapter 5

Spenser's Icon of the Past

Fiction as History, a Reexamination

Spenser's image of the past is, as critics have long recognized, a complex and sometimes self-contradictory construct. As Thomas M. Greene points out, "Spenser uses the word *antique* in many different senses, so that the meaning of the phrase *antique world* is not always consistent or clear." Andrew John Fichter emphasizes the dynastic theme in Virgil, Ariosto, Tasso, and Spenser, observing that it "brings into focus what must be considered one of the most basic elements of epic from Virgil onward, its consciousness of history." Michael O'Connell both challenges and qualifies traditional concepts of the "historical allegory" of *The Faerie Queene;* he considers the "historical dimension" of the poem primarily in terms of contemporary Elizabethan history rather than the remote past. In this chapter I shall reexamine Spenser's uses of the past in *The Faerie Queene* against the background of his references to remote antiquity in his romance epic and several of the minor poems, and in the context of Italian Renaissance theories of the relationship of the heroic poet's subject matter to historical fact or invented fiction.[1]

1.

The extent of Spenser's knowledge of sixteenth-century critical theory is uncertain. Graham Hough has suggested that although "we do not know what Spenser had read of this Italian criticism," it seems "clear from the structure of *The Faerie Queene* itself, and even clearer from the arguments used in the Letter to Raleigh, that he was aware of the general direction of ideas."[2] Spenser's

This chapter was published, in somewhat different form, in *The Huntington Library Quarterly* 55 (1992) : 535–58. It is reprinted by permission of the Henry E. Huntington Library.

lost book *The English Poete* had been written before the publication of *The Shepheardes Calender*. (E. K. mentions it in the Argument of the October Æglogue and states his intention of publishing it.) The qualifying adjective in the title may be significant. This was not, apparently, a *De Poeta;* the book may have been concerned largely with problems of language, versification, and style—the specific problems that confronted a poet writing in English—rather than with general theories of mimesis and allegory, genre and structure. Although Spenser must have "done his homework" for this treatise, citing poets and perhaps critics and theorists, there is no indication that he endeavored to revise or expand it after 1579. In war-ravaged Ireland, moreover, he must have had limited access to the books on poetic theory and criticism recently published in Italy. Tasso's *Dell' arte poetica,* though written earlier, appeared in 1587, only two years before the letter to Raleigh, and could hardly have exerted much influence on the basic design of *The Faerie Queene*.[3] The more extensive *Discorsi del poema eroico* were first published in 1594, between the publication of the first three books of the romance and the appearance of the last three books. On the other hand, Tasso's "Allegoria" of the *Jerusalem Delivered* had been included in the 1581 editions of the poem, and Spenser may well have read it. While still in England, he could have encountered two of the principal theoretical treatises on the romance, which had endeavored to defend and elucidate its principles as an altogether new and distinct genre, unknown to Aristotle. Written in 1549, Giraldi Cinthio's *Discorso intorno al comporre dei romanzi* had been published in 1554, and Pigna's *I romanzi* appeared during the same year.[4]

Spenser's familiarity with Italian epic and romance has been traced primarily through source studies. In addition to Ariosto's *Orlando Furioso* and Tasso's *Jerusalem Delivered*, the *Faerie Queene* shows the influence of Tasso's early epic *Rinaldo*, Boiardo's *Orlando Innamorato,* and Trissino's *Italia Liberata*. Among allegorical interpretations of Ariosto's romance, Spenser could have encountered the commentaries of Porcacchi, Fornari, and Toscanella. Noting affinities in particular with Porcacchi, Hough suggests that Spenser "read Ariosto in the manner of the Italians of his time" and that "in reading Ariosto as he did" he must "have become completely habituated to *discontinuous* allegory, which can be picked up and dropped at will; and to a conception of allegory that is often enough fulfilled by the simplest moral implications drawn from a pre-existing romantic tale."[5]

In the letter to Raleigh, Spenser did not distinguish between epic and romance, nor did he use the term *heroic poem;* instead he spoke of "historicall" poets, including Ariosto in this category along with Homer and Virgil and

Tasso. It is to this class of poem that *The Faerie Queene* (scarcely less "historicall" on the literal level than either of the romance-epics on Orlando) belongs.

In describing his poem as "a continued Allegory, or darke conceit," Spenser was referring to a level of meaning and a mode of presentation rather than to a literary genre. (The allegorical mode was, of course, common to lyric and pastoral, drama and satire, as well as to epic.) It is significant, however, that all of these "historicall" poems had been subjected to extensive allegorical interpretation. Ariosto had occasionally directed the reader to a hidden sense, and his commentators had supplied a more detailed and comprehensive allegorical analysis. Tasso had allegorized his historical fiction himself, assimilating the conquest of Jerusalem to moral theology; in the *Discourses on the Heroic Poem* he would treat allegory as a "continued metaphor."[6] Allegory was like night and darkness; hence it should be used in mysteries and in "mysterious poems" like the heroic poem. Although the enigma was not always identical with allegory, Aristotle had employed the former term in the latter sense, and the enigmas and symbols of Pythagoras were essentially allegorical. There was no part of the *Commedia* (Tasso continued) that was not allegorical; in his commentary on his *canzoni* Dante had distinguished the literal from the moral, allegorical, and analogical senses: the third and fourth conducing respectively to the contemplation of "interior" and superior things.

Of Spenser's "historicall" poets only one—Tasso—actually drew his material from authentic history, and Tasso felt thoroughly at liberty to alter and rearrange his materials, restructuring the action through characters and episodes of his own invention. Without Ismeno and Argante, without Clorinda and Erminia, without Armida and her sensual paradise, without the episode of the enchanted wood, *Jerusalem Delivered* would have been an altogether different poem. Though the siege of Jerusalem was a historical fact, and though Godfrey and Tancredi, Peter the Hermit and certain other personae possessed historical authority, the action itself was largely organized through fictive episodes and imaginary characters. Tasso's actual subject matter was in large part the conventional material of romance, although he subjected it to classical principles of epic structure and especially to the criterion of unity of action. The material of Homer and Virgil belonged largely to prehistory; even according to the dubious chronological schemes of antiquity, Elissa of Carthage could never have met the adventurous Trojan. The material of both of the romance-epics on Orlando was almost entirely fictitious. Despite a tenuous basis in history (Charlemagne *had* fought against the Saracens; Roland and several other characters in the romance had actually existed), the action and most of personae were the inventions of Boiardo and Ariosto or of earlier poets. Although Ariosto pretended to rely on the authority of Turpin—as Chaucer had affected dependence on "Lollius" for the story of Troilus—both the *Innamorato* and the *Furioso* professed to recount tales never told before. Indeed, as critics have suggested, it was the novelty and impropriety of representing the legendary Roland—zealous defender of the faith—in the atypical role of the lover that had attracted Boiardo in the first place. Hitherto the motif of chivalric love had been associated largely with the Arthurian rather than with the Carolinian legends, and the madness of Roland (aside from its association with medical theory—*hereos*—with the erotic furor of Platonic tradition, and with Pulci's representation of the hero's insane jealousy) was strongly reminiscent of the madness of Lancelot.

The tradition of "historicall" epic, as Spenser apparently conceived it, afforded ample license for the poet's own inventions; it is possibly significant that he did not allude to Lucan, whom many Renaissance critics regarded as too much of a historian to deserve the title of poet.

In this context, the relationship between Spenser's moral and historical vision—between on the one hand a comparatively stable realm of ethical absolutes and on the other an essentially fictive antiquity for which he claims historical truth (along with the historical and political realities of his own age, which he does not claim to represent directly but merely to shadow allegorically)—merits further exploration. Variable, shifting, and ambiguous, the interrelationships inhering among all four of these worlds—the world of ideas, the real England of Elizabeth, the largely legendary Britain of Arthur as it had been represented in chronicle and romance, and the imaginary realm of the poem itself—cannot be explained by Renaissance theories of imitation and allegory, or by romance conventions (for Spenser's imaginary world is as unique, as distinctive, and as complex as that of Ariosto), but they must nonetheless be examined against this background.

2.

As an imitative art, poetry "has for its end the presentation of an image."[7] Spenser's "antique Image" is at once verbal picture and example, historical fiction and allegory; and he describes it in all of these terms or in near equivalents: "mirror" or "pourtraict," "Pageaunt" or "patterne," "type" or "shadow," "vele" or "showes." Moreover, it is specifically a *heroic* image, and as heroic poetry it has glory as its end: the presentation of heroic virtues in action, the idealization of British antiquity, and the glorification of the reigning monarch and her government. The quest of the pattern hero for Gloriana the Faerie Queene shadows the magnificent (or magnanimous) man's pursuit of glory.

At its projected end the various, sometimes erratic lines of the story would apparently have converged at Gloriana's court, where the quests had been initiated in the first place. The "famous antique history" is a medium for praising past and present.

Like many other heroic poets (or 'poets historicall,' as Spenser usually calls them) he places his actions in a remote and legendary antiquity: he selects a legendary yet possibly historical prince as his chief pattern hero; he glorifies the ancestry (also largely legendary) of his ruler. Furthermore, like several of his predecessors, he has adapted the ancient myth of the Elysian fields and the isles of the blessed to the exaltation of his own country and the heroization of its knighthood. Metaphorically at least, he has placed the shadows of his patrons and other British worthies in a poetic Elysium: "Elyzas blessed field, that *Albion* hight." This is hardly Virgil's Elysium, and (as Gabriel Harvey suggests) it depends on a series of puns: Eliza—Elysium, "faire Iland"—"Faery-land."[8] But it apparently exploits the traditional association of this myth with glorified heroes.

Spenser describes his romance as "history" or "historicall fiction," and for its matter turns to "the historye of king Arthure." He associates himself with Homer and Virgil, Ariosto and Tasso as a "Poet historical"(*PW* 407–8). The term "history" is ambiguous, however, and may refer to a narrative ("story") of either true or false events, to actions of real or imaginary persons, or to a mixture of fiction and historical fact. Spenser apparently exploits all of these senses and perhaps deliberately blurs them, thereby softening the line between fact and fable. When he contrasts the historiographer and the "Poet historical," it is the method or order of narration that he is primarily emphasizing rather than (like Philip Sidney in *The Defence of Poesie*) the contrast between true and feigned examples.[9] It is in this context that he discusses the "beginning" or "wel-head" of his "History"—the initiation of the separate quests at Gloriana's feast—and this, of course, is his own fictional invention.

By "historicall fiction" Spenser could mean merely a narrative of his own inventing; and by "Poet historical" he may mean simply an epic or narrative poet. Yet he may also be hinting at a historical basis underlying the fictions of classical and modern epic. With the possible exception of Rinaldo, all of the epic heroes mentioned in the Letter to Raleigh were commonly regarded as historical personages, however much their exploits had been transformed by legend or by the conscious fictions of their poets. Significantly, in discussing "Historicall Poesie," George Puttenham had stressed its mixture of truth and fable and the persuasive force of the feigned example, citing Homer and Xenophon as instances. Example is "but the representation of old memories, and like successes happened in times past"; and historical poesy presents "as it were in a glasse the lively image of our deare forefathers, their noble and vertuous maner of life." Yet "more and more excellent examples may be fained in one day by a good wit then many ages through mans frailtie are able to put in ure. . . . And you shall perceive that histories were of three sortes, wholly true, and wholly false, and a third holding part of either." Thus Homer "wrate a fabulous or mixt report of the siege of Troy and another of *Ulysses* errors or wandrings"; Xenophon (Puttenham continues) wrote a "fained and untrue" history of "the childhood of *Cyrus* . . . for example and good information of the posteritie."[10] Spenser similarly portrays the imaginary youth or *enfances* of his hero through an invented fiction.

Behind the fictional image of Arthur's period lies the more ancient Britain of the eponymous conqueror; behind Brutus and his companions lay the legendary city of Troy. Having set his story chronologically in the early Middle Ages, at the period of the last flowering of Celtic Britain, Spenser can look simultaneously back to the heroic age celebrated by Homer and Virgil and forward to the age of Elizabeth. He can emphasize the links between Homer's Troy, the Roman empire, and Troynovant (London); by stressing the Trojan ancestry of his heroine Britomart, he can also strengthen the links between his own romance and that of Ariosto. (In Ariosto's *Orlando Furioso* both Ruggiero and Bradamante, the fictional ancestors of the Este family and thus the forebears of the poet's own patrons, are of Trojan descent.)

Although this "antique history" reflects much the same antiquarian interest that Spenser had displayed in *The Ruines of Time,* it is fully as anachronistic as the Carolinian France of Ariosto and Boiardo. Like his Italian predecessors, he imitates the chivalric ethos of late medieval romances at a time when medieval military and social conventions were already obsolescent or obsolete, although they might still adorn a court festival, a masque, or a joust. Despite the difference in chronological and geographical setting, the milieu of *The Faerie Queene* is much like that of *Orlando Furioso,* and its characters frequently observe some of the same chivalric conventions (albeit more seriously) in love and war.

In the latter part of the sixteenth century, the distinction between epic and romance and the relative merits of Ariosto and Tasso were hotly debated in Italy, and this controversy involved, among other things, the relationships between historical fact and poetic invention.[11] Did the poet have the right to exploit a feigned and imaginary geography? Should he imitate an action based on history or on an imaginary action of his own devising? Should he invent the names of his principal personages or imitate historic individuals? In

Della poetica in generale, Benedetto Varchi "held that the 'feigned and fabulous' was the proper field for the poet." Giraldi Cintio, recognizing three distinct forms of heroic poetry—the epic and two forms of romance—held that the biographical romance dealt "preferably with an historical subject, whereas the noblest writers of the more purely romantic form, dealing with many actions of many men, have invented their subject matter." Castelvetro maintained that "the matter of poetry should be like the matter of history and resemble it, but it ought not to be the same." Nevertheless, he believed that "the man who forms the plot of a tragedy or an epic taken from history with real and true names is not the less to be esteemed a poet than the maker of a plot containing only imaginary things." Jacopo Mazzoni maintained (against Castelvetro) that the poet might resort to fictitious geography: "the things he considers unsuitable, namely, the feigning of new countries, new peoples, and new kingdoms, and the altering and falsifying of the source and course of rivers, the site of countries, and the quality of other things in nature, are . . . wholly proper and fitting to the poet, since they are credible and marvelous." In *Discorsi dell' Arte Poetica,* Tasso argued that "the subject of the heroic poem must be historical" and that "the material must be neither too ancient nor too modern. . . . The times of Charlemagne and Arthur are accordingly best fitted for heroic treatment."[12]

The salient characteristics of Spenser's fictive image of the past invite comparison with the principal issues debated by these and other sixteenth-century Italian theorists and critics.[13] Though some of the more important treatises appeared too late to influence his own poetic method, they frequently centered on controversies that he could have encountered in earlier works. They deserve mention here, not as specific influences on Spenser's poetics but as part of the larger and more general context in which his poetics can be profitably studied.

As a self-avowed rival of Ariosto, Spenser feels free to portray many actions by many different persons and also to invent not only the "wel-head of the History" (the initiation of the quests) but also the greater part of the quests themselves, Arthur's search for Gloriana, and most of the "Accidents" (as he terms them). The actions that Spenser is imitating, and the individuals who perform them, are for the most part his own inventions or adaptations of the inventions of other poets. A few (Arthur, Arthegall, Saint George, etc.) had a tenuous basis in legend. Spenser's "antique history" is fabulous, and so are his topography and geography: "Sith none, that breatheth living aire, does know, / Where is that happy land of Faery" (*FQ* 2.proem.1).

Spenser usually maintains the pretense that he is indeed writing historical fact, just as Chaucer had claimed to follow Lollius on the Trojan War *(Troilus and Criseyde)* and Ariosto had pretended to follow the chronicle of pseudo-Turpin. He addresses his muse as though she were an archivist in the Public Records Office: "Lay forth out of thine ever lasting scryne / The antique rolles, which there lye hidden still, / Of Faerie knights and fairest *Tanaquill*" (*FQ* 1.proem.2). Like the old man Eumnestes ("good memory") in the castle of Alma, Spenser's muse is a custodian of British (and Faery) antiquities; significantly, she is also chief of the nine daughters of Memory. (Though several commentators have connected her with Calliope, the muse of epic poetry, most have identified her with Clio, the muse of history.) Like Homer and other epic poets, Spenser calls on his muse to relate events beyond man's wit and memory, but he also pretends on occasion to be basing his story on records preserved in the archives of Faery land. He invokes Clio, who ennobles "The warlike Worthies, from antiquitie" in her "great volume of Eternities," to recount Elizabeth's ancestry (*FQ* 2.3.4). For the catalog of nymphs at the wedding of the Thames and the Medway, he again asks the aid of his muse: "To whom those rolles layd up in heaven above, / And records of antiquitie appeare, / To which no wit of man may comen neare" (*FQ* 4.11.10). For the assembly of the gods on Arlo hill he turns to Clio (or conceivably Urania) for inspiration: "for, who but thou alone, / That art yborne of heaven and heavenly Sire, / Can tell things doen in heaven so long ygone; / So farre past memory of man that may be knowne" (*FQ* 7.7.1–2; Cf. Clio in 7.6.37). On the other hand, he may pretend to consult antiquarian records. Thus the story of the begetting of Belphoebe and Amoretta is mentioned in "antique bookes" (*FQ* 3.6.6). Similarly, he unfolds the "antique race and linage ancient" of the Titaness Mutability, "As I have found it registred of old, / In *Faery* Land mongst records permanent" (*FQ* 7.6.2).

On occasion Spenser cleverly deflects against his accusers the argument that he is writing mere fiction instead of historical fact: "That all this famous antique history, / Of some th' aboundance of an idle braine / Will judged be, and painted forgery, / Rather than matter of just memory" (*FQ* 2.proem.1). Later, however, he suggests that his fictive image of the past provides a more truthful image of real virtue than contemporary reality can do. The courtesy of the present age is "nought but forgerie, / Fashion'd to please the eies of them, that pas, / Which see not perfect things but in a glas"; it is merely "fayned showes . . . , / Which carry colours faire, that feeble eies misdeeme" (*FQ* 6.proem.4–5). Spenser's contemporaries had applied the same language, favorably or pejoratively, to the poet's imitation or "counterfeiting"; and elsewhere Spenser describes his own poetic method in similar terms. The poet's fiction (he is obliquely arguing) provides a more faithful image and example of virtue and truth than does historical reality—but with at least one notable exception: the person of Queen Elizabeth.[14]

Spenser's "antique history," his "antique Image" of an idealized national past, thus provides exemplary patterns of moral and public virtues, but also eulogizes contemporary individuals who are themselves exemplary figures. Through its central conceit (the correspondence between Eliza's England and Gloriana's Faeryland) it brings the distant and legendary Britain of Arthur into juxtaposition with contemporary England, not only "comparing the times past with the present" (in Puttenham's phrase) but also contrasting them, and shadowing the one in and through the other. Yet Spenser's attitude toward these analogies between past and present is often variable and equivocal. Alternately, he may contrast the genuine virtues of antiquity with the vices and counterfeit virtues of the degenerate present, or claim to be shadowing present realities through his idealization of the past.

Spenser's antiquity is, however, a composite image, drawing on a wide range of diverse and sometimes contradictory values: antiquity as a topos (commonplace) of nobility, whether of a family, a nation, or an institution; the revived interest in British antiquities (associated in *The Ruines of Time* with the researches of William Camden, "the nourice of antiquitie"), together with the humanist veneration of classical civilization; the concept of nature's decay and the belief that mankind had been nobler, wiser, and stronger in earlier ages; and the heroic tradition itself. The classical epic and the modern romance usually turned to the remote past for their subject matter, placing their actions in an obscure and legendary heroic era and sometimes comparing or contrasting it with still earlier ages or with the present. Thus Homer's Nestor had extolled the dead heroes of the siege of Thebes above the living warriors of the siege of Troy. Boiardo and Ariosto had endowed several of their heroes and heroines with Trojan ancestry and sometimes with Trojan arms as well. Yet, conversely, the heroic past could also serve to eulogize the present. The action of the *Aeneid* points forward to the age of Augustus and the imperial destiny of Rome; Ariosto *(Orlando Furioso)* and Tasso *(Gerusalemme Liberata)* glorify the Este family and its fictional or historical ancestors.[15] Much of the *Aeneid* is aetiological myth, depicting the origins of the Roman people from Latin and Trojan stock, of the feud with Carthage, of Italian place-names, of many of the patrician families of Rome, and of Roman rites and ceremonies.

As antiquarian fiction this epic of Rome is Janus-faced; like Spenser's epic of Britain, it looks simultaneously toward the remote origins and future destinies of a state, a people, and an empire.

Nevertheless, the antiquity that Spenser evokes as an ideal standard is not closely localized in time. Although centered on the age of Arthur, it comprehends the Golden Age of Saturn, the age of deified heroes like Bacchus and Hercules and Osiris, the heroic ages of Greece and Palestine and Italy, and even the age of Socrates—and Spenser often moves freely between them. At the beginning of the fifth book (Justice) his standard is the Golden Age: "So oft as I with state of present time, / The image of the antique world compare, / When as mans age was in his freshest prime, / And the first blossome of faire vertue bare, / Such oddes I find twixt those, and these which are, / Me seemes the world is runne quite out of square" (*FQ* 5.proem.1). In the legend of temperance the mores of Arthurian antiquity are explicitly contrasted with those of the earlier era. In denouncing avarice, Sir Guyon appeals to the example of the Golden Age ("The antique world, in his first flowring youth"); and, in reply, Mammon scoffs at "the rudeness of that antique age," arguing that Sir Guyon, living as he does "in later times," must "wage / Thy workes for wealth, and life for gold engage" (*FQ* 2.7.16–18). In other instances, however, the antique mores thus idealized are those of Arthur's age or a more generalized antiquity (*FQ* 1.9.1–2, 1.12.14, 3.1.12–13, 4.8.29–33). Thus Britomart—herself portrayed as a contemporary of Arthur—surpasses all other martial heroines of ancient times in "warlike puissance" just as Elizabeth surpasses all other great women in wisdom (*FQ* 3.2.2–3). Comparing Britomart with women of earlier ages—Penthesilea, the Amazon who had fought at Troy; the Hebrew heroine Deborah, who had slain Sisera; Virgil's woman-warrior Camilla, who had slain Orsilochus—Spenser asserts that none of these, or "all that else had puissance" can compare with Britomart "Aswell for glory of great valiaunce, / As for pure chastitie and vertue rare" (*FQ* 3.4.1–3). In thus extolling the "goodly usage of those antique times" (*FQ* 3.1.13), Spenser is following the precedent of the *Orlando Furioso* but usually disregarding the characteristic Ariostean irony (*Orlando Furioso* 1.22, 13.1, 36.1–10, 46.102).

On the one hand, antiquity affords patterns of virtue—temperance, concord, love, justice, courtesy, female valor—with which the present age cannot compare. Spenser must accordingly model his exemplary images on the mores of the past rather than on those of the present age: "Let none then blame me, if in discipline / Of vertue and of civill uses lore, / I doe not forme them to the common line / Of present dayes, which are corrupted sore, / But to the antique use, which was of yore" (*FQ* 5.proem.3). On the other hand, the present offers at least one model superior to those of the past, inasmuch as Queen Elizabeth provides an example surpassing those of antiquity. Thus Spenser does not need to fetch "Forreine ensamples" of chastity from Faeryland, for this virtue is already enshrined in Eliza's own breast: "form'd so lively in each perfect part" that one need only behold "the pourtraict of her hart" (*FQ* 3.proem.1). Again, though the present age cannot compare with "plaine antiquitie" in courtesy, antiquity itself cannot afford "so faire a patterne" of this virtue as Elizabeth (*FQ* 6.proem.4–7). Similarly, though her fictional ancestress Britomart surpasses all other heroines in martial valor, Elizabeth excels in wisdom and affords an even more illustrious example of chastity (*FQ* 3.2.3, 3.4.3). The *Faerie Queene* is thus a "mirrhour" wherein the queen may behold her own face, her own realms, and her own great ancestry—all shadowed in "this antique Image" (*FQ* 2.proem.4). Over and beyond the dispersed images of the virtues in their knightly patrons, and their collective or composite image in Prince Arthur, the poem purports to be a moral icon of the queen herself, reflecting as in a looking glass the invisible virtues of which she herself is the perfect "ensample."

On the surface, Spenser's "antique history" treats the matter of Britain, just as the romance-epics of Boiardo *(Orlando Innamorato)* and Ariosto *(Orlando Furioso)* had handled the matter of France—though in fact the matter of all three poems was in large part the poet's own invented fiction. In the strictest sense, Spenser claims to be recounting the "gentle deeds"—the "Fierce warres and faithfull loves"—of "Knights and Ladies" belonging to the time of Prince Arthur (*FQ* 1.proem.1), just as Ariosto had described "the ladies, knights, arms, amours, courtesies, daring enterprises" that had occurred "at the time when the Moor" had invaded France to avenge on Charlemagne the death of the Saracen king Troiano (*Orlando Furioso* 1.1). Nevertheless, Spenser frequently alludes, directly or obliquely, to earlier and later events and to other "matters," biblical or classical or modern. It is significant, however, that Spenser exploits the commonplace of inexpressibility both to praise the queen and to emphasize his own allegorical method. To portray the perfection of Elizabeth's heart defies the skill of "living art" and "life-resembling pencill"; and, since the poet cannot "figure" the queen's portrait plainly, he can only "shadow" it obliquely and obscurely through "colourd showes," fitting "antique praises unto present persons" (*FQ* 3.proem.1–3). Too dazzling for naked vision, Elizabeth's glory must be screened from the common gaze under the veil of allegory, made visible and endurable by shadowy types and symbols (*FQ* 1.proem.4, 2.proem.5).

Finally, Spenser's "antique Image" demands not only a conscious archaism in manners (which he achieves partly through imitating Ariosto's chivalric society, partly through drawing on a wide range of medieval materials, French and English and Italian), but also an archaic language and style. In this context, E. K.'s comments on the language of *The Shepheardes Calender* are apposite. He defends Spenser's "auncient words" on the grounds of not only rustic decorum but also grace and "auctoritee," and by the example of Livy. Those "auncient, solemne wordes" he insists are "a great ornament" both in Livy and Sallust. For Livy had labored "to set forth in hys worke an eternal image of antiquitie," while Sallust had discoursed of matters "of gravitie and importaunce" (*Shepheardes Calender,* epistle). For his own fictional image of British antiquity, Spenser has deliberately cultivated an "antique" idiom as his medium.[16]

3.

Like Arthur's vision of Gloriana and Britomart's vision of Artegal, Spenser's poem is a mirror; but—as in the speculum of Saint Paul and the cave world of the Platonists—the reflections themselves are enigmas: types and shadows of the real. The relationships between the poet's images, Elizabeth's court, and the persons and events of antiquity are ambivalent and equivocal. The antiquity he describes is a fictional image of the present. He professes to write as a "poet historicall," but with the exception of occasional references to British and English history, he draws his materials largely from his own imagination or from the fictions of other poets. Antiquity is a model for the degenerate present:

> O goodly usage of those antique times,
> In which the sword was servant unto right. (*FQ* 3.1.13)
> . . . .
> So oft as I with state of present time,
> The image of the antique world compare . . . ,
> Me seemes the world is runne quite out of square,
> From the first point of his appointed sourse,
> And being once amisse growes daily wourse and wourse. (*FQ* v.proem.1)
> . . . .
> Let none then blame me, if in discipline
> Of vertue and of civill uses lore,
> I doe not forme them to the common line
> Of present dayes, which are corrupted sore,
> But to the antique use, which was of yore. (*FQ* 5.proem.2)

The "antique age yet in the infancie / Of time, did live then like an innocent, / In simple truth and blamelesse chastitie," faithful in love and void of guile.

But when the world grew old, it grew progressively worse ("warre old"), bold in all manner of iniquity (*FQ* 4.8.30–32). All values are now reversed. Fair is foul and foul is fair (*FQ* 4.8.32). Virtue is called vice; vice is "now hight vertue, and so us'd of all; / Right now is wrong, and wrong that was is right" (*FQ* 5.proem.4).

To the realities of the present age, Spenser transfers the accusations that critics had leveled against the fictive images of poetry. The falsehood lies not in the poet's images of the true virtues of antiquity but in the vicious practices of his contemporaries and their confusion of false semblance with truth. Even though the "present age" *seems* to abound in exemplars of courtesy,

> Yet being matcht with plaine Antiquitie,
> Ye will them all but fayned showes esteeme,
> Which carry colours faire, that feeble eies misdeeme. (*FQ* 6.proem.4)

In comparison with the true courtesy of ancient times, that of the present

> . . . is nought but forgerie,
> Fashion'ed to please the eies of them, that pas,
> Which see not perfect things but in a glas:
> Yet is that glasse so gay, that it can blynd
> The wisest sight, to thinke gold that is bras.
> But vertues seat is deepe within the mynd,
> And not in outward shows, but inward thoughts defynd. (*FQ* 6.proem.5)

The opposition between truth and its deceptive counterfeit—Una and Duessa, the true and the false Florimel—underlies the epistemological structure of the entire poem.

Saint Paul had applied the image of the speculum to the soul's obscure and enigmatic apprehension of spiritual things while in the body and in this world; Cicero applied it to comedy, and a host of writers applied it to the poetic icon. Spenser transfers it to the court. With this praise of antiquity he associates a wide variety of topoi: the innocence of the Saturnian and Hesiodic golden age as classical myth had depicted it and of man's paradisal state before the Fall, the motifs of the decay of nature and the world upside down. Antiquity itself had long been a commonplace for eulogy: an argument for the dignity and nobility of an art or an institution, a nation and religion, or a family. In praising a man, the epideictic orator frequently began by landing his ancestors. In an age still obsessed with the idea (if not the reality) of gentillesse, when the nobility of blood lines and "old richesse" was undermined by other social forces, and nobility itself was subjected to ethical redefinition, the appeal to antiquity as a nobility topos was conventional, and no less conventional were its moral applications. Gentle blood must prove itself worthy of its high descent by noble deeds and manners, the virtuous exploits of a noble heart. This concern, shared by British and Continental writers, is reflected in the abundant courtesy books, the numerous manuals for "forming" or educating the gentleman, the genealogical catalogs that adorned the epics and romances of the period, and the mad scramble for coats of arms and patents of gentility at the Herald's Office. The Shakespeares and the Miltons were thus "engentled," and in Florence the young Milton could pass as a "nobile inglese."

The humanistic glorification of Greco-Roman antiquity—exemplary in arms as well as in arts, in private virtues as in public duties, and in the defense of political freedom as in empire; superlative indeed in everything except religion—was paralleled by the glorification of the national past in northern Europe.[17] To the study of British and English history antiquarians had transferred the critical techniques that humanist scholars had applied to classical antiquity. The praises that Horace and Juvenal and other Roman poets had bestowed on the plain manners and severely disciplined morality of the early Romans in comparison with the decadent present had been applied to English society. The gentry now forsook their country estates for the city; in the country they no longer offered the old hospitality. The lord and lady of the manor had ceased to dine in hall with their dependents and with strangers. English yeomen had lost their skill at the long bow. They could hardly win another battle of Agincourt. Court and clown alike neglected the poet.

Ancestor worship is inevitable, especially if one is praising a monarch, and the circuitous route by which a Welsh dynasty had assumed the crown of England and Ireland, with a titular claim to the throne of France, made it virtually inevitable also that a "poet historicall" should in some way exploit the "Tudor myth" and the queen's British descent. Though there were obvious alternatives—the victories of the Duke of Richmond, the exploits of Brutus, the legendary deeds of Brennus and Belinus and Arviragus—Spenser elected to set his story in the period of Arthur, but also (with the exception of genealogical references and a few other allusions) to base his arguments on other sources than the legendary materials of pre-Saxon Britain. Though Prince Arthur himself belongs to the matter of Britain, his conventional exploits are not described here. Even though Gloriana (or Tanaquill) is herself a fay, she has little in common with the Fata Morgana of the Arthurian cycle. Her position and significance in the poem derive, on the whole, rather from her assimilation to Elizabeth, along with the assimilation of Elizabeth to Diana, and of Diana as goddess of the chase and sovereign of woodland nymphs to the fairy queen. (In medieval tradition Diana often rides with Oberon or Arthur or with other legendary figures in the nocturnal hunt.) The Order of the Garter, in turn, is assimilated to the Knights of Maidenhead; and the first adventure is appropriately assigned to Saint George (the only "historical" personage among the major characters other than Prince Arthur), patron saint of the Order and of the English nation. Faeryland itself, traditionally located underground like Virgil's Elysian fields but now transferred to the surface of the earth, shadows the court and realm of Eliza: a Tudor Elysium.

The real world of the present, Spenser maintains, is too corrupt to provide patterns and exemplars of the moral virtues: for these, the poet must look to British antiquity, to the age of Arthur. But there is one notable exception, Queen Elizabeth herself:

> But where shall I in all Antiquity
> So faire a patterne finde, where may be seene
> The goodly praise of Princely curtesie,
> As in your selfe, O soveraine Lady Queene,
> In whose pure minde, as in a mirrour sheene,
> It showes (*FQ* 6.proem.6)

It is from the queen that the poet must derive this virtue, returning it to her again in a poetic tribute that displays her own portrait.

Similarly, the decay of "loyall love" is converted to Elizabeth's praise. A few transplantings of this once glorious flower, miraculously "preserv'd . . . In Princes Court," may chance to sprout again,

> Dew'd with her drops of bountie Soveraine,
> Which from that goodly glorious flowre proceed,
> Sprung of the auncient stocke of Princes straine,
> Now th'onely remnant of that royall breed. (*FQ* 4.8.33)

In Belphoebe the poet is portraying Elizabeth's chastity, in Gloriana her rule, shadowing her portrait "in colour showes" and fitting "antique praises unto present persons."

4.

Spenser simultaneously retains the pretense of writing a true history of the past and an allegorical representation of the present through his image of the past. Hostile critics, he foresees, will regard this "famous antique history" as merely "painted forgery" instead of "matter of just memory," accusing him of vouching "antiquities, which no body can know." Nevertheless, the elusive land can be found "By certaine signes here set in sundry place":

> And thou, O fairest Princesse under sky
> In this faire mirrhour maist behold thy face,
> And thine owne realme in land of Faery,
> And in this antique Image thy great auncestry. (*FQ* 2.proem.4)

Gloriana is the "true glorious type" of Elizabeth; but as a historical poet Spenser claims to be writing more than allegorical fiction, and he invokes Clio the muse of history instead of Calliope. Elsewhere in the poem, his major characters prefer history to fancy.

Spenser has thus accommodated the Platonic ideas, the history of the past, the metaphor of the poem as mirror, and the theory of allegory to the praise of the queen. The Ideas of courtesy, chastity, and the other virtues are mirrored in her own pure mind. She herself, in turn, is too glorious for mortal sight, and he can present to his readers only a mirror image or a portrait veiled in shadows. As with the glories of heaven, so dazzling and divine an object can be contemplated only through the dark glass of symbol and allegory. Nevertheless, he reserves this type of encomium primarily for the queen. Other contemporaries he eulogizes obliquely as exemplars of the virtues of the antique age, using the idealized past as a mirror for celebrating the heroic virtues of a few men and women in the decadent present.

These invented fictions of antiquity are thus validated, so to speak, by their oblique reference to contemporary persons and events. Just as Virgil had eulogized Augustus, Maecenas, and others through allegorical allusion, the *Faerie Queene* is a gallery of idealized portraits of the worthies of Elizabeth's own kingdom—arrayed in masque-costumes to be sure, but nonetheless recognizable to themselves and their contemporaries. The epic is simultaneously an Elizabethan hall of Fame—a kind of *coelum britannicum* exalting the queen and her court to the skies—and a "moral cosmos" inhabited by thinly disguised virtues and vices. Through a more consistent application of the principles of moral and historical allegory to the fantasy world and indeterminate causality of the romance, Spenser has fashioned (as Sidney had expressed it in another context) a second, more perfect nature. Here historical allusion is absorbed by fiction and assimilated to an ethical pattern. The "feigned" poetic exemplar transforms and idealizes the historical example by bringing it into closer conformity with a hierarchy of paradigms; the images in the mirror are the "realized" vision of a moral imagination.

Indeed the moral structures of *The Faerie Queene* are often clearer and more coherent than either the pattern of incidents or the historical allegory. In some instances the personae themselves are little more than abstractions on horseback, virtues and vices in armor or skirts. On other occasions they are described through concrete but symbolic detail, in the manner of iconographical manuals and medieval personification allegories. Alternately, they may be characterized by their actions and discourse or by the emotions they display. At times their roles are governed less by their ethical significance than by narrative contexts or by biographical or historical circumstances: the careers of the living individuals whom the poet is shadowing.

The mixture of precision and imprecision in this work—precise detail and ambiguous reference, or vice versa—is apparent also in the treatment of place. No one knows where this "land of Faerie" lies, Spenser observes. Perhaps some future explorer will rediscover it. Its location and boundaries, its connection with England and Wales, its geographical features are deliberately left indeterminate: the ground for a varied and sometimes unpredictable succession of pageants, backdrops, and actions.

To achieve a comparable variety in setting and mise-en-scène Boiardo and Ariosto had been compelled to roam three continents, shifting the action from Paris to the Hebrides, the forest of Ardennes to Albracca and Africa and the sphere of the moon. Tasso's epic was more localized. The central event occurs at the holy city, but the scene moves to Egypt and Syria, to Armida's castle by the Dead Sea, and to the Fortunate Isles. In all three of these poems such shifts in scene are partly due to the ecumenical nature of the war—Christian Europe versus the Islamic powers of Asia and Africa—but it is also specifically associated with dereliction of duty. The paladins *ought* to be at Charlemagne's side in Paris, the crusaders with Godfrey at Jerusalem; instead they are pursuing Angelica, or have already been seduced by Alcina, Armida, or some other fay or sorceror.

Spenser drops this geographical background almost entirely,[18] except for veiled allusions to Britain and to the Continent and occasional episodes like the marriage of the Thames and the Medway. Instead he creates his own imaginary realm: a "nowhere" that shadows the dominions of Elizabeth. This is his equivalent of Utopia, his image of an archetypal realm whose pattern, if not laid up in heaven, is at least shadowed in faeryland. The indeterminate setting is complemented, moreover, by the apparently fortuitous and unpredictable adventures that interrupt the knights' respective quests. Meeting by chance, they continue their journey together. A path forks, and they choose different routes. Ladies are mysteriously abducted and must be searched for. Confronted by a scene of violence, one knight pursues the villain; the other remains behind to minister aid and comfort to the victim—or to pursue her himself. Nevertheless, in many instances the seemingly unpredictable evolution of the plot is more apparent than real. In the central books, where the influence of Ariosto's technique is more significant, the sequence of episodes is less subject to chance than in either of the *Orlando* epics; in the other books of Spenser's epic the action is more firmly controlled by the moral allegory.

Against this indeterminate background—a landscape and a plot that seem to be in perpetual flux—the sharp definition often given to the description of persons and places (the allegorical houses, the symbolic landscapes, the characteristic details of feature and costume and gesture) brings into clearer focus both the visual image and the concept (or concepts) that it shadows. The conventional *attributa personarum* are assimilated not only to the characters themselves but also to the universals of which they themselves are symbols and patterns. This is a decorum of idea; in developing it the poet's method approaches at times that of the iconographer.

The chiaroscuro that is so notable a feature of Spenser's poem involves a similar opposition between the indefinite, the indistinct, the indeterminate, and an ideal clarity; like other aspects of the poem, his treatment of this motif is conditioned by both Platonic and Christian metaphors of light and darkness. Beauty, virtue, and glory are too radiant for mortal eyes to endure. Like the sun of the intellectual world, these dazzle the sight; one must screen one's vision in order to behold them. (One may compare Spenser's method with Dante's more systematic development of this motif in the *Paradiso,* at the conclusion of the *Purgatorio,* and in the *Convivio.* As Beatrice fixes her eyes on the sun [symbol of the supreme Good], the poet beholds it mirrored in her eyes [that is, by the demonstrations of theology, the only science that can confer knowledge of true blessedness]. As the act of the intellect precedes that of the will, one must know the supreme Good in order to love it, and the narrator is thus led gradually upward to his true happiness through successive stages of contemplation and devotion.)

The conventions of chivalric romance, the glorification of antiquity, and the archaistic vocabulary reinforce one another, distancing the poem still further from the present. The language itself helps to foster the illusion of antiquity; although the medieval decorum that Spenser constructs is both artificial and anachronistic, it could nevertheless strike his readers as plausible. He speaks of his style as rustic, but this apology is susceptible to several interpretations: it is an elaboration of the style he had developed in his Æglogues and in association with the persona of Colin Clout, the shepherd lad; he wrote much of his epic in rural Ireland; his vocabulary retained older words no longer fashionable but still current in rural areas. An "antique" language was appropriate for an image of the "antique age."

Yet there were other considerations. The languages of Homeric and Virgilian epic appeared to be artificial constructions. (The oral tradition behind the epics of Homer, which would account for its mixture of dialects, was still unsurmised.) Moreover, the humanist concern for pure Latinity had stimulated concern for the purity and integrity of the English tongue, and, in Spenser's eyes, Chaucer provided a model of linguistic purity, a language still uncontaminated by inkhornisms and barbarisms. His writings were a "well of English undefyled," a "pure well-head of Poesie." This image is interesting not only for its bearing on language, but also for its association with poetic inspiration. Spenser is suggesting a native English alternative to the springs and fountains of Parnassus and Helicon and the inspiration of classical poetry.[19]

Spenser's linguistic archaism serves in a degree to lend both decorum and verisimilitude to his fictive image of "antiquity." Its materials—persons, events, settings—allegedly belong to the time of Arthur; just as the manner in which he describes them consciously evokes the chivalric world of late medieval and Renaissance fiction (a world in which the heroes fight against Saracens rather than heathen Angles and Saxons), he attempts through his archaic language as well as through extensive use of classical, French, and Italian proper names to enhance still further the affinities between his own romance world and those of his medieval and Renaissance predecessors. He is also endeavoring to establish more firmly what he regards as the native English poetic and linguistic tradition, adopting toward the language and poetry of Chaucer much the same attitude that Renaissance Italians had held toward the Tuscan verse of Dante and Petrarch and Boccaccio.

Moreover, his deliberate archaism also had significant parallels in the epic language of Homer and Virgil and in the romance tradition. In northern Italy the material of the Carolinian cycle had circulated widely in Franco-Veneto; in the eyes of Renaissance critics, Homer and Virgil had created an artificial language appropriate not only to their lofty subject matter—so remote from the common and the ordinary—but also to its archaic character, set in remote and legendary antiquity.[20]

Lacking a real understanding of the linguistic contexts of Homeric epic and its relation to oral tradition, Renaissance critics, like many of their classical precursors, regarded the Homeric vocabulary as an extreme example of poetic license. Instead of confining himself to one language and one character of style (Tasso observed), Homer had tried to mix all of them. Not content with the vocabulary of his own time, or of Greece itself, he had borrowed archaic words from the ancients and foreign terms from the barbarians. Nor did he leave these as he had found them; he had abbreviated them, lengthened them, and otherwise transmuted them at will. In addition, he had minted new words, imitating the voices of stream and forest, wind and fire and sea, metals and stones, beasts and birds. Homer was the first to employ the word *bombous,* to apply the epithet *mormuronta* to streams, to speak of arrows as *klaxontas* and waves as *boonta.* Virgil had likewise used certain archaic words borrowed from Ennius and other early poets, and various terminations reminiscent of the barbarians, but he had exercised great judgment and art. Like Homer, he had mixed the forms and characters of style, but had made his transitions gradually and by stages—like the tiers in a theater—not abruptly and precipitously.[21]

5.

In *The Faerie Queene,* the eulogy of the past serves both to extol and to depreciate the present. One encounters similar techniques in Spenser's minor poems. In the *Complaints,* the glories of antiquity often serve as a mutability topos or as an argument for deploring the ignorance and depravity of the modern age. In *The Ruines of Time,* the city of Verulam ("Verlame") laments the passing of her ancient glory, altogether forgotten except by Camden, "the nourice of antiquitie," who "hath writ my record in true-seeming sort." From this theme she passes to the praise of Sir Philip Sidney and the Earl of Leicester and the superiority of poetry to architectural monuments in bestowing enduring fame. In *The Teares of the Muses,* each of the nine sisters decries the neglect of learning by all classes of contemporary society. The nobility, Clio complains, neither patronize wisdom nor seek it themselves. Priding themselves on illustrious ancestry and heraldic arms, they feel no desire to emulate the virtuous deeds of their forebears. Consequently, future generations will have no knowledge "Of things forepast, nor moniments of time"; all that is worthy in this world must perish in obscurity and oblivion. Calliope similarly laments the decadence of the nobility. Contemptuous of learning, no longer zealous for "worthie deeds," they do not "care to have the auncestrie / Of th' old Heroes memorizde anew, / Ne doo they care that late posteritie / Should know their names."

Colin Clouts Come Home Againe eulogizes the queen herself and certain other individuals—Sidney and Raleigh, the countesses of Pembroke and Derby and other ladies of the nobility, such contemporary poets as Daniel and Alabaster— but couples this praise with general censure of "Courtiers schoolery." Admittedly there were exceptions; among them were "many persons of right worthie parts." But all the rest "do most-what fare amis, / And yet their owne misfaring will not see."

To these minor poems the evocation of antiquity may serve an elegiac function, providing opportunities for lamenting the former greatness of a vanished civilization or for accentuating the degeneration of contemporary nobles from the heroic virtues of their remote ancestors. These pejorative comparisons of the present age with the past also recur in *The Faerie Queene,* but here the primary emphasis falls on the glorification of the present queen and her realm. Spenser's romance-epic reveals a tension between the heroic mode and that of the complaint, as well as an ambiguous relationship toward his own times as an object of both praise and blame. On the whole, his poem is Janus-faced, extolling equivocally both past and present; shadowing the present in an icon of the past, it glorifies Elizabeth and her kingdom by simultaneously praising her illustrious forebears and the ancient glories of her nation while affirming her superiority to the exemplars of the past.

One of the major challenges confronting a heroic poet of the Renaissance was the task of re-creating a heroic age and linking it effectively with his own age. Although more than a few epic poets selected subjects from recent history,[22] all of the "Poets historicall" commended by Spenser (both "antique" and modern) had centered their epic actions on the distant past. He himself situates his heroic age in British antiquity—the times of Arthur—just as Ariosto had centered his own romance epic on the heroic age of Charlemagne and his paladins. It is by no means fortuitous that Spenser's allusion to the "goodly usage of those antique times" (*FQ* 3.1.13) consciously echoes Ariosto's exclamation on the "gran bontà de' cavallieri antiqui" (*Orlando Furioso,* canto 1) or that Merlin's prophecy of the "royall virgin" and other "famous Progeny" (*FQ* 3.3) who shall spring from the union of Britomart and Artegall is deliberately modeled on Melissa's prophecies concerning the future descendants of Bradamante and Ruggiero, ancestors of the illustrious house of Este (*Orlando Furioso,* canto 3).

Finally, like other epic poets, Spenser also evokes images of still earlier heroic ages—the glories of ancient Troy and of Rome the second Troy, while exalting the splendors of the "third kingdome" Troynovant (*FQ* 3.9.44). Similarly, although Artegall as "Champion of true Justice" shadows Lord Grey of Wilton, Spenser extols him by associating him with the divine heroes or even remoter heroic ages, with Bacchus and Hercules and Osiris (*FQ* 5.1.1–3, 5.7.21–23):

> Though vertue then were held in highest price,
> In those old times, Of which I doe intreat,
> Yet then likewise the wicked seede of vice
> Began to spring which shortly grew full great,
> And with their boughes the gentle plants did beat.
> But evermore some of the vertuous race
> Rose up, inspired with heroicke heat,
> That cropt the branches of the sient base.

As a "poet historicall," Spenser exploits a wide variety of devices to link the remote past with the present. He resorts to aetiological myth, as in the fable of Diana's curse on the Irish nymph Molanna (*FQ* 7.6.40–55). He recounts "the famous auncestries / Of my most dreaded Soveraigne" through the medium of the chronicle histories of British kings and Elfin emperors that Prince Arthur and Sir Guyon peruse in the house of Alma (*FQ* 2.10). He uses the devices of vision and prophecy (*FQ* 3.3, 5.7.21–23). Finally, he shadows the present in a fictive image of the past through techniques that have been variously labeled as typological or allegorical. As in Ariosto's romance, where the fictitious exploits of Bradamante and Ruggiero celebrate the antiquity and nobility of the house of Este, Spenser's historical fiction extols the antiquity and nobility of the British nation and its ruling dynasty, glorifying the poet's monarch and the worthies of her realm by shadowing them in an icon of a national heroic age.[23]

Chapter 6

The "Platonic Telescope"

Narrative and Moral Focus in The Faerie Queene

The Mutability cantos have sometimes been regarded as a kind of epilogue to Spenser's romance. Centered on the conflict between perpetual change and an underlying stability and continuity of essence, they recapitulate a recurrent motif not only in *The Faerie Queene* but also in much of Spenser's minor poetry. Appropriately, they conclude with the anticipation of eternity, the perpetual Sabbath of rest.

One of the attractions of this view is that it bestows perfection and completeness on an incomplete and imperfect poem; this appeal has been enhanced by the symbolic decorum of the number seven. Even though he could not specifically correlate the individual books of the poem with any of the six days of creation or the six ages of the world, the critic could hardly overlook the seductive analogy between both of these chronological schemes and the poem as it appeared in the 1609 Folio: the six completed units of the poet's symbolic image of the world, rounded off by an incomplete seventh unit treating the relation between time and eternity and concluding with an anticipation of "that Sabaoths sight." The very incompleteness and imperfection of this final section might indeed be regarded as symbolic. (As a reader alert to number symbolism might recall, the twenty-fourth unit of the *Epithalamion,* which would round off the sequence of hours, was likewise incomplete. The marriage between the poet and his bride had not yet been consummated. Neither had the final and perpetual union between Christ and the church.)

Although one cannot regard them as an epilogue, the concluding stanzas of the Mutability cantos nevertheless provide a convenient point of departure for analyzing Spenser's imaginary faeryland: a world that is represented not only in perpetual flux but also through shifting and variable modes of vision. In these respects it resembles not only the romance world of Ariosto but also the world of Ovid's *Metamorphoses*—a poem frequently compared to the romance in its variety and marvels, and often extolled by the apologists of the romance and faulted by its opponents. A world of shadows, constantly changing and moving, continually in the process of becoming, subject to illusion and deception, the land of faerie corresponds (as the poet may have intended) to the Platonic realm of appearances, the realm of becoming and opinion. The fixed and constant elements in the poem are the ideal realities toward which it directs its readers— the moral universals and absolutes that the narrator is shadowing. In contrast to this ultimate realm of being and knowledge, the world of ideas, the techniques whereby he shadows them and his modes of representation and vision are themselves constantly altering, subject to mutation and transformation. Just as the sequence of incidents and characters and landscapes is perpetually moving and changing—"flowing" is the term many critics prefer—his modes of visualizing, of "apperceiving" the idea, are constantly shifting, varying in distinctness and clarity. He sees reality through adjustable lenses, so to speak— now dimly, now clearly; now in concrete and detail, now as bald abstractions; now enigmatically, now realistically—in variable and shifting focus. This is not Tesauro's "Aristotelian telescope," but it is, in a sense, a sort of "cannochiale platonico."[1]

In Spenser's imaginary world, as in the real world, change and vicissitude possess not only moral and political implications and historiographical and metaphysical significance, but also epistemological and aesthetic value. The world of becoming and perpetual flux was also the realm of mere appearances of truth, easily subject to illusions and deceptions and associated with opinion rather than true knowledge of being. The history of the world was a chronicle of vicissitudes; the empires of the mind, like the fortunes of monarchs, were subject to change and decay. In contrast to the heavens (and Mutability challenges this point, as did Donne), all sublunary things are mutable and transient. Families and nations degenerate from the virtues of their founders. Substance remains stable, through its succession of changing accidents, but it is invisible. The true constants are God himself, the unmoved prime mover, his laws inscribed in the books of Scripture and nature, the truths of revealed theology, and the essential principles of moral philosophy. The latter are as applicable to the England of Elizabeth as to the Britain of Arthur; they remain, indeed, the fixed points of reference in the poet's indeterminate and fluid landscape.

The incoherence of Spenser's plot structures has, I think, been much exaggerated; but it is nevertheless true that the shifting pattern of analogies and contrasts between the structures and narrative modes of the different books is paralleled by the shifting and changing focus of his modes of visualization. This depends on not only the diverse mimetic and symbolic techniques he employs to convey his ideas but also the clarity with which he himself had envisioned them to begin with. In some instances the concepts themselves appear to have conditioned his presentational techniques; in other cases, the reverse appears to be true. In actuality, one cannot really distinguish between them; more significant are the methods whereby he encouraged the reader to infer his meaning from and through his images.

Thus in the Malbecco episode (as Graham Hough, Rosemary Freeman, Kathleen Williams, and other critics have observed)[2] Spenser shifts through successive stages from fairly realistic imitation in the direction of personification allegory. Initially, Malbecco is not simply and specifically a jealous husband; he is also old and miserly. He displays the characteristic traits of the comic *senex* married to a young and beautiful wife: avarice, impotence, reclusiveness, jealousy. In the course of the action, even these simple traits of character are brought into dramatic opposition. At the time of his wife's elopement his character has not yet become absolutely fixed; like the proverbial donkey between two bundles of hay, he is torn between contrary passions: his jealous love of his money and his jealous love for his wife. It is only later that the scales are tipped in Hellenore's direction. From a man torn between two kinds of jealous love, Malbecco becomes successively the "character" or "type" of the jealous cuckold and finally Jealousy itself.

In his representation of ethos Spenser may alternately transform an abstract concept into a particular man or woman, or the living creature into the abstract idea. He can present the same concept—alternatively or associatively— as landscape, architecture, and persona. He presents the triumph of Truth over Error through Saint George's victory over the monster and through his successful exit from the wandering wood, accompanied by Una. He conveys the ideal of temperance alternately through the house of Medina, the house of Alma, Guyon's combats with Pyrochles and Cymochles as representatives of wrath and lust, the temptations of Mammon and Phaedria and the sirens, and his destruction of Acrasia's bower. In the latter episode, moreover, the sorceress and her dwelling are correlative and complementary symbols. The ivory wall is suggestive of false dreams. The "wanton wreathings" of the arboreal porch, with its "embracing vine," the "lascivious armes" of golden ivy, and (not least) the cunning mixture of nature and art— these are symbolic of the charms of the accomplished *meretrix* herself (*FQ* 2.12.50–61).

In other instances Spenser may analyze a general concept into various sub-species and depict these symbolically through different personae: true and false religion or genuine and counterfeit holiness; true and false courtesy and nobility; faithful and unfaithful friendship; the true equity of Artegall and the false distributive justice of the egalitarian giant. In the central books, the variety of types and modes of love portrayed range all the way from "greedy lust" and the abominations of Argante and Sir Ollyphant to chaste and pure devotion. They include loyal and faithless lovers, jealous lovers, unrequited lovers, patient and indignant lovers, settled affection and the malady of Hereos, lovers' complaints, and both virtuous and adulterous love.

1.

Since the books on love and friendship are more heavily indebted to Ariosto than are other sections of Spenser's romance, it may be useful to compare his views on love and war as epic themes with those of Ariosto and Tasso. Ariosto had chosen arms and amours as his argument:

> Of Dames, of Knights, of armes, of loves delight,
> Of curtesies, of high attempts I speake. . . .
> (Le donne, i cavallier, l'arme, gli amori,
> Le cortesie, l'audaci imprese io canto. . . .) (*Orlando Furioso* 1.1; translation from
> Sir John Harington, *Orlando Furioso,* ed. Robert McNulty [Oxford, 1972])

This was the traditional subject matter of romance; Virgil had professed to sing of "arms and the man," with no allusion to amours, and Tasso had retained this formula in his epic of the first crusade ("Canto l'arme pietose e'l capitano.").[3] The proposition of Spenser's romance-epic combines the Virgilian with the Ariostean formula. Adapting the opening formula attributed to Virgil ("Ille ego, qui quondam gracili modulatus avena")[4] to his own progress from pastoral to epic poetry ("Lo I the man, whose Muse whilome did maske"), he follows Ariosto in his concern with dames as well as cavaliers, loves no less than arms. He will "sing of Knights and Ladies gentle deeds," which have remained too long unsung. "Fierce warres and faithfull loves shall moralize my song" (*FQ* 1.proem.1). The analogy with Ariosto and Tasso—and with Boiardo—would have been heightened if he had ever represented Gloriana's wars against the Paynim king as a full-scale war. As the poem now stands, there are no actual wars, no massed armies, no large-scale invasions. Instead, there are individual combats, individual quests, a few stray Saracens, and an occasional besieged castle. On the other hand, *faithful* loves do in fact "moralize" his romance, in comparison with the *Orlando Furioso*. Ariosto's heroes and heroines drink too freely and too indiscriminately from the fountains of love and hate in the forest of Ardennes, switching allegiance accordingly. Yet there are notable exemplars of fidelity in Bradamente, Isabella, and other heroines. Primarily, however, Spenser "moralizes" the persons and events of his fable by associating them with specific ethical categories.

Spenser's idealization of love and friendship as chivalric virtues, no less appropriate for the knight than martial fortitude, invites comparison with Tasso's views on this subject. In his *Discourses on the Heroic Poem,* Tasso endeavored not only to subject the romance to the laws of epic but also to appropriate romance materials—love, enchantments, courtesies—for the heroic poem, which had been traditionally centered on exploits of arms. The eristic techniques whereby he argued these points need not concern us, but it is significant that (like Spenser) he was disposed to "moralize" the passion of love: asserting the nobility of love and friendship through Platonic topoi and through commonplaces of moral theology. His initial syllogism runs something like this: the most beautiful things befit the heroic poem; love is a most beautiful thing; therefore, love is an appropriate epic argument. Again, love and wrath are the two major passions according to the Platonists. (Compare the roles of Pyrochles and Cymochles in Spenser's allegory of temperance.) Homer regarded Achilles' wrath as a passion proper to a hero and hence to the heroic poem; therefore, love is also a suitable epic subject. Indeed the love of Helen was "most noble" and "most beautiful," even though immoral; in Isocrates' opinion, all the beauty and grace of Homer's epics had sprung from Helen's beauty. Moreover, love was not merely a passion and movement of the sensitive appetite (according to Saint Thomas Aquinas) but a "most noble" habit of the will. Thus actions accomplished for love were heroic beyond all others, and both love and friendship (compare books 3 and 4 of *The Faerie Queene*) were appropriate subjects for the heroic poem. As a chivalric virtue, "honest" or noble love was a habit of the will. The subject matter of the heroic poem (whether one called it epic or romance) was essentially "the arms and amours of heroes and wandering knights."[5]

Like Milton, Tasso and Spenser were writing in the context of an essentially pedagogical theory of poetry. The former was concerned with "l'idea d'un perfetto cavaliere";[6] the latter aimed "to fashion [i.e. model] a gentleman or noble person in vertuous and gentle discipline." Just as earlier "historicall" poets—

Homer and Virgil, Ariosto and Tasso—had "ensampled a good governour and a vertuous man," Spenser proposes to represent the "private morall vertues" in Prince Arthur and the public virtues in Arthur the king (*PW* 407). In his earlier plans for a national epic, Milton had similarly considered "what king or knight before the conquest might be chosen in whom to lay the pattern of a Christian hero" (*CP* 668–69). These are, in a sense, the poetic counterparts of the various prose works devoted to the idea of the orator, the prince, the courtier, the governor, or the gentleman—paradigms developed in antiquity by Xenophon and Cicero and Quintilian and emulated in the Renaissance by Castiglione and Erasmus, Elyot and Peacham and others.

Spenser does not only depict aspects of a general concept through different personae. Conversely, the same persona may shadow a variety of types and ideas. In Spenser's hands, a number of literary analogues and ectypes are transformed and subsumed in a new creation. In Acrasia and her bower, for instance, the reader immediately recognizes Circe and her Renaissance granddaughters Alcina and Armida. It is not simply that the poem itself is in continuous process, constantly changing and evolving or dissolving, but that the relation between symbol and referent, image and idea, and the dual relationship of Spenser's "types" to literary "prototypes" and to moral and spiritual "archetypes" is represented in diverse ways. On the one hand, his symbolic "referents"— derived from a variety of sources and contexts and accommodated to the structure and texture of a new romance—are themselves integral parts of larger "systems" or structures external to the poem, but nevertheless relative to it: to the structures of moral philosophy and theology, to the structures and conventions of Elizabethan society, to the pattern of recent events in Britain and on the Continent, and to the more comprehensive patterns of the history of England and of the church. Spenser has transformed and assimilated these materials—much as he has transmuted the materials, images, and phrases borrowed from other poets—yet in many instances the significance of his symbols, the coherence of certain clusters of events, and their interpretation depend largely on structures implicit in history or in moral philosophy.

On the other hand, in his adaptation of passages from other writers, Spenser not only accommodates them to his own narrative and doctrinal structures and descriptive modes but also often treats them in a manner strikingly at odds with that of the original poet. In other instances, however, these may retain much of the same meaning and value that they had possessed in the original— though to what extent he intended to evoke the original context is sometimes uncertain and variable. In certain contexts he is content merely to display this borrowed plumage; in other contexts he is deliberately calling attention to the changes and improvements he has made. Thus Acrasia's bower gains in significance through the reader's awareness of parallels with Ariosto's Alcina and Tasso's Armida and Homer's Circe. Spenser could expect an educated reader to associate his monster Error with Hesiod's Echidna, to recognize the analogies between his Britomart and Ariosto's Bradamante, to compare the fugitive Florimel with the fugitive Angelica and her false counterpart with the false Angelica of Italian romance and the false Helen of classical myth. He might also have intended an analogy between the twelve knights of the quest and the twelve paladins of the Carolinian cycle, and between Arthur's role and the twelve labors of Hercules. Yet he would scarcely have expected his audience to recognize all such adaptations. In his own age the imitation of authors was a standard pedagogical technique in humanist grammar schools; Continental theorists were still debating the relative superiority of modern romances and classical epics as models for imitation; though some of Spenser's imitations and borrowings are indeed allusive references to earlier poems, it would be a mistake to interpret them consistently in this way.

The clownish young man who undertakes the first quest in *The Faerie Queene* is patently reminiscent not only of Piers the Plowman, but also of the young Perceval, though the chivalric parallel is overshadowed by the theological import of Spenser's imagery. As portrayed in the letter to Raleigh, "unfitte through his rusticity for a better place," George the plowman was essentially the natural or earthy man, not yet an heir of heavenly glory. It was not until he had put on "the armour of a Christian man" and the cross of the heavenly man that he "seemed the goodliest man in al that company, and was well liked of the Lady" (*PW* 408). The ecclesiastical associations of the plowman in Langland's poem (Luke 9:62) are relevant to Spenser's theme (*FQ* 1.10.66), as is Langland's image of Christ in Piers's armor advancing to joust at Jerusalem. On his first appearance at Arthur's court and on his early quests Percival, the knight of the Grail, had been a kind of chivalric schlemiel; country-bred and ignorant both of the use of arms and of the principles of courtly manners, he had made virtually every possible blunder, including the signal failure to ask the crucial question concerning the Grail. We do not see this facet of his character in Spenser's poem, though he is easily beguiled and misled; but it is implicit in the letter to Raleigh.

Although the opening stanzas of the poem evoke the conventional iconography of the Saint George legend, this has been both moralized and transformed. The red cross belongs traditionally to Saint George, but the Pauline armor converts the knight into a type of the *miles christianus* (the "Christian Warrior"). The "line" that links the Lady to "a milke white lambe" belonged traditionally to the scene of the dragon fight itself. The lamb and the lady are tied together as intended victims of the monster. Spenser has introduced them in an altogether different and largely figurative context, as symbols of Christ the sacrificial Lamb of God and his bride the true church. Subsequently he expresses these ideas through different symbols, as George himself becomes a type of Christ and the bridegroom of the church. In the fight with the dragon the hero is simultaneously George and the type of the Christian warrior, but his combat is also assimilated to Saint Michael's war with the dragon in the Apocalypse, to the Passion of Christ, and to the exploits of the monster-quellers of myth and romance. After delivering Una's parents (the king and queen who shadow Adam and Eve), they are betrothed, but must wait for six more years before consummating their marriage (*FQ* 1.12.18, 19).

If this detail was indeed intended symbolically, it could be an oblique compliment to the queen, wishing her the felicity of a sixty-year reign. If one were to interpret it in terms of the six world ages, the most plausible chronological schema would seem to hinge on the doctrine (developed by several Protestant theologians) that before their deaths Adam and Eve had been justified by faith in their future redeemer and that accordingly the church and the essentials of the Protestant faith were almost as old as mankind.[7]

2.

Since Spenser's romance remains incomplete and his final designs for its structure uncertain, his critics, like those of Ariosto, have sometimes stressed other kinds of unity and coherence than formal unity; especially unity of tone and atmosphere. His pictorial imagination, his aesthetic "distancing" and detachment, the "visionary" and "dream-like" qualities of his poem are topoi as proverbial as Ariostean irony and the *sorriso ariostesco* (the "Ariostean smile"). Alternatively, they have emphasized its blending of diverse emotional tones and styles; the poem is a *concordia discors,* a harmony achieved out of variety. Like the pleasure gardens of Armida or Atlante's castle, *The Faerie Queene* is an illusion wrought by magic, a phantasm; the reader may wander through its halls and parterres without asking how it was actually constructed, what it was built of, or what if anything it actually means.

This is not altogether begging the question, for it is usually for pleasure rather than for instruction that one reads *The Faerie Queene;* among its principal attractions are its variety not only of plots and characters but also of tone and technique; its shifts from one mode of visualization to another; its mingling of clarity and ambiguity; its combinations of blurred and distinct outlines, of *sfumato* and *evidenza*. Its chiaroscuro effects are not limited merely to the imagery of light and shadow, in which its author excelled, but to the changing relationships between sense and idea, the fictive images and the universals to which they refer. In some instances its personae are merely mute abstractions; the poet simply names them without describing them. In other cases (such as Phantastes and the Seven Deadly Sins) they are given characteristic features and garments and gestures, or symbolic companions and steeds. In other contexts (such as Ate and Despair, Elissa and Perissa, Pyrochles and Cymochles) they may both speak and act. Mingling with these are personae who are not personifications but who nevertheless represent stock types of character; Braggadocchio and Trompart, Paridell and Hellenore are conventional figures of comedy. Talus derives from allegorized myth, but he is essentially little more than a thinly disguised personification of judicial execution. The knights of the quest are exemplars and patrons of the several moral virtues, but they are both more and less than ethical symbols. Since the moral virtues themselves are habits of the will, perfected by exercise, their patrons—or most of them—must struggle to achieve and to maintain them. Spenser's characters are engaged accordingly in a perpetual battle against various forms of temptation; on occasion some of them fail when put to the test. Redcrosse apostatizes from the true faith. Even the inflexible Artegall allows pity to obstruct justice, and he must pay the consequences; through the mercy he shows to Radigund, the unfortunate knight whom he had rescued is captured once again and put to a vile and ignominious death. The majority of these figures are types and examples—the temperate or continent man, the chaste woman, the just magistrate, the courteous gentleman, the warfaring and wayfaring Christian, the loyal but jealous lover—rather than actual symbols or personifications of these virtues.

Other characters—Matilda, who adopts the infant rescued from the bear; the shepherds and brigands of book 6—are not strictly part of the moral allegory, though they are not without moral significance. (The shepherds for the most part display a natural courtesy; unlike the ambitious gentry at court, they are content with their lot and station.) Similarly, although Scudamour and Amoretta are lovers, indeed "types" of the lover, they do not need to be interpreted allegorically. Their tormentors, on the other hand, belong to a different level of reality, for they are not human beings at all, but passions of the mind. The enchanter Busyrane is a figure of Tyrannic Love. The blacksmith Care is a personification; his Pythagorean smithy, an allegory.

3.

Like other poets of his age, Spenser mixes allegorical and mimetic techniques; recent critics have commented with justice on tendencies to confuse the two modes.[8] If one were to insist on the essentially metaphorical nature of allegory—on the quality of *otherness*—one would have to exclude all the personifications (except those endowed with symbolic attributes) as well as most of the stock character types, such as Paridell and Braggadocchio. Renaissance commentators themselves often used the term loosely, without distinguishing clearly or consistently between different kinds of poetic exempla. The exempla might include personifications, myths, historical persons and events, and incredible or realistic fictions. Merely by descriptive or narrative elaboration, personifications could be readily developed into allegories; realistic presentations of character, depicted in accordance with the principle of decorum, might easily become moral examples and types—the good governor, the faithful lover, etc.—or "Ideas" of virtue or vice.[9]

Though historical and personal allusions through the medium of allegory are frequent, they are sometimes elusive, and their relation to the moral allegory is likewise ambitious. Gloriana and Belphoebe shadow the "two persons" of Elizabeth, public and private: "the one of a most royall Queene or Empresse, the other of a most vertuous and beautifull Lady." The one mirrors "her rule"; the other "her rare chastitee." Spenser portrays "her kingdome in Faery land," her courtiers and ministers as faery knights or as Britons, and London as Cleopolis. Nevertheless, Mercilla also shadows at least one facet of Elizabeth's rule; under the name of mercy the poet is portraying her justice, and under the head of justice both her domestic government and her foreign policy. The knights of the quest—St. George (presented as a faery knight, but actually an Englishman), Sir Guyon, Sir Scudamour, Sir Artegall, Sir Calidore—are under Gloriana's jurisdiction. The British knights—Prince Arthur, who is in quest of the Faerie Queene and the princess Britomart, who is in quest of Artegall—are lovers, each in search of an unknown beloved, and under no command except their own. Yet Scudamour fails in his quest, and the task of delivering Amoretta falls to Britomart. Gloriana herself bears no direct relation to the assistance that Artegall bestows on Borbon, to Arthur's enterprise against Geryoneo on Belge's behalf, or to his defeat of the Souldan (an episode often interpreted as an allusion to the Spanish Armada). Arthur has not yet met the Faery Queen, and it is at Mercilla's court that he undertakes the defense of Belge. Artegall is indeed under Gloriana's command, but his commission is to deliver Irena (simultaneously Erin and Peace) from Grantorto. The regal glory of Mercilla's court is portrayed in imagery that Spenser might have applied to Gloriana's court and her Panthea and Cleopolis if he had ever reached the final book of his romance.

Although these historical allusions serve to glorify the queen, her government, and the poet's own country and its religion, they also provide a vehicle for social and political criticism, intermixed with personal references. The veil of allegory could thus function as protective coloring or camouflage, as it had frequently done in satire. Even though Spenser was not overdisposed to caution, though his satiric allegory was sometimes so thinly veiled that it brought him into difficulties with powerful individuals at court and in other countries, it is significant that in his letter to Raleigh he professed to be safeguarding himself against "gealous opinions and misconstructions" by disclosing his intent (PW 407). In particular, he explicitly points out the personae in whom he was shadowing the queen. He would eventually conclude his poem—at least as it appeared during his own lifetime—on a note of bitterness, evoking the not uncharacteristic motif of complaint.[10] His poem had already experienced the envenomed fangs of the Blatant Beast: "some wicked tongues did it backbite,/ And bring into a mighty Peres displeasure." The great, it would seem, did not want to be instructed or corrected. They preferred the pleasure of flattery, to have their ears tickled: "And seeke to please that now is counted wisemens threasure" (FQ 6.12.41).

4.

Several of Spenser's minor works similarly exploited allegory as a medium for commenting on contemporary events and as a vehicle both for praise and for political and ecclesiastical criticism: The Shepheardes Calender, Mother Hubberds Tale, and Colin Clouts Come Home Againe. In the first of these, the edge of the satiric references to conditions within the Church of England had been blunted to a considerable extent by E. K.'s gloss (Shepheardes Calender, May, July, and September AEglogues). The transparent references to Archbishop Grindal and to Bishop Young of Rochester are ignored; Algrind is simply "the name of a shepheard," and Roffy is identified merely as "The name of a shepehearde in Marot his AEglogue of Robin and the Kinge." Criticism of the more conservative and anti-Puritan elements within the English clergy is explained by the glossator as allusions to the Church of Rome.

Spenser converts his translation of Virgil's *Culex* into an allegorical medium. *Virgils Gnat* serves as a "riddle" for his personal complaint to and against the Earl of Leicester: "Wrong'd, yet not daring to expresse my paine, / To you (great Lord) the causer of my care, / In clowdie teares my case I thus complaine / Unto your selfe, that onely privie are."[11] Virgil's poem purports to be nothing more than a miniature mock epic, a poetic *jeu d'esprit:* "Lusimus, Octavi, gracili modulante Thalia"; "omnis ut historiae per ludum consonet ordo / notitiae"; "quisquis erit culpare jocos Musamque paratus, / pondere vel Culicis levior famaque feretur."[12] On the surface, this is all that Spenser's translation appears to be: "We now have playde *(Augustus)* wantonly"; "th'whole history / Is but a jest"; and "who such sports and sweet delights doth blame, / Shall lighter seeme than this Gnats idle name."[13]

In this poem a gnat saves the life of a sleeping shepherd menaced by a treacherous serpent by stinging the man in the eye, but the insect is promptly killed by the shepherd for his pains. Later the ghost of the gnat appears to the shepherd in a vision, complains of his wrong, and laments his fate in the underworld. Spenser's *Visions of the Worlds Vanitie* are centered on an inversion of this motif. Although the poems are modeled on the visions of Petrarch and DuBellay, they are concerned neither with the death of a beautiful woman nor the ruin of a great empire but with the relationship between the small and the great. A gadfly stings a bull. A small bird feeds in the jaws of the crocodile. A fly destroys the eagle's brood. A swordfish pierces the throat of a mighty whale. A spider poisons a dragon. A cedar tree is blighted by a worm. An ant compels a stately elephant to cast down the golden tower upon his back. A goodly ship is stopped abruptly by the little fish called Remora. A wasp stings a lion. The Roman empire is saved by a goose. Meditating on "so great things by so small distrest," the poet learns "To scorne all difference of great and small," and concludes with an admonition to his readers "to love the low degree":[14]

> And if that fortune chaunce you up to call
> To honours seat, forget not what you be.

5.

Spenser's pictorialism, his visual imagination, his iconographic techniques are coins that have passed through the hands of critic after critic. Yet worn as they are, they are still legal tender, still valid currency. These aspects of his poetic method owe much to Ovidian tradition and to Spenser's master Ariosto, something (surely) to the detailed symbolic descriptions characteristic of the mythographies and iconographies of the Renaissance, and much to a critical heritage that had assimilated the poet's methods to those of the painter, the verbal to the visual icon. With its immediate appeal to the senses, its ability to impress simultaneously the imagination, the understanding, and the memory, and its alleged power over the emotions and the will, the pictorial image provided an analogue, if not a model, for the eidolon of the poet. Such comparisons had been traditional in European literature virtually from the beginning; there was a substantial element of truth in Simonides' metaphorical definition of the sister arts: a speaking picture, a silent poem. Homer's description of Achilles' shield and its Hesiodic analogue, the shield of Herakles, were imitated by Virgil and later poets. The Sophists had made extensive use of literary icons, similar to *The Tablet of Cebes,* as pedagogical aids. The classical iconographers and their medieval and Renaissance successors drew upon poets as well as painters and sculptors for their descriptions of gods and heroes and personified concepts such as the liberal arts or the virtues and vices; the poets in turn consulted the iconographers. The pictorial aspects of Ovid and Virgil—and in particular their images of mythological figures and personifications—were assimilated by both poets and painters. Although we cannot know how much of this critical theory Spenser had read firsthand, he was almost certainly familiar with Sidney's *Apology* (he refers to Gosson's unlucky treatise in an early letter to Harvey [*PW* 635]), and he would have encountered many of its basic principles indirectly in poetry and in art. Moreover, he was probably familiar (as Rosemary Freeman has argued) with some of the emblem literature of the Renaissance.

It is scarcely surprising, therefore, that critics have stressed the "painterly" qualities of his verse, or—in view of its diversity and variety—that they should compare it to pictorial styles diversified enough to raise the eyebrows and hackles of any art historian. At one moment *The Faerie Queene* is a medieval tapestry; now a mannerist fresco; now an oil painting by Giorgione or Titian or some other Venetian artist. Now Raphael, now Gozzoli or Ghirlandaio, now Uccello. Now the Vinci of "The Madonna of the Rocks," now Albrecht Dürer—or Hieronymus Bosch.

Such comparisons are a tribute to Spenser's ability not only to combine a wide range of materials—classical, medieval, Renaissance—but also to assimilate without obvious incongruity or discord a variety of modes of representation.

As critics have noted, the different books create their own special decorums; they establish contexts, not only moral and thematic but also affective and atmospheric; what would probably be discordant in book 1 can be made to seem not unfitting in the third and fourth books or in book 6. Redcrosse and Guyon would have been less tolerant than Sir Satyrane of the peccadilloes of the Squire of Dames (*FQ* 3.3). Scudamour would hardly have wrecked the Bower of Bliss—certainly not so unceremoniously. Calidore would have found a fitting reply to the welcome of Genius and Excesse. It would be hard to imagine him "disdainfully" upsetting the porter's bowl and breaking his staff, or dashing the maidservant's welcome cup to the ground. He would surely have been more scrupulous than Guyon and the Palmer about entering a lady's bower without invitation and without knocking. If by chance he had obtruded so rashly upon her privacy, he would (one suspects) have handled the embarrassing situation with habitual tact. It would be equally difficult to picture Guyon's reaction to the temple of Venus, where Scudamour meets his Amoretta, or to the dance of the Graces and the hundred maidens (*FQ* 6.10), which Calidore inadvertently interrupts. On the other hand, in delivering the homicidal Phedon from Furor, Sir Guyon and the Palmer merely lecture the young man on the merits of temperance; Artegall would surely have turned him over to his iron henchman for execution.

In these different contexts, Spenser can accommodate the influence of Ariosto and Malory to that of Virgil and Tasso: assimilating to the heroic poem the techniques or materials of the fabliau, the saint's legend, the morality, the love lyric, the complaint, the pastoral idyll, the Alexandrian and chivalric romances, the masque and the pageant. In his own way Ariosto had achieved a similar mixture. The names that Spenser assigns to his characters—a linguistic gallimaufry of Greek and Latin, French and Italian and Celtic—recall the onomastic practices of the medieval and Renaissance romances, exotic and heterogeneous. There are few English proper names among them, and they suggest the range of allusions—literary or historical or moral—that he is endeavoring to evoke. Isis's chapel and the garden of Adonis suggest the pagan mysteries fashionable in Renaissance Italy. The houses of Temperance and Holiness recall the figurative castles of the morality play and medieval allegory. The palace of Lucifera, reminiscent in some respects of Chaucer's house of Fame, also recalls medieval representations of Fortuna's dwelling, a tradition that had already influenced Chaucer's poem. The goddess Nature of the Mutability cantos derives from Alain de Lille through Chaucer's *Parliament of Fowls:* the divine council is inherited from classical epic. Mutability's formal complaint reflects the conventions of medieval and Renaissance judicial allegory; before some symbolic court, held by Nature or Love or Wisdom, or by Jove or Apollo, the suppliant presents a complaint or a petition, and sometimes pleads his case with all the resources of forensic oratory. The procession of the months and seasons in the cantos has been termed Ovidian, but essentially it is a masque spectacle, a pageant. The personifications in the masque of Cupid—Daunger, Hope, Dissemblance, and the like—recall those of *The Romance of the Rose* and other erotic allegories. Duessa's hell-journey is a legacy from Virgil. The story of Cambell and Canacee is explicitly connected with Chaucer's Squire's Tale (*FQ* 4.2.32–34). With the procession of the Seven Deadly Sins, the reader is in Langland's world; with the house of Sleep, one is in the realm of the *Metamorphoses*. Though Venus's temple is chaster than most of its classical and medieval counterparts, the representation of love's spoils in the house of Busyrane recalls motifs in Chaucer's images of Venus's shrine and temple as well as in Petrarch's triumph of Love. Mirabella, cruel fair punished for scorning her lovers and abused by Scorn and Disdain, has offended in much the same manner as Ariosto's Lydia, but the details of her punishment bear a closer resemblance to the maltreated lady in the romance of Percival. With the Pastorella episode the reader is in the realm of Longus's *Daphnis and Chloe* and the *Aethiopica* of Heliodorus; Ariosto had already adapted the motif of the brigands for his story of Olimpia. The Malbecco episode, which burlesques the seduction of Helen of Troy, has been called a fabliau; in this respect it resembles Ariosto's tale of Giocondo, which Harington had allegedly translated for the amusement of Elizabeth's maids of honor. Braggadocchio and Trompart—*miles gloriosus* (braggart soldier) and scheming servant—are essentially the *alazon* and *eiron* of classical comedy.

As in Ariosto's *Orlando,* the diverse elements are sometimes juxtaposed and their contrasts emphasized, but more frequently they are fused and combined. They achieve variety and on occasion a fine surprise, but they rarely give the impression of being a mosaic or a collage. There are mosaic and inlay, to be sure—the topographias and chronographias, the descriptions of persons and houses, paintings and processions, are for the most part insets—but one does not see them as medallions in the narrative action; nor do the diverse elements of which some of them are composed seem inappropriate. If there is inherent incongruity or contradiction, it is often deliberate: an integral part of the decorum of the concept or the character. And though the method is often carefully controlled—as in the opening canto of the poem—the result frequently seems natural rather than an effect of conscious artifice. Instead of cosmatesque work, one is confronted with what appears to be the variable and fortuitous patterns in veined marble.

The solvent that enables Spenser to assimilate materials so diverse in origin and in quality—leaving him free to restructure them according to his personal taste, the comparatively loose requirements of his narrative, and the somewhat stricter demands of his moral allegory—is, on the whole, the mode of the chivalric romance, even more than its technical conventions. His "antique" world is itself a fiction, located somewhere in an "unreal" space and time, between classical antiquity and contemporary society and able to participate in both. In this respect it resembles to an extent the heroic world of classical epic: a world that never existed in reality and that bore only a remote resemblance either to the realities of Mycenaean Greece as archaeologists now conceive them or to the Greece of Homer's contemporaries. With each successive phase in the evolution of classical civilization—the development of history and moral and political philosophy, a written literary tradition and systematic poetic theory, changing attitudes toward the older religion and its mythology, and established exegetical techniques—the world of Homeric epic not only became progressively distanced from contemporary society but also underwent profound changes in the process. This was likewise the case with the matter of Britain and France in the romances. The Orlando of Boiardo and Ariosto and Pulci is as distant from the Roland of the *Chanson* as is the latter from the Hruodlandus slain by the Basques at Roncevaux. In Orlando's case, the literary historian is able to some extent to trace the development from a historical incident through the *chanson de geste* to romance. In the case of Arthur, on the other hand, valid historical testimony is lacking; except for the brief allusions in Gildas and Nennius there is little evidence for the development of the Arthurian legend before the fabulous history of Geoffrey of Monmouth. When we first encounter Arthur in literature he is already a romance hero, already well established in the domain of myth and romance. In both cases the virtual absence of an authentic historical tradition and antiquarian knowledge, and the interaction of oral tradition with literary fiction, encouraged the creation of a never-never land belonging largely to the imagination, a heroic world unlike the present and governed not by historical fact but largely by the conventions of the romance.

6.

The "unreal" space and time and the shifting modes of visualization in Spenser's romance have led critics to categorize it, along with Ariosto's poem, as a "mannerist" work. Though this label is not altogether satisfactory, it nevertheless underlines the "nonclassical" aspects of both poems as well as their exploitation of changing perspectives and shifting angles of vision. In the strictest sense, however, the term would seem to be inappropriate; neither poem is really a "reaction" against Renaissance classicism. Though the principles of classical structure had established themselves among the erudite, they had not won acceptance either among the people or among the greater part of the gentry. Unlike mannerist painting and architecture, the sixteenth-century romance, especially as Spenser treats it, represents a partial—though only a partial—accommodation of romance structures to those of classical epic. These are, significantly, concessions to classical principles, not reactions against them. Tasso would carry this development a stage further in his own epic, endeavoring to subject the varied materials and chivalric ethos of the romance to neo-Aristotelian canons; for his pains he has been labeled "baroque."

Spenser's image of heroic antiquity is essentially a charade, a "spectacle"; the prominence of processions and masques in the poem, or of paintings like those in the house of Busyrane, is an integral part of this spectacular mode. Having completed his own quest, Redcrosse refers to Guyon's quest as the next of the several spectacles: "But you, faire Sir, whose pageant next ensewes" (*FQ* 2.1.33). This is a ceremonial performance, as studiedly and festively archaic as a Renaissance fête or joust: those court solemnities at which the pageantry and ritual of medieval warfare and chivalric love continued to be cherished and preserved long after they had lost any direct relevance to the social and military realities of the time. The poet's own contemporaries, and the virtues or vices he associates with them, are in masque costume or in tilting armor, complete with heraldic bearings and heroic or amorous *devises*. At the same time, motifs derived from classical antiquity are likewise medievalized, as in the romances of Chaucer and Boccaccio and in medieval painting. Though patently reminiscent of Polyphemus, the cannibal who holds Amoretta and Aemilia captive belongs to the romance world of Ariosto rather than to Homer's epic milieu. Paridell and Hellenore live in a different world from that of their classical prototypes: a society with a different kind of sophistication and a different sense of the comedy of manners. The Paris and Helen of the *Iliad* might retreat to her chamber when by every standard of heroic conduct he ought to be on the battlefield instead, but it would be difficult to picture them at Menelaos's table making assignations by wine cups and after-dinner fruits. Spenser's satyrs are medieval woodwoses. They have virtually forgotten the god Dionysos and the delights of the vine; they are more apt to pursue mortal women than nymphs. They would be more at home in the milieu of Renaissance masques and pastorals and romances than in the myths of classical antiquity.

The tonal modulations of Spenser's poetry and its techniques of visualization embody qualities that many Cinquecento Italians especially valued in the romance, in lyric and pastoral, and in painting: sweetness and softness *(soavità)*, smoothness, grace, and "prettiness" *(piacevolezza* and *vaghezza),* chiaroscuro effects, and *sfumato* and *morbidezza.* They also reflect the contemporary interest in variety of materials, and of corresponding adjustments of style, within the same poem. Both Scaliger and Tasso had discussed the mixture of styles in the *Aeneid;*[15] though Spenser may not have seen their treatises, he would nevertheless have been alert to stylistic variations in Virgil's epic as well as in those of Ariosto and Tasso. He would also have been sensitive to the different kinds of mixture that these poets had achieved—as well as to the distinct tone and flavor *(gusto)* of his own romance. Through his choice of vowels or consonants and through his manipulation of verbal cadences, he tries to suggest harshness *(asprezza)* as well as smoothness, rapidity as well as languor. Like Ariosto, he feels free to introduce the comic. The moral dialectic in his poem, moreover, with its sharp opposition between logical contraries, encourages the use of the grotesque (symbolic of the ugliness of evil) as a foil to the beauty of virtue. Alternatively, smoothness and sweetness of discourse, when applied to evil, could emphasize both its seductive charm and its falsehood, enhancing the element of illusion.[16]

The flexibility of the romance—not tied to a single action or setting and moving freely between court and countryside, castle and forest—made it easier to represent social extremes and to combine heroic with pastoral conventions. The introduction of such contrasts owed much to the Greek romances, but they were also to some extent present in classical epic. The disguised Odysseus dwells with a faithful swineherd. Aeneas visits the Arcadian king Evander, whose people lead a life of rustic simplicity at the wooded site of the future city of Rome. In Tasso's epic Erminia takes refuge among shepherds. In Sidney's Arcadian romance, which he apparently regarded as a heroic poem, a royal family retires to the countryside to dwell among shepherds. In Ariosto's romance, the princess Angelica disguises herself as a shepherdess and dwells for a time in a shepherd's cottage with her lover Medoro. The Renaissance pastoral drama, on the other hand, had included shepherd kings among its personae, and, through the proximity of field and pasture and woodland, much of the apparatus of

sylvan mythology: nymphs and fauns and satyrs, the goddess Diana, and such
rural divinities as Silvanus, Faunus, and Pan.

Once the knight-errant of romance, or his lady, enters the forest, they cross
a threshold of reality; they are now within an indeterminate world that may
prove neither menacing nor idyllic. They can conceivably encounter hostile
or friendly knights and hermits and satyrs, monsters and savages or merely
shepherds and foresters. Or they may meet with witches and fays, with Artemis
herself or with some other sylvan deity. Braggadocchio and Timias meet an
ectype of Diana (Belphoebe). Calidore's quest brings him into the open fields,
where he falls in love with Pastorella; while wandering the fields and woods
he beholds the nymphs and Graces dancing. A savage man befriends Serena.
In the same book other savages attempt to sacrifice Serena for a cannibal feast;
earlier, Amoretta had been seized by a lustful and cannibalistic savage. Timias
and Serena are healed by a holy hermit; yet the apparently holy hermit who
shelters Una and Redcrosse is a disguised sorcerer and promptly betrays both
of his guests. Una is befriended and adored by satyrs; others of the same species
ravish Hellenore and the mother of Sir Satyrane. And when Florimel ventures
into the forest, she must take to her heels to escape the lusts of a forester, a
witch's son, and a hyena-like beast that "feeds on womens flesh."

7.

What is chiefly missing in Spenser's epic-romance is the heroic ethos of
classical epic as it appears in Achilles and Hector and Ajax and (in a very
different way) in Virgil's Turnus and Aeneas and in Milton's Satan. Yet in view
of the genre and materials of *The Faerie Queene,* this was virtually inevitable.
Spenser's fictive milieu, like the literary species he had preferred, was medieval
rather than classical—an idealized British antiquity instead of the idealized
prehistory of Greece and Rome. Its ethos, similarly, is chivalric and medieval—
the idealized medievalism of the Renaissance romance—rather than the kind
of heroism celebrated in classical epic or (for that matter) in early Teutonic
heroic poetry. For all the swordplay and bloodletting, the open manslaughter,
there is (with few exceptions) little sense of the actual imminence of death. The
sense of doom that pervades the *Iliad* is wanting, and with it the peculiarly
tragic quality of Homeric and early Germanic heroism: the dark luster of
a short and strenuous life of dedicated bloodshed that promises the hero a
posthumous survival as a name long after he himself has descended to the

shadows of the underworld. Like the wrath of Achilles, this is incompatible not only with Christian ethics but also with classical moral philosophy, and Milton himself could approximate it only by developing his fallen archangel as an antihero, a false counterpart of true heroism. Heroic wrath could not be fitted into a systematic schema of moral philosophy; in Spenser's system the ethical counterpart of Achilles would be Pyrochles.[17]

The notable exception in Spenser's romance is the Redcross knight. Unlike most of the other heroes of *The Faerie Queene,* he attains something like heroic stature largely because he possesses an inner life and is therefore subject to moral conflict. Fallible, easily deceived by false appearances, subject to pride and despair, he must struggle to achieve holiness. Though this is not the old Homeric heroism,[18] it appears both more human and more heroic than the kind of struggle depicted by Spenser's immediate predecessors. It is also perhaps a more plausible image of moral heroism than Tasso could achieve in Godfrey of Bologne.

The conventions of Renaissance chivalric romance did not lend themselves readily to the representation of spiritual drama, nor were they intended to do so. Their appeal, and the interest of the author and his audience, lay elsewhere, and in the kinds of things they attempted to represent they sometimes did very well. If Spenser succeeds in adapting them to this end, he does so by assimilating them to a different tradition: the spiritual combat against the world, the flesh, and the devil.

The motif of the holy war, so prominent a theme in chivalric romance, tended to externalize the conflict. The spiritual enemies are without, and they can be overcome by sheer physical strength and superior gladiatorial and equestrian skills, assisted on occasion by divine grace. The poet must expend his energies and skills on describing arms and armor, horses and tents, the exchange of boasts and insults, and especially the details of combat: seeking to avoid monotony in his descriptions of the shock of engagement, the broken lances and falling riders, the blows delivered or received. These are in a sense the clinical techniques of the surgeon and the play-by-play commentaries of the sportscaster transferred to the skirmishes of a Morris dance.

There is a subjective dimension also, to be sure; in the romances of Boiardo and Ariosto it is primarily erotic. Any religious subjectivity is usually subordinated to amatory passion and sentiment. Tasso's Godfrey, on the other hand, like the protagonist of *Paradise Regained,* is so rational and devout a hero, so egregious an exemplar of the "good governor" and the responsible commander, that he shows little evidence of either spiritual struggle or strong moral conflict.

In contrast to such almost perfect heroes, the Redcrosse knight, inexperienced and unexercised in arms, untried by temptation, is significantly imperfect. As the type of the *miles christianus,* subject to sin but also to repentance, he is in the process of *becoming* the perfect man, the saint. The action of the first book—centered on the pristine sanctity originally possessed by Adam, obscured by sin, and restored through Christ the second Adam—portrays the hero's progressive, though unsteady, growth and development toward Christian perfection: the renewal of the divine image in the inner man.

In several respects, moreover, Redcrosse's quest differs significantly from those of his fellows, and these differences give to this knight and his *aristeia* not only a different meaning but also a different heroic quality from those of the other knights. In the first place, holiness itself, or sanctity, is essentially a spiritual or theological virtue; it provides a foundation for the other virtues, treated in later books. In Spenser's ethical system, conditioned by Reformed theology, the practice of the various moral virtues must depend largely on spiritual regeneration and on justification by faith. As a virtue belonging to the regenerate and the elect, holiness may apply to all classes of society; it is not restricted to the gentleman, the courtier, or the magistrate. George, like Milton's Adam, is Everyman fighting against his ghostly foe, and the nature of his enemy also gives him a different heroic dimension from that of the other knights of the quests. Satan is a more formidable foe than slander or incontinence or tyrannical love, or than fury or jealousy. He is also more deadly than the Saracens confronted by Boiardo's paladins and several of Spenser's own knights (including Redcrosse himself), for the annihilation he threatens is more than physical death: it is the death of the soul.

The effect that Spenser achieves results largely from the meaning and nature of the quest, but also from the more coherent and logical structure of the plot of this book. Though most of the extant books of his poem open with a quest and end with its accomplishment, there is usually little sense of urgency; progress toward this end is leisurely and interrupted by frequent distractions and alternative enterprises. Although there are a beginning and an end to the action, the middle is often diffuse. In book 1, the distractions are closely related to the theme of the quest, serving as "delaying actions" in the development of the plot; moreover, the sequence of events is usually logical on the narrative level as well as the level of moral allegory. As the narrative shadows in large part the traditional stages of regeneration and in some degree the course of the English Reformation, there is inherent logic and probability in the intellectual structures underlying the sequence of events, and the narrative order is itself logical insofar as it moves toward or against the fulfillment of the quest. If this is to be frustrated or delayed, the knight must be parted from his guide; the poet accomplishes this through a single agent, Archimago, who simultaneously deludes both the lady and her protector and sends them on their separate ways. Though their paths are not strictly parallel (Redcrosse acquires a false glory at Lucifera's court; Una wanders in the wilderness, an errant damsel), there are nevertheless analogies between them. At the outset of her wanderings, Una is beguiled by a false Redcrosse, just as Redcrosse had been deluded earlier by the apparition of a false Una. Both suffer the violence of the Saracen Sansjoy, and both are assisted and ultimately reunited by Arthur. The seduction of the Redcrosse knight by a false faith (Fidessa-Duessa), which concludes with his own captivity, counterpoints the guidance of the true faith (Una), which culminates in his own act of deliverance. The actions that lead directly to the goal of the quest or away from it are thus centered on two princesses, representatives of rival faiths and rivals for his affections—and also analogous both to the rival females in the Choice of Hercules and to the true and false Helens of mythology. With few exceptions, all lines in the poem tend to focus either on Duessa and bondage or on Una and the hero's deliverance of paradise.

The heroic image also gains in force through Spenser's treatment of the dragon fight. This is not just a more formidable monster than the Blatant Beast or Error or the hyena who pursues Florimell, but an altogether different kind of antagonist from Sansloy and Sansjoy. Redcrosse's duels with the latter are conventional chivalric combats—moralized or theologized, but depicted much in the manner of Boiardo or Ariosto. A Satan portrayed as a Saracen knight— arrayed like most of the personae of Renaissance romance—would have been a less terrifying figure than the dragons of classical myth and Germanic or Celtic legend or the dragon of the Apocalypse. However dangerous a beautiful witch or a bookish enchanter might be, their power resided in their magic, not in physical prowess; a hero like Odysseus might overcome them through supernatural aid and his own cunning or by some kind of magical talisman, or he might even put them to death. Nevertheless, he would rarely regard them as appropriate antagonists in heroic combat. Neither Guyon nor Britomart fights the enchanter, and Bradamante engages only in a mock combat. Of all the personae in the romance, only Sansloy (and then through a mistake) ever comes to blows with Archimago. (Hypocrisy could not, of course, be defeated by force.)

If Archimago serves as a type of Satanic fraud, the dragon, for all his grotesqueness, provides a more forceful image of Satanic power. He seems very much "flesh and blood," to be sure, and for a suggestion of the "mystery" of iniquity one would look rather to the disguised sorcerer. Nevertheless, through the rich mythical and heroic traditions associated with the dragon fight, through Spenser's narrative and descriptive detail, and through his manipulation of apocalyptic imagery, the Redcrosse knight acquires yet another heroic dimension, which distinguishes him from other heroes of the quest. He seems indeed to be challenging the powers of evil, the "hideous strength" of the preternatural, and to face indeed the peril of imminent death. This impression may perhaps be intensified rather than dissipated if one recognizes in the knight's adversary the power who had once warred with angels—the ruler of "the darkness of this world," and that "spiritual wickedness" on high, against which the spiritual combatant must clothe himself in "the whole armour of God" (Eph. 6:10–17)—and if one perceives in this mortal combat the deadly peril of the human soul.

The majority of Spenser's heroic exemplars—whether Magnificence or Temperance or Justice—experience little inner conflict. Britomart may temporarily give way to jealous rage, suspicion, and grief. She may compare her passion for Artegall to an imposture and a festering sore; she may sulk or fall into tantrums like a child. Nevertheless, her chastity is never really imperiled. Love may disturb the tranquillity but not the purity of her mind. Unlike Scudamour, she is unseared by the flames of Busyrane's castle, and in contrast to Amoretta, she is completely safe from the enchanter's spells. Artegall may err once on the side of pity (John Knox would have been more inflexible in his opposition to the "monstrous regiment" of the Amazonian queen), but he learns his lesson painfully. Unlike Arthur and Mercilla, he shows no compassion for Duessa: "But *Artegall* with constant firme intent / For zeale of Justice was against her bent."

Even when separated temporarily from his Palmer, Sir Guyon experiences little difficulty in controlling his anger and desire. He is in firm command of his "irascible" and "concupiscible" faculties; at most his Platonic chariot may waver slightly. (He would never receive a ticket for "driving under the influence.") He is not vulnerable to the transports of passion and imagination, and if he seems pedestrian, it is because he is consistently rational. Indeed, he loses his symbolic steed very early in the story—significantly to the swaggering Braggadocchio, who can control neither his aspiring imagination nor his cowardly fear, his vainglory nor his lust—and he patiently follows the Palmer (Reason) on foot.

Nevertheless there is moral conflict of a sort, and this exercise of the will is necessary if Guyon is to resist the charms of Acrasia. On his Odyssean voyage to her Circean bower, he is tempted to ease the sorrow of a lamenting maiden, but is overruled by his guide; the Palmer counsels him against "womanish fine forgery" and "foolish pitty." As they pass the bay of the sirens, his senses are "softly tickeled" by their strange harmony and he bids the boatman "row easily" so that he may hear their "rare melody"; but he is immediately dissuaded by the Palmer's "temperate advice." As they enter the park of the sorceress, Guyon admires its "faire aspect . . . , yet suffred no delight / To sincke into his sence, nor mind affect, . . . / Bridling his will and maistering his might." Though he is immune to the charms of the landscape, he is not invulnerable to the beauty of the bathing maidens; he betrays the signs of "kindled lust," and is promptly rebuked by his guide.

In Guyon's combats with Furor and with Pyrochles and Cymochles, the struggle is almost entirely externalized; his own temper of mind is not jeopardized by the madness of wrath or lust. In this psychomachia he is consistently the exemplar of Temperance: the resolute will guided by Reason and triumphant over the irrational passions. The moral allegory is clear enough, and appropriate; but as a persona Sir Guyon is largely immune to the passions he is subduing, if not quelling. It is only when we take these several personae ensemble—Guyon, the Palmer, the two passion-demented brothers—that we behold an image of internal conflict, a single man at war with himself. In this respect there is an analogy with Tasso's allegorical key to the relationships between Godfrey, Rinaldo, Tancredi, and the two hermits.[19] Interpreted in terms of faculty psychology, they represent the human soul, the revolt of the irrational faculties against reason, and the restoration of rational control and natural justice through divine grace. This is also true of the besieged house of Temperance where there is perpetual warfare against the temptations of the senses, but continual peace, harmony, and order within. (Spenser's figurative castle presents in fact a significant contrast to Poe's schizoid house of Usher; in Poe's story there is no assault from without, the tarn mirrors the house itself and its nearly invisible fissure, and the disintegration originates and proceeds from within the symbolic mansion of the mind.) In Alma's castle of temperance Prince Arthur and Sir Guyon remain overnight—the virtues of magnificence and temperance indwelling in the well-governed body and soul; but it is left to Arthur, as magnanimity or greatness of mind and soul, to rout the temptations that beset the five senses.

Although Spenser exploits the Pauline and Gregorian metaphors of spiritual combat and trial in both of these episodes, he not only externalizes the moral conflict but also distributes it among a cluster of personae. With Saint George the case is usually otherwise. Even though the spiritual combat is externalized, it is also concentrated in the persona of the hero himself. The enemies without are also the enemies within.

Chapter 7

Moral Fiction in Milton's Epic Plot

In this final chapter I shall reexamine Milton's neoclassical epic largely in terms of the contrast that it affords to Spenser's romance-epic, stressing the impressive differences between these heroic poems in the light of significant contrasts in Renaissance literary theory and practice between these genres. These poems belong essentially to diverse but overlapping literary traditions— traditions that were subject to heated controversy but that were recognized by Renaissance poets and literary theorists alike. Behind Spenser's epic lies the "Ariostean" tradition of the romance (or romance-epic) as defined in the treatises of Giraldi Cinthio and Pigna; behind Milton's heroic poem lies the tradition of the Renaissance neoclassical epic modeled on Homer and Virgil and elaborated theoretically in treatises by Tasso and other neo-Aristotelian critics. Milton's epic can serve as a kind of foil for setting off the principal values of Spenser's romance, and vice versa.

Yet just as Spenser's poem subsumes other traditions besides those of epic and romance, Milton's poem cannot be reduced to a single epic stereotype or generic formula. On the contrary, within the framework of the neoclassical tradition it comprehends a wide range of other literary traditions. Among these, as scholars have recognized, are the traditions of classical, medieval, and Renaissance drama.[1] In discussing some of the affinities between *Paradise Lost* and the morality play, I have placed primary emphasis on their common focus on the drama of the temptation of Mankind and the degree to which this focus has affected the structure of Milton's epic of the Fall.

In his three major poems, Milton selected a subject based on what he regarded as biblical history. These subjects, however, were sufficiently remote in time, and the "historical" facts sufficiently ambiguous and cursory, to allow him ample freedom to invent and reorganize details and incidents, and in some instances persons, in order to construct a plot that would conform to his conceptions of epic and tragic poetic theory and of epic and tragic literary tradition. By means of such fictive inventions he might amplify his material and structure his plot in accordance with the cardinal principles of probability, verisimilitude, and the marvelous. In these respects he conformed fairly closely to the views expressed by Torquato Tasso and Edward Phillips on the relationship between the poet's choice of a historical subject and his license to invent and feign.[2] As a matter of fact, Edward Phillips's remarks on this subject in *Theatrum Poetarum* were, in all probability, largely influenced by Milton himself and thus constitute significant evidence of the poet's own literary theory.

Milton's dramatic notes and sketches in the Trinity College manuscript, as well as his tragedy *Samson Agonistes,* reflect much the same attitude as his epic poems toward the much debated relationship between historical material and poetic fiction. The dramatic plans include notes for dramas on British and Scottish history, but the great majority of these dramatic sketches are centered on biblical subjects. Elsewhere, in *The Reason of Church Government,* he considered writing an epic based on secular rather than sacred history ("what king or knight before the conquest might be chosen in whom to lay the pattern of a Christian hero"), but this subject was sufficiently remote in time to allow him freedom in inventing and arranging his material (*CP* 668–69). Though Milton's eventual decision to draw the arguments of both of his epics from biblical history marked a departure from the tradition of national heroic poetry in the Renaissance and from the conventional epic argument of martial combat, he nevertheless possessed significant predecessors in the tradition of "divine" poetry based on the Judeo-Christian Scriptures.[3]

Milton's attitude toward poetic fiction in the epic was, however, ambiguous. Among his many objections to the epic and romance tradition was its flagrant exploitation of fictive subject matter, "fabl'd Knights / In battles feign'd" (*PL* 9.30–31). Nevertheless, Milton felt free to draw on classical myth and on the fictitious materials of epic and romance for comparisons and contrasts. In *Paradise Regained,* the military forces of the Parthian king in Ctesiphon are compared with the armies of Boiardo's romance-epic *Orlando Innamorato:*

> Such forces met not, nor so wide a camp,
> When *Agrican* with all his Northern powers
> Besieg'd *Albracca,* as Romances tell,
> The City of *Gallaphrone,* from thence to win

> The fairest of her Sex, *Angelica,*
> His daughter, sought by many Prowest Knights,
> Both *Paynim,* and the Peers of *Charlemagne.*
> Such and so numerous was thir Chivalry. (*PR* 3.337–44; *CP* 513n)

Similarly, the forces of the fallen angels are compared to the heroes of classical epic and Arthurian and Carolinian romance:

> . . . For never since created man,
> Met such imbodied force, as nam'd with these
> Could merit more than that small infantry
> Warr'd on by Cranes: though all the Giant brood
> Of *Phlegra* with th' Heroic Race were join'd
> That fought at *Thebes* and *Ilium,* on each side
> Mixt with auxiliar Gods; and what resounds
> In Fable or *Romance* of *Uther's* Son
> Begirt with *British* and *Armoric* Knights;
> And all who since, Baptiz'd or Infidel
> Jousted in *Aspramont* or *Montalban,*
> *Damasco,* or *Marocco,* or *Trebisond,*
> Or whom *Biserta* sent from *Afric* shore
> When *Charlemain* with all his Peerage fell .
> By *Fontarabbia.* Thus far these beyond
> Compare of mortal prowess, yet observ'd
> Thir dread commander. (*PL* 1.573–89)

Elsewhere in *Paradise Lost,* Milton makes extensive use of mythological illusions. In Satan's flight through "the World's first Region," the stars seem

> . . . other Worlds . . . , or happy Isles,
> Like those *Hesperian* Gardens fam'd of old (*PL* 3.562–68)

In Paradise itself

> . . . Universal *Pan*
> Knit with the *Graces* and the *Hours* in dance
> Led on th' Eternal Spring.

To emphasize the beauty of the Garden of Eden, Milton compares it with actual places paradoxically associated with false myths and legends or wrongly identified as Paradise:

> . . . Not that fair field
> Of *Enna,* where *Proserpin* gath'ring flow'rs
> Herself a fairer Flow'r by gloomy *Dis*
> Was gather'd, which cost *Ceres* all that pain
> To seek her through the world; nor that sweet Grove
> Of *Daphne* by *Orontes,* and th' inspir'd
> *Castalian* Spring might with this Paradise
> Of *Eden* strive; nor that *Nyseian* Isle
> Girt with the River *Triton,* where old *Cham,*
> Whom Gentiles *Ammon* call and Lybian *Jove,*
> Hid *Amalthea* and her Florid Son,
> Young *Bacchus,* from his Stepdame *Rhea's* eye;
> Nor where *Abassin* Kings thir issue Guard,
> Mount *Amara,* though this by some suppos'd
> True Paradise under the *Ethiop* Line
> By *Nilus* head, enclos'd with shining Rock
> A whole day's journey high, but wide remote
> From this *Assyrian* Garden (*PL* 4.266–85)

In the foregoing instances, as in Milton's evocation of classical myths in his catalog of devils under the names of Gentile gods (*PL* 1.376–521) and his critique of the Hephaestus myth (*PL* 1.738–51), the poet endeavors to make the characters, places, and events that he is describing seem more vivid—and more real—through comparison with the fables of myth and fable and romance. It is significant, however, that even in dismissing Gentile fable in the account of Mulciber, he does not hesitate to invent his own fictions concerning this angel's architectural works in Heaven and in Hell. At times Milton chooses to emphasize the dichotomy between truth and fiction; on other occasions, he blurs such distinctions. He feels free to link Heaven and the world with a golden chain reminiscent of Homer's *Iliad* (*CP* 257n, 603n), to connect the cosmos and Hell with a fictive causeway across chaos, to invent the names of many faithful and unfaithful angels alike, and (as Samuel Johnson observed) to assign active roles in the epic plot to the personified abstractions Sin and Death. In the same way he can simultaneously heighten both the visual image of Sin and her moral significance by drawing on classical myths of Echidna and other serpent-women and melding them with the myth of Scylla and with viper lore.

The frequently hostile attitude expressed toward fable and romance in *Paradise Lost* provides a striking contrast to Milton's earlier praise of the materials of fable and romance in Thyrsis's speech in *Comus* (lines 513–19) and in the *Apology for Smectymnuus.* In the latter work he had praised "those lofty fables and romances, which recount in solemn cantos the deeds of knighthood founded by our victorious kings, and from hence had in renown over all Christendom" (*CP* 694).

The apparent dismissal of the romance tradition in the opening lines of book 9 of *Paradise Lost* occurs, however, in a complex defense of Milton's potentially controversial subject against the tradition of both classical heroic poetry and medieval or Renaissance romance—against, in fact, the prevailing traditions in heroic poetry. His tragic argument, he asserts, is "Not less but more Heroic" than the arguments of the three major classical epics—the *Iliad,* the *Odyssey,* and the *Aeneid.* Again, reiterating the heroic character of his theme ("this Subject for Heroic Song"), he emphasizes his personal distaste for a military subject:

> Wars, hitherto the only Argument
> Heroic deem'd, chief maistry to dissect
> With long and tedious havoc fabl'd Knights
> In Battles feign'd; the better fortitude
> Of Patience and Heroic Martyrdom
> Unsung.

This censure might apply not only to medieval and Renaissance romance (and romance-epic) but also to classical heroic poetry and to such modern epics as Tasso's *Gerusalemme Liberata.* Nevertheless, though certain details in the following lines may fit the races and games of classical epic, most of the references in this passage are properly applicable to the tradition of the chivalric romance:

> . . . or to describe Races and Games,
> Or tilting Furniture, emblazon'd Shields,
> Impreses quaint, Caparisons and Steeds;
> Bases and tinsel Trappings, gorgeous Knights
> At Joust and Tournament; then marshall'd Feast
> Serv'd up in Hall with Sewers, and Seneschals;
> The skill of Artifice or Office mean,
> Not that which justly gives Heroic name
> To Person or to Poem.

The fabulous character of the knights and battles of romance is (it appears) merely one of the details that, in Milton's opinion, make the subject matter of the romance tradition decidedly inferior in heroic qualities to his own "higher Argument."

Despite his misgivings about the romance tradition, Milton nevertheless draws on this tradition not only for epic comparisons but also for his description of the Limbo of Vanities and for his proposal to pursue "Things unattempted yet in Prose or Rhyme" (*PL* 1.16). Similarly, though he sometimes brands classical mythology as a perversion of truth, he nevertheless adapts the Greek myth of Athene's birth for his account of the birth of Sin, combining it with biblical metaphors concerning the genesis of sin and death.

In Milton's "moral cosmos" (as Lawrence Babb has named it) the dramatic conflict between God and Satan involves not only a moral and spiritual struggle between good and evil agents but also an epistemological dichotomy between truth and falsehood.[4] Poetically, Heaven and Hell are rival polities engaged in a spiritual war for the possession of the world and the soul of Man—John Bunyan's "town of Mansoul."[5] In accordance with the conventions of the heroic poem—traditionally centered as it had been on martial combat—both of the contending forces in this narrative of spiritual warfare hold councils of war, enunciate contrary and competing strategies, engage in preliminary attempts to thwart the enemy's strategy, and ultimately carry out their major attacks and counterattacks. The world and its divinely appointed lord, Mankind, are the focus both of the Satanic strategy of temptation and moral conquest and of the divine strategy of redemption and deliverance. Like Homer's *Iliad* and Luigi Alamanni's *L'Avarchide, Paradise Lost* belongs to the siege tradition. Like Troy, or like the Castle of Perseverance in the morality play of that name, the Earthly Paradise and with it the soul of man are under siege by an implacable and crafty enemy; and, like Troy, the terrestrial paradise and its lord are (albeit temporarily) conquered.

In *Paradise Regained*, the central temptation ordeal is essentially a dialectical encounter between truth and falsehood. The Son of God enters "his great duel . . . to vanquish by wisdom hellish wiles"—those "stratagems of Hell, / and devilish machinations" (*PR* 1.173–81). "Girded with snaky wiles," Satan attempts to "subvert" his adversary through "Temptation and all guile" (*PR* 1.120–24) and through "well couch't fraud, well woven snares" (*PR* 1.97). Their first encounter unmasks Satan as a liar who falsely pretends to truth, and confirms his opponent's identity as God's living oracle. God has sent the Christ "Into the World to teach his final will, / And sends his Spirit of Truth henceforth to dwell / In pious Hearts, an inward Oracle / To all truth requisite for men to know" (*PR* 1.407–64). To Satan's offer of Parthian military power as a means to achieve the throne of David, "*Israel's* true King . . . Made answer meet, that made void all his wiles." As the poet comments, "So fares it when with truth falsehood contends" (*PR* 3.441–43).

This preliminary engagement between Christ and Satan serves as an introduction to the more extended temptation of the kingdoms of the world and provides a frame of reference for interpreting the various lures and threats whereby the devil will test the Messiah. The various goods of the active and contemplative lives pursued as ends or means by secular magnates—those "manlier objects"

> . . . such as have more show
> Of worth, of honor, glory, and popular praise;
> Rocks whereon greatest men have oftest wreck'd (*PR* 3.225–28)—

are, in a sense, prejudged (for the reader as well as for the epic protagonist) in the light of the character of the tempter and of the fact that they will be proposed by the archetypal liar. Although regarded as true goods in the eye of the world, these Satanic lures will be proven demonstrably false, as the Son systematically exposes their inherent deficiencies. The temptation of the kingdoms, as Milton will develop it, will be a dialectical duel in which the truth will be demonstrated and confirmed by juxtaposition with its contrary: falsehood or error. "Let her [Truth] and Falsehood grapple," Milton had exclaimed in *Areopagitica;* "who ever knew Truth put to the worse, in a free and open encounter" (*CP* 746). Trial "is by what is contrary," he had affirmed in the same treatise (*CP* 728); and elsewhere (in *Of True Religion, Haeresie, Schism, Toleration*) he would declare that "In *Logic* they teach, that contraries laid together more evidently appear."[6]

Christ's temptation is a trial of both intellect and will. Its dialectical process involves both logical disproof of Satan's arguments and moral rejection of the false or inferior goods that he proposes. This spiritual duel, wherein truth and falsehood contend, is (much like the Alithia and Pseustis of Theodolus's Eclogue) both an intellectual and a moral exercise, testing both the hero's wisdom and his strength of character.

In his dialogue with the Son, Satan is repeatedly foiled by his adversary's rebuttals, guided as they are by right reason. When his offer of secular wealth is rejected, he stands

> . . . confuted and convinc't
> Of his weak arguing and fallacious drift (*PR* 3.3–4)

When Christ similarly rejects the military might of Parthia, Satan again is struck dumb by his opponent's refutation of his arguments and rejection of his lures:

> Discover'd in his fraud, thrown from his hope,
> So oft and the persuasive Rhetoric
> That sleek'd his tongue, and won so much on *Eve,*
> So little here, nay lost. (*PR* 4.3–6)

In *Paradise Lost* also, the spiritual and moral warfare between Heaven and Hell is strongly conditioned by the dichotomy of truth and falsehood. Satan perverts Mankind by "false guile" and "glozing lies" (*PL* 3.92–93); He seduces his own followers with false promises and boasts (*PL* 4.83–86) and "with calumnious Art of counterfeited truth" (*PL* 5.694–704, 770–71). A "fraudulent Impostor" and hypocrite, he deceives even the archangel Uriel, the "sharpest-sighted Spirit of all in Heav'n" (*PL* 3.681–93). Resorting to a series of animal disguises to avoid detection in Eden, he tempts Eve initially in the form of a toad and subsequently—and successfully—in the body of a serpent. In his first temptation he endeavors

> . . . to reach
> The Organs of her Fancy, and with them forge
> Illusions as he list, Phantasms and Dreams.
> (*PL* 4.800–803)

In the second temptation he deceives Eve not only with flattery but also with downright lies about the Creator and his injunction and about the seemingly miraculous properties of the forbidden fruit. To Eve, "his persuasive words" seem "impregn'd / With Reason . . . and with Truth" (*PL* 9.737–38).

In this extended battle between truth and falsehood, Satan's deceptions do not remain unopposed. Courageously rebutting Satan's blasphemies, the loyal angel Abdiel refuses "To swerve from truth, or change his constant mind / Though single" (*PL* 5.902–3), and he is subsequently rewarded with divine approval:

> . . . who single hast maintain'd
> Against revolted multitudes the Cause
> Of Truth, in word mightier than they in Arms;
> And for the testimony of Truth hast borne
> Universal reproach. (*PL* 6.29–34)

An exemplar of zeal, Abdiel is also a suffering witness to truth and thus a model of "the better fortitude / Of Patience and Heroic Martyrdom."

Subsequently, encountering Satan in battle as "Idol of Majesty Divine," Abdiel challenges the Apostate to combat, arguing that he has already found Satan's "Reason . . . Unsound and false":

> nor is it aught but just,
> That he who in debate of Truth hath won,
> Should win in Arms, in both disputes alike
> Victor. (*PL* 6.101, 120–24).

Accusing Satan "Of erring, from the path of truth remote" (*PL* 6.173), Abdiel delivers a strong blow that forces the rebel angel to recoil "ten paces huge."

The angel Uriel belatedly detects Satan's fraudulent disguise when the devil's passions have "marr'd his borrow'd visage, and betray'd / Him counterfeit." (*PL* 4.114–25). Although Satan immediately disguises his emotions— "Artificer of fraud," practicing "falsehood under saintly show"—the sharp-sighted archangel is, on this occasion, no longer deceived, and he promptly alerts the angelic guard.

Soon afterward, Satan's first temptation of Eve fails when the angel Ithuriel unmasks the impostor with his spear:

> . . . for no falsehood can endure
> Touch of Celestial temper, but returns
> Of force, to its own likeness: up he starts
> Discover'd and surpris'd. (*PL* 4.810–14)

Thus apprehended by the angelic guard, Satan is escorted to Gabriel, who further exposes him as "a liar trac't" (*PL* 4.947–49).

In this holy war between Heaven and Hell, the infernal strategy of deception is consistently countered by the divine strategy of revelation, mediated by the angelic historian Raphael before the fall and the angelic seer Michael after Mankind's transgression. Through Michael's prophecy of the future course of the human race up to the ministry of Christ and the vicissitudes of his church, Adam experiences his "eyes true op'ning" (in contrast to the false illumination promised by Satan) and departs from Michael's revelation (and from Paradise) "Greatly instructed, Greatly in peace of thought" (*PL* 12.274, 557–58).

The archangel's prophecy has progressed "From shadowy Types to Truth" (*PL* 12.303) and to the illumination of the Paraclete:

> . . . but from Heav'n
> Hee to his own a Comforter will send
> The promise of the Father, who shall dwell
> His Spirit within them, and the Law of Faith
> Working through love, upon thir hearts shall write,
> To guide them in all truth. (*PL* 12.485–90).

The plot of *Paradise Lost,* like that of Milton's minor epic, hinges on an epistemological conflict between true and false wisdom, divine truth and infernal falsehood—between the true Image of the Father, Christ the Logos, and Satan, "Idol" of divine majesty. Throughout both epics the devil conforms to his characterization in Scripture (John 8:44) as "a liar, and the father" of lies. Moreover, his strategy of deception and illusion is shared by all the forces of Hell. All are deceived, either by their revered leader or by their own folly and fallacious reasoning. All are alienated from the Right Reason that Milton associates consistently with the Messiah, the Son of God. In the infernal council Belial reveals himself as the archetypal sophist. All is "false and hollow," even though he can "make the worse appear / The better reason," uttering "words cloth'd in reason's garb" (*PL* 2.112–14, 226). Beelzebub's proposal to seek revenge against Heaven by seducing Mankind has been "first devis'd / By Satan, and in part propos'd" (*PL* 2.279–380). The arguments of other speakers in Pandaemonium cancel one another; Moloch's proposal of open warfare is exploded by Belial's arguments, and Beelzebub in turn rebuts the proposals of both Belial and Mammon. The pretensions of Hell are, as it transpires, self-refuting; falsehood stands exposed through its own fallacies.

In Milton's moral fiction the principal emphasis falls on the spiritual warfare between Hell and Heaven, which constitutes the background of his epic argument and the backbone of his plot. This involves (as Babb has recognized) a morally organized cosmology.[7] Heaven and Hell (and with them the thrones of God and Satan) occupy diametrically opposite positions in Milton's universe, with the newly created world and its human inhabitants occupying a position (almost though not quite intermediate) between them. In this structure John Demaray has found reminiscences of the masque; one may also find—particularly in the contrary strategies of Heaven and Hell toward Mankind—suggestive reminiscences of the late medieval morality play.

In Demaray's opinion, "Milton's spacious universe, with Eden at its core between the polarities of Satan's throne in Hell and God the Father's throne in Heaven, is to some extent an enormously elaborated reflection of the opposed seats of power and the other polarities of *Comus.*" *Paradise Lost* is "a theatrical epic of a unique kind that interweaves and fuses divine prophetic shows in eternity with a multitude of classical allusions, conventions, and patterned episodes, a work that partially transforms and yet remains daringly contained within a classical epic structure."[8]

Despite its conformity to classical and neoclassical norms of epic structure, *Paradise Lost* shows marked affinities with the mystery plays and moralities of medieval tradition. As Merritt Y. Hughes has observed, in Milton the "two main currents" of Christian drama "flow together—the medieval, native stream of the half-forgotten mystery plays and the contemporary continental revival of their tradition in Holland and Italy" (*CP* 174). The subject matter of Milton's heroic poem includes not only its announced argument the temptation and fall of man but also the entire course of history covered by the medieval mystery cycles, extending from the revolt of the angels and the creation of the world to the last judgment. Significantly, Milton adapts this material to the conventions of the epic genre, and the neo-Aristotelian insistence on a unified plot, by reorganizing this history into the familiar retrospective and prospective episodes of epic tradition and assigning the episodes respectively to Adam's angelic interlocutors Raphael and Michael.

In the York mystery cycle the first play begins with the creation of the angels and portrays the revolt and fall of Lucifer. The second play depicts the creation of the world, and the third play the creation of Adam and Eve. The Fall of Man is represented in the fifth play. The cycle concludes with the Last Judgment. The Chester cycle opens with the creation of the nine orders of angels, followed by Lucifer's rebellion and fall. The second play portrays the creation of the world and the Fall of Man. The cycle ends with Doomsday.

The characters in the *Ludus Coventriae* include *Angeli boni* and *Angeli mali*. This cycle begins with the creation of heaven and its angels, followed by the revolt and fall of Lucifer and subsequently by the creation of the world and man's own creation, temptation, and fall. This cycle too concludes with Doomsday. In the Wakefield cycle the initial action portrays the first five days of the creation of the world and Lucifer's rebellion and fall. These events are followed by the work of the fifth day, including the creation of man, and subsequently by man's temptation and fall. Like the other English mystery cycles, this sequence concludes with judgment.

Milton has apparently been influenced, however, not only by the tradition of the mysteries but also by that of the morality plays. Alice-Lyle Scoufos has called attention to the possible impact of the Chester play of Antichrist on Milton's *Comus* and on affinities between Milton's masque and the twelfth-century

Ludus de Antichristo, in which the Lady Ecclesia wanders the wilderness accompanied by Misericordia and Justitia.[9] Emphasizing the importance of the motif of the Four Daughters of God in the morality play *The Castle of Perseverance* as an element in the background of Milton's Ludlow masque, she concurs with Hughes on the influence of this motif on the celestial dialogue in book 3 of *Paradise Lost.* In Hughes's opinion, "The dramatic situation in Milton's dialogue is of a kind which he had sketched at some length, probably earlier than 1640, in the third of his four 'outlines for tragedies' on the theme of *Paradise Lost* in the Trinity College Manuscript. The scene following the prologue was to be a debate between Justice and Mercy on the question 'what should become of man if he fall.' " Arguing that the Son's "chivalrous response" in book 3 to the challenge presented by the devils' plot against man represents the influence of the morality tradition, Hughes cites the debate of the Four Daughters of God in *The Castle of Perseverance.* Although the debate might begin "with sharp contention among Mercy and Peace, Justice and Truth over the soul of Mankind as he lies on his deathbed, it regularly ended in the triumphant appeal of Mercy and Peace to God the Father in Heaven. God is merciful and seats Mankind at his right hand, where his Saviour also sits." In *Paradise Lost* Milton abandoned "the debate between Justice and Mercy over fallen Man in favor of a dialogue between the Almighty Father and the Son" and thus "found the way to a dialogue of distinct persons."[10]

In conformity with the Homeric and Virgilian model of the epic as interpreted by Renaissance critics, and with neo-Aristotelian theory, *Paradise Lost* exhibits a unified plot, portraying a single action, the Fall of Man. Milton's "whole Subject" according to the Argument of book 1 is *"Man's disobedience, and the loss thereupon of Paradise wherein he was plac't."* Stripped of its retrospective and prospective episodes, the narrative depicts the disobedience, judgment, partial regeneration, and expulsion of the protagonists (or "epic persons") Adam and Eve. The major deeds of Satan and the Son are oriented toward this central action, while other acts of these supernatural figures are assigned to interpolated episodes narrated by the angelic messenger. Thus the actions of the three (or four) principal characters in Milton's drama serve to further the single crucial action announced in the poem's *propositio.*

Moreover, as the *propositio* indicates, the poem is doctrinally centered on the Adam-Christ parallel, on the complementary relationship between the disobedience of the first (and "earthy") man and the obedience of the second (and heavenly) man.[11] The first Adam forfeits Paradise; the second Adam will (in the words of *Paradise Regained*) found "A fairer Paradise . . . For *Adam* and his chosen Sons" (*PR* 4.613–14.)

With this focus on the temptation of a central mankind figure, *Paradise Lost* recalls the tradition of the late medieval morality play and its recurrent protagonists Mankinde and Everyman. In *Mankind* the protagonist (Mankinde) is perverted by such tempters as Mischeff, New-Guise, Nowadays, Nought, and the devil Titivillus, but counseled and delivered by Mercy. Moreover, Mercy informs Mankinde that he must resist the "temptacion of the flesch . . . ,/ For ther is ever a batell betwixt the soull and the body: / *Vita hominis est militia super terram.*" This passage from Job (7:1) had been interpreted in Christian exegetical tradition as a reference to the spiritual warfare that the faithful soul must wage against evil and to the ordeal of temptation.[12]

A closer parallel to the dramatic situation in Milton's epic occurs, however, in *The Castle of Perseverence*. In *Paradise Lost* the representatives of mankind (Adam and Eve) occupy a central position between Heaven and Hell and are the objects of temptation and counseling by evil and good angels respectively. Similarly, in *The Castle of Perseverance* the cast of characters includes "HUMANUM GENUS, *et cum eo* BONUS ANGELUS *et* MALUS ANGELUS."[13] Before the dramatic action begins, the second Vexillator informs the audience concerning the relationship of these good and evil angels to Mankind:

> The case of oure cominge, you to declare,
> Every man in himself forsothe he it may find;
> Whou Mankinde into this werld born is ful bare
> And bare schal beried be at his [l]ast ende.
> God him gevith t[w]o aungel[ys] ful yep and ful yare,
> The goode Aungel and the Badde, to him for to lende.
> The Goode techith him goodnesse; the Badde, sinne and sare.[14]

In this morality Mankinde initially occupies a central position in the playing area or *platea*. According to the stage plan, the castle "standeth in the midst of the place," and "Mankind's bed shall be under the Castle, and there shall the soul lie under the bed till he shall rise and play." The positions of the scaffolds, moreover, in the stage plan "appended to the Macro manuscript" involve moral and spiritual contrasts and distinctions, although there is no specific scaffold for Hell. The scaffold for Deus is situated in the east, diametrically opposite to the scaffold of Mundus in the west. The remaining three scaffolds belong to Flesh in the south, Covetous in the northeast, and Belial (appropriately) in the north.[15]

The *bonus angelus* and *malus angelus* subsequently reappear as the Good Angel and Evil Angel of Marlowe's *Doctor Faustus*. As David Bevington has observed, "Shorn of its happy ending, the morality plot . . . provided a formula for tragedy that was to be of immense importance" to Marlowe's drama.[16]

In Lawrence Babb's opinion, Milton "has invented many scenes and events and a great deal of dialogue, but there is less invention in *Paradise Lost* than one might suppose."[17] In presenting his moral fictions, the poet resorts on occasion to personification allegory, as in the instance of Sin and Death and the powers of the Abyss and indeed in the case of Mammon (Riches). More frequently, however, he prefers to rely on the techniques of moral characterization, especially in portraying the vices of his infernal angels and in representing in Adam and Eve idealized, though fallible, examples of man and woman. The main plot of *Paradise Lost,* as well as the interpolated narratives of Raphael and Michael, functions as moral exemplum, as do the plots of his brief epic and his unique tragedy.

Both of his epics, moreover, are centered on the symbolism of Paradise (the Earthly Paradise, the "paradise within," and the celestial paradise) as the state of human (or angelic) felicity or beatitude. Traditionally not only ethics, but politics and theology as well, had as their end or final cause the felicity of man. In Arminius's words, "The end of Theology is the blessedness of man; and that not animal or natural, but spiritual and supernatural. It consists in fruition, the object of which is a perfect, chief, and sufficient Good, which is God."[18] After man's fall and loss of original happiness, Michael's revelation in the final books of Milton's poem promises him a higher and more enduring beatitude. Through divine instruction and through regeneration, Adam and Eve may attain a spiritual felicity superior to the earthly happiness that they have lost through sin.

Like Milton's major epic, *Paradise Regained* in turn is centered on the Adam-Christ parallel and on the ideal of the *summum bonum* and the true felicity of man—on the antithesis between "the happy Garden . . . By one man's disobedience lost" and "Recover'd Paradise to all mankind, / By one man's firm obedience fully tried / Through all temptation, and the Tempter foil'd . . . / And *Eden* rais'd in the waste Wilderness" (*PR* 1.1–7). The ethical dialectic of this poem mimes the method of moral philosophers and theologians in endeavoring to achieve knowledge of the highest good and true happiness by rejecting false notions of the *summum bonum* and inferior conceptions of felicity. Thus the "pattern of systematic rejection which Milton employs in his treatment of the Second Temptation" in *Paradise Regained* is "a standard method of Western ethical tradition. His hero demonstrates his knowledge of the *summum bonum*, his insight into the nature of the 'public good' and what is 'best' and 'happiest' for mankind, through a process of negation already well established in classical and Christian approaches to the highest good."[19] In elaborating the biblical accounts of the temptation of the kingdoms of the world, Milton provides a comparatively succinct yet comprehensive recapitulation of the methodology of classical and Christian moral philosophy in approaching the definition of the true end and beatitude of man. Appropriately, this dialectical drama between Christ the God-man (or *theanthropos*) and the prince of this world is also reminiscent of the respective roles of the "mankind figure" and the mundus figure in the morality play. Milton has assimilated this motif, borrowed from medieval drama, along with Protestant metaphors of spiritual warfare, to the epic tradition of rival gods and the contention of celestial and infernal powers and to the epic convention of antithetical councils of war.

Epilogue

In the previous pages I have considered some of the techniques whereby Milton and Spenser ("his Original")[1] exploited the resources of invention and illusion in developing the poetic eidolon as a vehicle for what they regarded as ethical and historical truth. Examining these techniques against the background of Renaissance literary theory and the practice of such poets as Tasso, DuBartas, and other Renaissance or late medieval writers, I have attempted to reassess the significance of Renaissance conceptions of the relations between epic and romance for two major poets of the English Renaissance. By analyzing the Renaissance poet's carefully crafted persona—his self-image as divinely inspired bard—I have endeavored to revalue the views of twentieth-century critics and to demonstrate the importance of conscious fiction over biographical or autobiographical fact in the poet's treatment of the literary devices that John T. Shawcross has aptly associated with "the metaphor of inspiration."

Of paramount importance in the poetry of Milton and Spenser were the opportunities that Renaissance poetic afforded for mediating the distinctions between fictive invention and moral and historical "fact" through the resources of exemplum and allegory, through traditional or newly invented (or reinvented) "myth," through allusive techniques of simile and metaphor, and through adding conscious fiction to historical subject matter (or ethical doctrine) to create a plausible, coherent, and affectively powerful poetic fable.

Despite manifest (and manifold) differences between their major poems, Spenser and Milton both wrote against the background of an epic tradition that, in theory and practice alike, involved an ambiguous and shifting relationship among the deliberate fictions of the poet, the commonplaces of moral philosophy (and, on occasion, political or indeed theological doctrine), the accepted "truths" of history, and the apparent truths of historical legend.

This epic tradition was, however, both complex and ambivalent, embodying not only a varied and multiple diversity of potential models and principles but also numerous inconsistencies and indeed contradictions. Milton and Spenser differed widely in their relationship to the principles of classical epic and Renaissance romance and in their attitudes toward the literary principles of verisimilitude and probability, the element of the marvelous, and the relationship of poetic narrative to allegory. They also diverged significantly in their development of the topos of the divinely inspired bard.

The interval that separated Spenser from Milton—the age of Elizabeth from that of the Commonwealth and the Restoration—inevitably and radically affected the attitudes these poets displayed toward literary models and the body of epic theory. Milton distanced himself much further than Spenser from the romance genre and from Ariosto as an epic predecessor and potential model. He was far closer to classical (and neoclassical) prototypes, to the tradition of neo-Aristotelian poetic theory in general, and to Tasso's theories of heroic poetry in particular. He was, moreover, much more concerned with achieving verisimilitude and probability in the construction and motivation of his epic plot. Furthermore, in selecting an epic subject, he chose as his argument an event that he regarded as a historical fact—even though (ironically, for the modern reader) this event belonged essentially to the realm of religious myth rather than to history.

Milton was, to be sure, too independent and (to echo a Romantic commonplace) too original a poet to be strictly bound by the poetic theory that he had inherited and that he had formerly hailed as "that sublime art" which teaches the "laws" of the various literary genres. Nevertheless, he was far more influenced by these principles and by the body of Renaissance neo-Aristotelian critical theory than Spenser—writing in an earlier age—had been.

* * * * *

Milton's narrative method relied primarily on an argument based solidly on what he regarded as scriptural verity, biblical history fleshed out and augmented by his own fictive inventions, and by his own "feigning" of probable circumstances. Spenser's method stood in striking contrast: it depended on an unabashed fiction—the poet's own invention of Gloriana's twelve-day feast and the various individual quests that this occasion called forth, the conceit of Prince Arthur's personal quest for the Faerie Queene, and the fictive ancestry of the poet's sovereign figured through his invention of the romance of Britomart and Artegall. Even though Milton's "historical" argument, the disobedience and fall of man, acquired heightened significance and topical relevance through the analogy with England's recent apostasy—the failure of the Commonwealth experiment and the betrayal of "the good old cause" by the restoration of the Stuart monarchy at the very time when *Paradise Lost* was in the process of composition—the historical validation of Milton's poetic fiction depended largely on his selection of a biblical event as subject. In contrast to Milton's method, Spenser had validated his own fictive inventions by shadowing contemporary or near contemporary persons and events through the resources of what is generally labeled "historical allegory." The vicissitudes of the Reformation in England, the rivalry between Elizabeth and Mary Stuart and between the Anglican and Roman Catholic communions, the Elizabethan policy in Ireland, the Spanish armada, warfare in Belgium and France, and other contemporary events were figured allegorically through the poet's own invented myths. In Spenser's fictional Faeryland, his monarch could behold an image of her own realms and her own friends and enemies. Mediated through the resources of historical allegory, these persons and events constituted the actual historical validation of the poet's fictions. (Paradoxically, Spenser's overt historical validation—the pretext that he had derived his materials from historical records under the guidance of Clio, muse of history—was itself a deliberate and manifest fiction.)

Milton and Spenser diverged significantly in their exploitation of the resources of allegory. Milton's limited use of this trope was restricted largely to such elements as the personification allegory of Sin and Death, in contrast to Spenser's more extensive resort to the technique of the "dark conceit." In his presentation of ethical, political, or theological values and concepts, Milton consistently placed greater emphasis on the methods of the narrative exemplum than on those of allegorical fiction.

In their treatment of the commonplaces of poetic inspiration, invocations of the muse (or muses), and the persona of the bard, one detects underlying and ultimately unresolvable ambiguities in the practice of both poets. Spenser pretended to relate events of the remote past at the dictates of his muse, even though he was actually alluding to recent persons and events. Milton in turn maintained the fiction that he was writing at the dictation of his own heavenly muse and under the inspiration of the Spirit. It remains, however, problematic and uncertain how far and how seriously he intended his adaptation of this literary commonplace to be accepted by his readers. What *is* certain is that in recent years not a few critics have interpreted his treatment of this venerable poetic convention too literally, and that some of them have carried their interpretations of his resort to the bardic voice and the fiction of the poet-prophet (or *vates*) beyond the bounds of reason and literary tact.

Milton never abandoned his youthful dedication to the concept of a masterwork not "to be obtained by the invocation of Dame Memory and her Siren daughters, but by devout prayer to that eternal Spirit who can enrich with all utterance and knowledge" (*CP,* 671). Yet throughout his long career as poet and prose controversialist he was never so rash as to believe that his discourse had been dictated verbatim by God himself or that (*pace* DuBartas) he was essentially a "penman" of the Holy Spirit.

Notes

Introduction

1. Among related studies the reader may consult the following books: William Nelson, *Fact or Fiction: the Dilemma of the Renaissance Storyteller* (Cambridge, Mass., 1973); Joseph Anthony Wittreich Jr., *Visionary Poetics: Milton's Tradition and His Legacy* (San Marino, Calif., 1979); John Demaray, *Cosmos and Epic Representation: Dante, Spenser, Milton and the Transformation of Renaissance Heroic Poetry* (Pittsburgh, 1991); S. K. Heninger Jr., *Touches of Sweet Harmony: Pythagorean Cosmology and Renaissance Poetics* (San Marino, Calif., 1974); Heninger, *The Cosmographical Glass: Renaissance Diagrams of the Universe* (San Marino, Calif., 1977); Heninger, *Sidney and Spenser: The Poet as Maker* (University Park, Pa., 1989); Kenneth Gross, *Spenserian Poetics: Idolatry, Iconoclasm, and Magic* (Ithaca, N.Y., 1985); David Lee Miller, *The Poem's Two Bodies: The Poetics of the 1590 "Faerie Queene"* (Princeton, 1988); James Nohrnberg, *The Analogy of "The Faerie Queene"* (Princeton, 1976; reprinted 1980). Examining "the way in which Spenser's poem is gradually shaped by an analogy of inner and outer government" (xi), Nohrnberg discusses the relation between epic and romance, poetry as a species of "sophistic," allegory, the representation of time, and related subjects. See also Paul J. Alpers, *The Poetry of the "Faerie Queene"* (Princeton, 1967).

For discussions of Milton's relationship to Spenser see John D. Guillory, "John Milton," *The Spenser Encyclopedia*, A. C. Hamilton (Toronto, 1990), 473–75; and Guillory, *Poetic Authority: Spenser, Milton, and Literary History* (New York, 1983). Guillory cites, inter alia, Harold Bloom, *A Map of Misreading* (New York, 1975); Patrick Cullen, *Infernal Triad: The Flesh, the World, and the Devil in Spenser and Milton* (Princeton, 1974); Angus Fletcher, *The Prophetic Moment: An Essay on Spenser* (Chicago, 1971); Richard Helgerson, *Self-Crowned Laureates: Spenser, Jonson, Milton, and the Literary System* (Berkeley and Los Angeles, 1983); A. Kent Hieatt, *Chaucer, Spenser, Milton: Mythopoeic Continuities and Transformations* (Montreal and London, 1975); Thomas E. Maresca, *Three English Epics: Studies of "Troilus and Criseyde," "The Faerie Queene," and "Paradise Lost"* (Lincoln, Nebr., 1979); Richard

Neuse, "Milton and Spenser: The Virgilian Triad Revisited," *ELH* 45 (1978): 606–39; and Colin Burrow, *Epic Romance: Homer to Milton* (Oxford, 1993).

2. See inter alia Isabel E. Gamble MacCaffrey, *"Paradise Lost" as Myth* (Cambridge, Mass., 1959).

3. See John T. Shawcross, "The Metaphor of Inspiration in *Paradise Lost*," in *Th' Upright Heart and Pure: Essays on John Milton Commemorating the Tercentenary of the Publication of 'Paradise Lost'*, ed. Amadeus P. Fiore, O.F.M. (Pittsburgh, 1967), 75–78.

4. On Milton as prophet and visionary, see Joseph Anthony Wittreich Jr., *Visionary Poetics: Milton's Tradition and His Legacy* (San Marino, Calif., 1979); and Wittreich, " 'A Poet Amongst Poets': Milton and the Tradition of Prophecy," in Wittreich (ed.), *Milton and the Line of Vision* (Madison, Wisc., 1975), 97–142; William Kerrigan, *The Prophetic Milton* (Charlottesville, Va., 1974); John Spencer Mill, *John Milton, Poet, Priest, and Prophet: A Study of Divine Vocation in Milton's Poetry and Prose* (Totowa, N.J., 1979); Michael Lieb, *Poetics of the Holy: A Reading of "Paradise Lost"* (Chapel Hill, N.C., 1981).

5. Maurice Kelley, "Milton and the Third Person of the Trinity," *Studies in Philology* 32 (1935): 221–34; James Holly Hanford, *A Milton Handbook*, 3d ed. (New York, 1939), 194n. See Milton's discussion of the Holy Spirit in *Complete Prose Works of John Milton*, vol. 6, *The Christian Doctrine*, ed. Maurice Kelley, trans. John Carey (New Haven and London, 1973), 281–98.

6. James Holly Hanford, "That Shepherd, Who First Taught the Chosen Seed: A Note on Milton's Mosaic Inspiration," *University of Toronto Quarterly* 8 (1939): 403–19.

7. William B. Hunter, *The Descent of Urania: Studies in Milton, 1946–1988* (Lewisburg, London and Toronto, 1989), 31–32.

8. Jackson I. Cope, *The Metaphoric Structure of "Paradise Lost"* (Baltimore, 1962), 156–59.

9. William J. Grace, "Orthodoxy and Aesthetic Method in *Paradise Lost* and *The Divine Comedy*," *Comparative Literature* 1 (1949): 173–74, 174n. Kerrigan, *The Prophetic Milton*; see the review by Mary Ann Radzinowicz in *Renaissance Quarterly* 29 (1976): 458–61.

10. Mary Ann Radzinowicz, *Toward "Samson Agonistes": The Growth of Milton's Mind* (Princeton, 1978), 350–64.

11. Barbara Kiefer Lewalski, *"Paradise Lost" and the Rhetoric of Literary Forms* (Princeton, 1985), 25, 30.

12. Hunter, *Descent of Urania,* 32; Lewalski, *"Paradise Lost" and the Rhetoric of Literary Forms,* 30, 291n; John M. Steadman, *Milton's Biblical and Classical Imagery* (Pittsburgh, 1984), 114–20.

13. John N. King, *English Reformation Literature: The Tudor Origins of the Protestant Tradition* (Princeton, 1982), 446–48, 455–56.

14. Debora K. Shuger, *Sacred Rhetoric: The Christian Grand Style in the English Renaissance* (Princeton, 1988), 48, 67, 69, 111, 183–84, 235, 237, 245. See also Jameela Lares, "Milton and the Rhetoric of Religious Controversy" (Ph.D. diss., University of Southern California, 1994).

15. See *The Oxford English Dictionary,* 2d ed., vol. 12 (Oxford, 1991). *s.v.* "prophecy," "prophesy," "prophesyings," and "prophet." See also M. M. Knappen, *Tudor Puritanism: A Chapter in the History of Idealism* (Chicago, 1939), 253–55; Michael Walzer, *The Revolution of the Saints: A Study in the Origins of Radical Politics* (Cambridge, Mass., 1965), 98–99; J. F. McGregor and B. Reay, eds., *Radical Religion in the English Revolution* (Oxford, 1984), 57–62, 121–32, 136–39.

16. For Milton's relationships to contemporary radical thought, see Christopher Hill, *Milton and the English Revolution* (New York, 1977), 93–116. For more on Milton's "conservative" views on the art of poetry, see John M. Steadman, *Milton and the Renaissance Hero* (Oxford, 1967); and John M. Steadman, *The Wall of Paradise: Essays on Milton's Poetics* (Baton Rouge, La., 1985).

17. See Lily Bess Campbell, *Divine Poetry and Drama in Sixteenth-Century England* (Cambridge, 1959).

18. See John M. Steadman, *The Lamb and the Elephant: Ideal Imitation and the Context of Renaissance Allegory* (San Marino, Calif., 1974), 71–105. For a different perspective see Mindele Anne Treip, *Allegorical Poetics and the Epic: The Renaissance Tradition to "Paradise Lost"* (Lexington, Ky., 1994).

Chapter 1

1. Cf. Dante's *Paradiso,* canto 1. Dante invokes Apollo not only as patron of poetic inspiration and "divine virtue" but also (it has been suggested) as the sun and hence as a symbol for God himself. The poet prays to be inspired like the flayed Marsyas (a traditional symbol of spiritual ecstasis) so that he may relate to others his own memory of paradise. In *Inferno,* canto 2, he calls on the muses, on genius *(ingegno),* and on memory for assistance.

2. Torquato Tasso, *Discourses on the Heroic Poem,* trans. Mariella Cavalchini and Irene Samuel (Oxford, 1973), 112–13. In these quotations I prefer the literal translation "style" rather than "poetry."

3. Tasso, *Discourses,* 114.

4. Torquato Tasso, *Prose,* ed. Francesco Flora (Milano, Roma, 1935), 446–52.

5. Ibid., 452.

6. See George Coffin Taylor, *Milton's Use of Dubartas* (Cambridge, Mass., 1934); Campbell, *Divine Poetry and Drama;* and Campbell, "The Christian Muse," *Huntington Library Bulletin* 8 (1935), 29–70. In "L'Envoy" to *The Ruines of Rome,* Spenser turns from the eulogy of DuBellay to the praise of DuBartas and his "heavenly Muse."

7. *Comus,* lines 459–63.

8. Cf. the motif of Adam's visions and prophecies in pseudepigraphical tradition; see John M. Steadman, *Milton's Epic Characters: Image and Idol* (Chapel Hill, N.C., 1968), 72–81; J. M. Evans, *"Paradise Lost" and the Genesis Tradition* (Oxford, 1968).

9. The manner in which DuBartas and his muse participate figuratively in the events and elements that he is describing is a somewhat pedantic elaboration of a conventional poetic conceit. Thus in book 4 of the *Georgics,* where Virgil treats the cultivation of the vine, the poet invites Bacchus to join him in treading the grapes.

10. Cf. Leah Jonas, *The Divine Science: The Aesthetic of Some Representative Seventeenth-Century English Poets* (New York, 1940).

11. Cf. Tasso's suggestion that the great poet is called divine inasmuch as he resembles the creator of the universe in his own works ("operazioni"); Allan H. Gilbert, *Literary Criticism: Plato to Dryden* (New York, 1940), 500–501.

12. See also Shakespeare's allusion to "the prophetic soul / Of the wide world dreaming on things to come," in Sonnet #107.

13. See Kathleen Williams, "Milton, Greatest Spenserian," in *Milton and the Line of Vision,* 25–55; Williams, "Vision and Rhetoric: The Poet's Voice in *The Faerie Queene,*" *ELH* 36 (1969): 131–44; Joseph Anthony Wittreich Jr., "Prophecies," in *Spenser Encyclopedia,* 559–60; Wittreich, "Visions," in *Spenser Encyclopedia,* 722–23; Thomas Hyde, "Vision," in *Spenser Encyclopedia,* 721–22; Fletcher, *The Prophetic Moment.*

14. Cuddie continues, "Thou kenst not *Percie* howe the ryme should rage./ O if my temples were distaind with wine, . . . How I could reare the Muse on stately stage." E. K. comments that Cuddie "seemeth here to be ravished with a Poeticall furie. For . . . the verse groweth so big, that it seemeth he hath forgot

the meanenesse of shepheards state and stile." Elsewhere in the dialogue Pierce praises Cuddie's ability to inspire his audience with rapture: "Seemeth thou dost their soule of sence bereave." In his gloss, E.K. cites classical authorities on the "secrete working of Musick . . . in the myndes of men" and the power of harmony.

15. *Virgil,* ed. H. Rushton Fairclough (2 vols.; London and New York, 1916, 1918), vol. 2, 372–73.

16. Statius similarly calls on Clio in the *Thebaid,* inquiring which of the heroes at the war she will present to him first ("quem prius heroum, Clio, dabis?"). The poet has already invoked the muses and addressed Domitian. His invocation is interesting both for its allusions to poetic fury ("Pierius . . . calor," "Pierio . . . "oestro") and for its inversion of the Homeric formula of asking the muse to sing the tale, beginning at a particular point in the story. Perhaps mindful of Protagoras's objection to Homer's invocation as too much like a command, Statius deferentially asks his muses to command *him:* "unde iubetis / ire, deae?" (Where do the muses order the poet to begin?) Similarly, Statius is at Clio's command: it is she who will decide the order in which she will present the heroes. See *Statius,* trans. J. M. Mozley (2 vols.; London and New York, 1928), vol. 1; *Thebaid,* book 1, lines 1–45.

With Spenser's frequent appeals to Clio, the muse of history, as the *inspiratrix* of his romance-epic (*FQ* 1.proem.2; 3.3.4; 7.7.37), one should contrast his resort to Calliope, the muse of epic poetry, for his myth of Faunus and Diana and the union of Molanna and the Fanchin in the Mutability cantos (*FQ* 7.6.37): "Meane while, O *Clio,* lend *Calliope* thy quill."

In the second of the Mutability cantos (*FQ* 7.7), Spenser has shifted this theme from the mythical union of Molanna and the Fanchin to the dispute between Jove and Mutability for dominion over the heavens. The poet is at his muse's command—not she at his behest—and he accordingly invokes his muse for the higher flight appropriate to his argument:

> Ah! whither doost thow now thou greater Muse
> Me from these woods and pleasing forrests bring?
> And my fraile spirit (that dooth oft refuse
> This too high flight, unfit for her weake wing)
> Lift up aloft, to tell of heavens King
> (Thy soveraine Sire) his fortunate successe. . . .
>
> Yet sith I needs must follow thy behest,
> Doe thou my weaker wit with skill inspire
> Fit for this turne; and in my feeble brest

> Kindle fresh sparks of that immortall fire,
> Which learned minds inflameth with desire
> Of heavenly things: for, who but thou alone,
> That art yborne of heaven and heavenly Sire,
> Can tell things doen in heaven so long ygone;
> So farre past memory of men that may be knowne.
>
> (*FQ* 7.7.1–2)

These are essentially the same topoi that Milton exploits in invoking his own heavenly muse; her celestial origin gives her the authority of an eyewitness to speak of heavenly things surpassing human wit and events too ancient for the memory of man. Of heavenly birth herself, she can elevate the poet's mind and discourse to the altitude demanded by his lofty theme.

17. In *Colin Clouts Come Home Againe,* Cuddie protests that, in his eulogy of Elizabeth, Colin has mounted too high for a pastoral poet: "Such loftie flight, base shepheard seemeth not, / From flocks and fields, to Angels and to skie." Cuddie in turn justifies this apparent breach of decorum by the inspiration of his lofty theme:

> . . . her great excellence,
> Lifts me above the measure of my might:
> That being fild with furious insolence,
> I feele my selfe like one yrapt in spright.
> For when I thinke of her, as oft I ought,
> Then want I words to speake it fitly forth:
> And when I speake of her what I have thought,
> I cannot thinke according to her worth.

Again, when Colin praises the "mightie mysteries" of pure love, Cuddie attributes his eloquence to divine inspiration:

> . . . it seems that some celestiall rage
> Of love . . . is breath'd into thy brest,
> That powreth forth these oracles so sage
> Of that high powre, wherewith thou art possest.
>
> (*PW,* 542–44)

18. See Hughes, *Complete Poems,* 95n, 505n; John M. Steadman, *The Lamb and the Elephant: Ideal Imitation and the Context of Renaissance Allegory* (San Marino, Calif., 1974), 125, 142; Steadman, "Herbert's Platonic Lapidary: A

Note on 'the Foil,' " *Seventeenth-Century News* (1972), 59–62. One might expect that a hymn to beauty would precede a hymn to love, inasmuch as it is conventionally the sight of beauty that awakens love.

19. Behind Spenser's denial of true love to "baseborne mynds" and his distinction between true love and lust lies the Platonic contempt of the multitude, whether conceived in metaphysical terms (the Many as opposed to the One), psychological (the sensual appetites and passions), ritualistic (the uninitiated in comparison with the mystoi or true initiates), epistemological (the majority of mankind, content with mere shadows of reality, in contrast to the philosopher), or political and social (the demos as distinct from the aristoi, and ochlocracy as contrasted with the rule of the one or few). Closely related are the Platonic (and Neoplatonic) contrast between the vulgar and the heavenly Venus (Aphrodite Pandemos and Aphrodite Urania) and their correlative Erotes, and the sharp distinction between true love and sensual lust. These distinctions were zealously adapted by the stilnovisti (who regard love as inseparably and exclusively associated with the noble or "gentle" heart) and by later poets, especially when writing in "elitist" contexts: for a literary clique, a prince's court, a learned readership, or an audience of amateurs and gentlemen. With the notable exception of shepherds or an occasional fisherman, the love of the peasant belonged to an altogether different species from that of the well born or the well educated.

Spenser elaborates this contrast between the earthly passion of the base-born and the purity of true love—along with the topos of love as a divine "infusion"—not only in the *Amoretti,* the *Four Hymns,* and *The Faerie Queene,* but also in Erato's complaint in *The Teares of the Muses.* Love was "wont to be schoolmaster of my skill" and the "matter of my song" (the muse laments), but "love devoyd of villanie or ill," no less "pure and spotles" than when he first sprang from God's bosom, "where he nests; / From thence infused into mortal brests."

Now, however, poets are inspired by a less celestial frenzy; they "rime at riot" and "rage in love" without knowledge of true love and "what doth thereto behove":

> Such high conceipt of that celestial fire,
> The base-borne brood of blindness cannot gesse,
> Ne ever dare their dunghill thoughts aspire
> Unto so loftie pitch of perfectnesse.

Neither Venus nor Erato, neither Amor nor the three Graces, shall ever again find entertainment at court or school, "For that which was accounted heretofore / The learneds meed, is now lent to the foole." The fool writes lays of love and is approved and applauded (*PW,* 484).

Chapter 2

1. Tasso, *Prose,* 474–75; Gilbert, *Literary Criticism,* 502.

2. See Jason Rosenblatt, "The Mosaic Voice in *Paradise Lost,*" *Milton Studies,* vol. 7, *"Eyes Fast Fixt": Current Perspectives in Milton Methodology,* ed. Albert C. Labriola and Michael Lieb (Pittsburgh, 1975), 207–32. As Rosenblatt observes, critics have recognized that "the role of inspired poet-narrator" in Milton's epic is "in some sense an artifact"; "critics have been especially attentive to those voices which Milton himself invented—the night bird, the blind bard, and the Christian poet who defines himself with reference to the characters in his poem." Rosenblatt cites Anne Davidson Ferry, *Milton's Epic Voice: The Narrator in Paradise Lost* (Cambridge, Mass., 1967); Louis L. Martz, *The Paradise Within* (New Haven, Conn. 1964); and William G. Riggs, *The Christian Poet in Paradise Lost"* (Berkeley and Los Angeles, 1972). See also Robert M. Durling, *The Figure of the Poet in Renaissance Epic* (Cambridge, Mass., 1965).

3. See Ferry, *Milton's Epic Voice.*

4. John S. Diekhoff, *Milton's "Paradise Lost," A Commentary on the Argument* (New York, 1946).

5. See Ferry, *Milton's Epic Voice,* for the relevance of this passage to Milton's *persona* as blind bard.

6. See Lily Bess Campbell, *Divine Poetry and Drama;* Campbell, "The Christian Muse," *Huntington Library Bulletin* 8 (1935): 29–70. In *Gerusalemme Liberata* (canto 1, stanza 2) Tasso invokes a heavenly muse, but does not explicitly refer to her as Urania. He implores her to inspire him with celestial ardors and to pardon him if he embellishes the truth and adorns his pages with other delights than those directly inspired by his celestial muse:

> tu spira al petto mio celesti ardori,
> tu rischiara il mio canto, e tu perdona
> s'intesso fregi al ver, s'adorno in parte
> d'altri diletti, che de' tuoi, le carte.

Opere di Torquato Tasso, ed. Bartolo Tommaso Sozzi, vol. 1, 2d ed., rev. (Torino, 1964; reprinted 1968). Sozzi comments that some commentators identify Tasso's muse with the Virgin, others with Urania, but that it is preferable to regard her as the Christian muse: "meglio, senza troppo specificare, la Musa cristiana" (p. 59n).

7. On the interpretation of Milton's muse, see William B. Hunter, *Descent of Urania* (Lewisburg, Pa., London, Cranbury, N.J., 1989). See also Steadman, *Milton's Biblical and Classical Imagery,* 73–120. The relationship of Milton's heavenly muse to the true God, the eternal Father, is analogous to the Olympian origin of the classical muses, sired either by Apollo or by Jove himself. Older than the universe, Urania possesses a longer memory than the daughters of Mnemosyne.

8. See Maurice Kelley, *This Great Argument: A Study of Milton's "De doctrina christiana" as a Gloss upon "Paradise Lost"* (Princeton and Oxford, 1941); Kelley, "Milton and the Third Person of the Trinity," 221–34; *Christian Doctrine,* 295.

9. See Steadman, *Milton's Biblical and Classical Imagery,* 114–20. Both Masson and Verity have distinguished two separate invocations, to the muse and the Spirit respectively. David Masson, ed., *The Poetical Works of John Milton,* vol. 3 (London, 1874), 114; A. W. Verity, ed., *Paradise Lost,* vol. 2 (Cambridge, 1929), 368, 370.

10. Milton's contrast between physical blindness and intellectual vision, his emphasis on purification, and the analogy he draws between himself and Orpheus would seem to acquire further significance when placed in the context of Renaissance Neoplatonic tradition. In an Orphic reference to love as "eyeless," Proclus perceived an allusion to the doctrine "that the highest mysteries must be seen without eyes and heard without ears," and both Pico of Mirandola and Agrippa of Nettesheim followed this interpretation; Orpheus had described love as blind "because he is above the intellect." According to Hermias's commentary on Plato's *Phaedrus,* "to close the eyes in initiation" is "no longer to receive by sense those divine mysteries, but with the pure soul itself." Beroaldus similarly credits Plato with the statement "that the eyes of the mind begin to see clearly when the eyes of the body begin to fail." See Edgar Wind, *Pagan Mysteries in the Renaissance,* rev. and enl. ed. (New York, 1968), 53–59.

The analogy that Milton suggests between himself and Moses, both inspired by the heavenly muse and both narrating the same hexaemeral material, is perhaps enhanced by the analogy between the blind poet and the prophet who was permitted a glimpse of the back parts of Deity and whose radiance was such, when he descended the mount, that he was compelled to wear a veil over his face.

11. On the "Book of Creatures" see Ruth Wallerstein, *Studies in Seventeenth-Century Poetic* (Madison, Wisc., 1950), 48–50, 183–216, and passim; cf. John G. Demaray, *Cosmos and Epic Representation.*

12. *On the Morning of Christ's Nativity,* lines 1–28.

13. *The Passion,* lines 1–4.

14. *Comus,* line 515.

15. Tasso comments on the poet's use of invocation and proposition in the middle of a poem as well as at the beginning (Tasso, *Prose,* 452). He also observes that poets are wont to invoke divine aid often at the beginning of their works, and sometimes in the middle or at the end (447).

16. Tasso, *Prose,* 448.

17. See Nora K. Chadwick and Victor Zhirmunsky, *Oral Epics of Central Asia* (Cambridge, 1969). On the image of the inspired poet in Homer and Hesiod, and its relation to prophecy, see Moses I. Finley, *The World of Odysseus* (London, 1964: rev. ed. Harmondsworth, 1972), 30–36. In the *Odyssey,* book 17, Eumaeus refers to "an inspired bard who can charm with his song." Finley comments that the word *thespis* literally means "produced or shown by a god" and that "*thespis* provides the necessary frame of reference for the opening line of the *Iliad*: 'Sing, goddess of the wrath of Peleus' son Achilles.'" In book 22, Phemius declares that he is "self-taught; the god has implanted in my heart songs of all kinds." Similarly, in book 8, Odysseus praises the bard Demodocus "whether it was the Muse, daughter of Zeus, who instructed you, or indeed Apollo. For you sing truly indeed of the fate of the Achaeans . . . as if you yourself had been present or had heard it from another." Moreover, as Finley observes, "Demodocus's precise knowledge had already been explained" earlier: "For so Phoebus Apollo had told him in prophecy."

In Hesiod's *Theogony,* Finley observed, "the simple invocation has become a full-blown vision and personal revelation." One day, as he was shepherding his flocks under Helicon, the muses, daughters of Zeus, appeared to Hesiod and "taught (him) glorious song." Declaring that "we know how to speak many false things as though they were true; but we know, when we will, to utter true things," they "gave me a rod, a shoot of sturdy olive, and breathed into me a divine voice to celebrate things that shall be and things that were aforetime; and they bade me sing of the race of the blessed gods that are eternally, but ever to sing of themselves both first and last." Finley comments that "Hesiod's divine voice sounds like a direct quotation of the description of the soothsayer Calchas, 'who knew things that were and things that shall be and things that were aforetime.'" (*Iliad,* book 1). "This close link between poetry and the divine knowledge of the past and future," he notes, also "found its personification in Orpheus."

18. Benjamin Jowett, trans., *The Works of Plato* (New York, n.d.), vol. 4, 287–88. In "Of Cato the Younger," Montaigne comments that it is easier to write poetry than to understand it. Although there is "a certain low and moderate sort of poetry, that a man may well enough judge by certain rules of art," the "true, supreme, and divine poetry is above all rules and reason." One discerns its beauty instantaneously like a flash of lightning; "it does not exercise but ravishes and overwhelms our judgment." From the *Ion,* Montaigne borrows the image of poetic enthusiasm as a divine magnetism: "The fury that possesses him who is able to penetrate into it would yet attract a third man by hearing him repeat it; like a loadstone that not only attracts the needle, but also infuses into it, the virtue to attract others." This is evident in our own theaters. Through the poet, transported "out of himself" by the "sacred inspiration of the Muses" and moved to anger or sorrow or hatred or other passions, the fury possesses the actor and through him the spectators. *Essays of Montaigne,* trans. Charles Cotton, ed. W. C. Hazlitt, vol. 1 (London, 1977), 286–87.

19. Spenser, *The Shepheardes Calender,* "Argument" to the October AEglogue. In his gloss on this poem, E. K. cites the first book of Plato's *De Legibus (Laws)* on "the first invention of Poetry" at "solemne feastes called Panegyrica." At these festivals "some learned man . . . would take upon him to sing fine verses to the people, in prayse eyther of vertue or of victory or of immortality or such like. At whose wonderful gift all men being astonished and as it were ravished, with delight, thinking (as it was indeed) that he was inspired from above, called him vatem." In commenting on Cuddie's line "O if my temples were distained with wine" (line 110), E. K. suggests that "He seemeth here to be ravished with a Poetical furie." See E. K.'s gloss on Cuddie's emblem, and Gilbert, *Literary Criticism,* 118, 237–38.

20. Gilbert, *Literary Criticism,* 445, 458, 667.

21. See Steadman, *The Lamb and the Elephant,* 150–56.

22. Ingram Bywater, ed. and trans., *Aristotle on the Art of Poetry* (Oxford, 1909), 49. Gilbert, *Literary Criticism,* 352; cf. 117–18. Elsewhere, as Gilbert notes, Aristotle refers to poetry as "inspired by the god" (*Rhetoric,* 3, 7, 1408b19). For Democritus's view that madness was necessary for great poetry, see Gilbert, 137–38. Like Castelvetro, Gerald Else emends the text; "the poetic art is an enterprise for the gifted [rather than] the 'manic' individual; for of these types the one is highly adaptable (sensitive), the other is eccentric and unbalanced." Gerald F. Else, *Aristotle's Poetics: The Argument* (Cambridge,

Mass., 1963), 486. Cf. Gilbert, 94, "the affair of the gifted man rather than of the madman, for men of the first kind can adapt themselves well but those of the second are beside themselves." Trissino interpreted Aristotle's statement as meaning "those who are moved by violent feeling *(furore)*" because they know "how to form the passions" (Gilbert, 216). S. H. Butcher retains the traditional interpretation: "a strain of madness," for "he is lifted out of his proper self" (Butcher, *Aristotle's Theorys of Poetry and Fine Art,* 3d ed. [London, 1902]).

23. Plato's categories of inspiration were familiar to many Renaissance poets and critics. Although overladen with myth—deities in whose divinity Plato himself may or may not have believed and whom his Renaissance admirers must necessarily regard as symbolic fictions at best—these distinctions are logical in their approach to the irrational, and they provide a convenient point of departure for discussing the topos of the inspired poet and frequent assumption of the roles of the inspired prophet and the inspired lover. Nevertheless, they are perhaps *too* logical—and they occur rather too late in the development of Hellenic society—to be altogether valid even for Plato's own culture. Virtually every divinity was invoked and worshiped with song. Most of them (including Zeus and Apollo) could either enlighten or deceive a man, sending true or false dreams and fostering true insights or illusions. Athene could illuminate the mind from within; Ares could inspire a man with martial fury no less irrational than the inspirations of Dionysos and Aphrodite. In addition, there were many other kinds of divine or demonic furor: the panic terror inspired by the goat-god; the madness inflicted by the Erinnyes; the inspiration of daimons, good or bad (such as the daimon of Socrates); the sudden blind folly inflicted by Ate.

24. In *Pharsalia,* book 1, lines 33–66, Lucan ironically invokes Nero instead of Apollo or Bacchus to "inspire my verse." Lucan, *The Civil War,* trans. J. D. Duff (London and N.Y., 1928).

25. *The Complete Poetry of Richard Crashaw,* ed. George Walton Williams (Garden City, N.Y., 1970), 216–17.

26. Traditionally, either Zeus or Apollo was regarded as the father of the muses.

27. *Virgil,* ed. H. Rushton Fairclough (2 vols.; London and New York; vol. 1 (1916), 28–33. Eclogue 4. Ludovico Ariosto, *Orlando Furioso,* cantos 34, 35.

28. Wind, *Pagan Mysteries in the Renaissance.*

29. In *Ad Patrem,* poetry is associated not only with the prophet and the priest but also with royal banquets (though significantly *before* gluttony and luxury

and intemperance had made their appearance). "By song Apollo's priestesses and the trembling Sibyl . . . lay bare the mysteries of the far-away future." Songs are composed by "the sacrificing priest at the altar," when he slays the bull and when he "consults the secrets of destiny" in its entrails. At the royal tables of antiquity, the bard sang of "the deeds and emulable achievements of heroes, and of chaos and of the broad foundations on which the earth rests, of the deities who once went creeping about in search of their acorn-food, and of the thunderbolt not yet sought out of the depths of Aetna" (*CP,* 83–84). In *L'Allegro,* Mirth is the daughter of love and wine (Venus and Bacchus); but in *Il Penseroso,* Melancholy is associated with abstinence:

> Spare Fast, that oft with gods doth diet,
> And hears the Muses in a ring
> Aye round about *Jove's* Altar sing.

30. One may compare Milton's image of sacred fury at the advent of Apollo with that of Virgil in the *Aeneid,* book 6. In her prophetic seizure the Cumaean Sibyl hails the presence of Apollo with the cry "deus, ecce, deus!" She becomes frenzied, seems taller, and speaks with a voice that no longer seems mortal: "et rabie fera corda tument, maiorque videri / nec mortale sonans, adflata est numine quando / iam propiore dei" (*Virgil,* trans. H. Rushton Fairclough [London and New York, vol. 1 (1916)], lines 46–51]. Not yet "brooking the sway of Phoebus," the prophetess *(vates)* storms wildly in the cavern (immanis in antro / bacchatur vates), if so she may "shake the mighty god from off her breast; so much the more he tires her raving mouth, tames her wild heart (fatigat / os rabidum, fera corda domans), and moulds her by constraint" (*Virgil,* vol. 1, lines 77–80). Virgil also refers to her furor and *rabida ora* ("mad countenance").

The poet's sacred rage could also be a topos for ridicule as well as praise. In the dedicatory epistle to *The Shepheardes Calender,* E. K. applies the imagery of prophetic and poetic madness pejoratively to the "rakehellye route of our ragged rymers," who "without reason rage and fome, as if some instinct of Poeticall spirite had newly ravished them above the meanenesse of common capacitie. And being in the middest of all theyr bravery sodenly eyther for want of matter, or ryme, or having forgotten theyr former conceit, they seeme to be so pained and traveiled in theyr remembrance, . . . as that same Pythia when the traunce came upon her.

Os rabidum fera corda domans &c." (Spenser, *Poetical Works,* 417–18).

For further discussion of Renaissance topoi associated with the conception of the poet as prophet or poetry as a divine frenzy, see Craig Kallendorf, "From Virgil to Vida: The *Poeta Theologus* in Italian Renaissance Commentary," *Journal of the History of Ideas* 56 (1995), 41–62.

31. Milton's early epicedic verse makes frequent use of the motifs of vision or flight. The flight itself, however, belongs to the deceased rather than the poet; the apotheosis motif, as well as visionary or prophetic elements, is conventional in this genre. Though one should not exaggerate the importance of these conventions in these poems, the fact that Milton chose them instead of other alternative techniques is nevertheless significant. In the *Third Elegy* (on the death of the Bishop of Winchester) the poet dreams that he is in heaven and sees and hears the welcome accorded the dead prelate by the angels. In the funeral verses on the death of the Bishop of Ely, on the other hand, he beholds no vision, but hears the voice of the dead man relating his translation to heaven by angels, "carried aloft, clear to the stars, like the venerable prophet of old [Elijah], charioteer of a fiery chariot, who was caught up to heaven." ("Vates ut olim raptus ad caelum senex.") Soaring beyond the moon and the sun through the planets and galaxy, "wondering often at my strange speed," the bishop's soul finally reaches the portals of Olympus. "But here I fall silent," for what mortal "can tell the delights of that place?" (*CP,* 25). Milton draws no analogy between Elijah as *vates* and the poet; in "The Passion" it is another visionary chariot (the chariot of Ezekiel's vision) that bears the poet to Palestine. Ariosto, on the other hand, borrows Elijah's chariot for Astolfo's ascent to the moon (canto 34). Ariosto is perhaps (like Milton) employing the flying chariot as a symbol of the act of contemplation.

32. In this poem, "At a Vacation Exercise in the College," as in the Fifth Elegy and other early works and as in the two epics themselves, the universal range of the poet's flight brings him perilously close to the sin of Eve. It was, in fact, by endeavoring to ascend to heaven and "see / What life the Gods live there" that she had ultimately fallen (in spite of rejecting Satan's initial temptation). There is little respect for the warning *noli sapere in alto* ("seek not to know too high"), in these early poems. Inspired, like Donne, with a hydropic love of learning, Milton could very well understand the sin of curiosity. If not the last infirmity of noble mind, intemperance in the appetite for knowledge was surely penultimate; it was a fortunate paradox that Milton's hunger for universal knowledge could eventually find expression in a universal epic centered on the temptation of forbidden wisdom.

Geography and cartography continued to fascinate Milton even in his blindness, and the geographical catalogues that are so characteristic a feature of both of his epics obviously delighted him even though he might introduce them in pejorative contexts. The scheme of education that he recommended was encyclopedic in scope; the cosmic range of the studies that he recommended (not without facetiousness) to his academic colleagues in the Third Prolusion is analogous to that of the poetic ambitions expressed (with something of the same mixture of idealism and fancy) in "A Vacation Exercise." Employing the same flight metaphor, he urges his auditors to roam the earth and the heavens. He exhorts them to "rove with your eyes over all the lands which are drawn on the map, to look at the places where the heroes walked of old," to "ascend Mount Aetna in eruption." They must then observe the manners of men and "well ordered governments of nations." They must examine the natures of all living creatures. They must study the hidden virtues of herbs and stones. "Nor should you hesitate . . . to fly into the heavens and contemplate the manifold shapes of the clouds," the sources of hail and snow and dews and thunderbolts, the stars and the course of the sun. "But your mind should not consent to be . . . circumscribed by the earth's boundaries, but should range beyond the confines of the world. Let it reach the summit of knowledge and learn to know itself and . . . those blessed minds and intelligences with whom hereafter it will enter into eternal fellowships" (*CP,* 606–7).

33. Milton's fiction is, in large part, a technical device enabling him to suggest obliquely the evangelical authority upon which his poem on the Passion is based. In *Paradise Lost,* the allusion to Moses and Genesis ("In the Beginning") serves a similar purpose. Yet the wheels of Ezekiel's vision were also a highly appropriate vehicle for a poet who pretends to be rapt in the Spirit, since it is the Spirit that moves them. "And they went every one straight forward; whither the spirit was to go, they went" (Ezek. 1:12); "and when the living creatures were lifted up from the earth, the wheels were lifted up. Whithersoever the spirit was to go, they went, thither was their spirit to go; and the wheels were lifted up over against them; for the spirit of the living creature was in the wheels" (Ezek. 1:10–20; cf. 21). In *Il Penseroso,* this is the vehicle of the cherub Contemplation.

34. See Michael Lieb, *Poetics of the Holy;* Lieb, "Ezekiel's Inaugural Vision as a Literary Event," *Cithara* 24 (1985): 22–39; Lieb, "Milton's 'Chariot of Paternal Deitie' as a Reformation Conceit," *Journal of Religion* 65 (1985): 359–77.

35. *Purgatorio,* canto 29.

36. This lost work was attributed to Aristeas of Proconnesos; see *Paulys Real-Encyclopädie der classischen Altertumswissenschaft,* new ed. (Stuttgart, 1896), vol. 2, cols. 826–27.

37. Plato, *Republic,* book 10; Cicero, *De re publica,* trans. Clinton Walker Keyes (London and New York, 1928), 260–83; Dante, *Inferno,* canto 20, lines 13–33; *Visio S. Pauli* (Halle, 1885), see also *L'Apocalisse di Paolo Siriaca,* ed. Giuseppe Ricciotti (2 vols.; Brescia, 1932. Ricciotti's book treats the cosmology of the Bible and its transmission down to Dante. That Dante's visionary journey through hell and purgatory and heaven was sometimes interpreted as a dream vision was discussed by Jacopo Mazzoni in his *Discorso in difesa della "Commedia" del divino Poeta Dante* (Bologna, 1572) and in *Della difesa della "Commedia" di Dante.* (The first three books of the *Difesa* were published at Cesena in 1587, but the remaining four books did not appear until 1688.) In the *Discorso,* Mazzoni declares that Dante pretends his fable is a journey that he actually took to the otherworld through extraordinary grace. In the *Difesa,* however, he revises this opinion, maintaining that Dante feigns the action occurs in a cataphoric ecstasy, in periods of interrupted visions and dreams. The tradition of Mohammed referred to is the prophet's *mi'raj* ("ladder") and the winged steed Buraq. In *Dante y el Islam* (Madrid, 1927) Miguel Asín Palacios discussed the possible influence of this and other Islamic traditions on Dante, but the issue remains controversial. See Harold Sunderland's translation and abridgment of Asín Palacios' book, *Islam and the Divine Comedy* (London, 1926). On the *Kitab al Mi'raj* see also José Muñoz Sendino (ed.), *La escala de Mahoma; traducción del árabe al castelano. latín y francés. ordenada por Alfonso X el Sabio* (Madrid, 1949) and Enrico Cerulli (ed.), *Il "libro della scala" e la questione delle fonti arabo-spagnole della Divina commedià* (Città del Vaticano, 1949).

38. See Dante, *Inferno,* canto 2, lines 7–9:

> O muse, o alto ingegno, or m'aiutate;
> o mente che scrivesti ciò ch'io vidi,
> qui si parrà la tua nobilitate.

Cf. Chaucer, *The House of Fame,* book 2, lines 524–27:

> O Thought, that wrot al that I mette,
> And in the tresorye hyt shette
> Of my brayn, now shal men se

> Yf any vertu in the be,
> To tellen al my drem aryght.

F. N. Robinson compares these lines with *Inferno,* canto 2, lines 8–9; *Paradiso,* canto 1, line 11; and *Paradiso,* canto 18, line 87. See *The Complete Works of Geoffrey Chaucer,* ed. F. N. Robinson (Boston, 1933), 891.

39. *On the Morning of Christ's Nativity,* lines 22–28.

40. See Louis L. Martz, *The Poetry of Meditation: A Study in English Religious Literature of the Seventeenth Century,* rev. ed. (New Haven, Conn., 1962); Barbara Kiefer Lewalski, *Protestant Poetics and the Seventeenth-Century Religious Lyric* (Princeton, 1979).

41. Lowry Nelson Jr., *Baroque Lyric Poetry* (New Haven and London, 1961). In both the Nativity Ode and "Upon the Circumcision," Milton's shifts in tense would seem to be closely correlated with his meditative or devotional techniques: his presence on the scene and his reflections on the significance of these events and their relationship to future or past events. Yet in view of the frequency with which his own contemporaries could alternate between preteritive forms and the historical present, or between the present and the future, when describing the same events, one should not overemphasize their significance in Milton's poetry.

It may be helpful to examine briefly the treatment of time in the first episodes of book 12 of *Paradise Lost.* In his prophetic survey of world history, Michael shifts with comparative ease and facility between past, present, and future tenses. Nimrod "Will arrogate Dominion" over his brethren. Men "shall be" his game, and he "shall be styl'd" a mighty hunter. With a crew, "whom like Ambition joins," he "shall find" the plain, where bitumen "Boils out" from underground. Of that stuff "they cast to build a city and a tower" that "may reach" to heaven; but God "Comes down" to see their city, and in derision "sets" a spirit upon their tongues to confuse their speech. Forthwith a hideous gabble "rises loud" among the builders; "each to other calls," and, thinking themselves mocked, "they storm" in rage. Great "laughter was in Heaven" to see the hubbub. Thus "was the building left / Ridiculous."

In his own comment on these events, Adam logically resorts to the past tense to describe the nature of the dominion that God had originally bestowed on man ("He gave," "He made") and the present to indicate the continuity of man's right of rule over beasts ("that right we hold"). He shifts into the present, however, to describe Nimrod's usurpation: "But this Usurper his encroachment proud / Stays not on Man; to God his Tower intends / Siege and defiance."

After returning to the future tense ("Thus will this latter, as the former World, / Still tend from bad to worse"), Michael describes the vocation of Abraham in the present ("voutsafes / To call by Vision," "he straight obeys," "firm believes," "leaves his Gods" and native soil. On this occasion, however, the shift to the present is rationalized by the fact that Michael as blessed seer actually beholds the future events that he is relating, although Adam cannot see them: "I see him, but thou canst not," "I see his Tents." Adam can still behold the geographical sites where these events will occur, however, as the angel indicates them to him ("each place behold / In prospect, as I paint them," "See where it flows").

In both of these episodes Milton resorts to the present partly for greater immediacy of presentation, but also to clarify the relationship of the events described to events anterior or subsequent to them. Thus Adam refers to Nimrod's usurpation in the present tense, but employs the past tense to refer to the kind of dominion that God had given him. Michael similarly refers to Abraham's vocation in the present, but resorts to the future to refer to Abraham's seed (a land which he "will show him," from him "will raise? A mighty nation," so that "in his Seed / All Nations shall be blest"). There is a rationale underlying these tense shifts, though Milton does not always preserve it.

42. Cf. Eusebius, *Praeparatio evangelica;* Don Cameron Allen, *Mysteriously Meant: The Rediscovery of Pagan Symbolism and Allegorical Interpretation in the Renaissance* (Baltimore and London, 1970), 10 and passim.

43. Cf. Donne, *Holy Sonnets,* 10, "Nor ever chast, except you ravish me." Richard Crashaw, "To . . . the Countesse of Denbigh Persuading her to Resolution in Religion, and to render her selfe without further delay into the Communion of the Catholick Church."

44. See E. M. W. Tillyard, *The Miltonic Setting* (Cambridge, 1938), 1–28; and *A Variorum Commentary on the poems of John Milton,* vol. 2, *The Minor English Poems,* ed. A. S. P. Woodhouse and Douglas Bush, part 1 (New York, 1972), 231–41. There is, one should note, a fundamental difference between Milton's poems and Burton's poem. Whereas Burton had juxtaposed the pleasures and the torments of melancholy, Milton confines himself to the pleasures alone. The basic opposition in his poems is the kind of pleasures that mirth and melancholy respectively offer.

The genealogies and associates of mirth and melancholy invite comparison with Milton's allusions elsewhere to diverse sources of poetic inspiration. The true ancestors of mirth, he suggests in *L'Allegro,* are not love and wine—powers that he elsewhere describes as inspiring the light elegy—but rather the spring itself: that furor whose power he had celebrated in his *Fifth Elegy*. In this poem Apollo had exhorted Aurora to arise and urge on the steeds of dawn; in her amorous supplications to the same divinity as god of the sun, the "wanton earth" ("Tellus lasciva") had associated the west wind with her in her appeals: "Look Phoebus, facile loves are calling to you and the winds of spring carry honied appeals. Perfume-bearing Zephyr gently fans his cinnamon-scented wings and the birds seem to carry their blandishments to you" (*CP*, 3a–40).

Melancholy's ancestry in turn reflects medical and astrological doctrine concerning the influence of the planet Saturn on black bile and the melancholy temperament, as well as the traditional association of both with the contemplative life and with genius and learning.

One should note the contrasting allusions to mirth and melancholy in *Comus*. In *L'Allegro*, Milton repeats but undercuts the myth of Euphrosyne's descent from Bacchus and Venus. Comus, on the other hand, is the son of Bacchus and Circe; his revels are closely associated with the rites of love and wine. The Lady deplores the "sound / Of Riot and ill-manag'd Merriment." Thyris, in turn, professes to have been "Wrapt in a pleasing fit of melancholy," meditating his rural minstrelsy. The enchanter dismisses the Lady's arguments as "but the lees / And settlings of a melancholy blood."

See Lawrence Babb, *The Elizabethan Malady: A Study of Melancholia in English Literature from 1580 to 1642* (East Lansing, Mich., 1951); Babb, *Sanity in Bedlam: A Study of Robert Burton's "Anatomy of Melancholy"* (East Lansing, Mich., 1959); Rudolf and Margot Wittkower, *Born Under Saturn: The Character and Conduct of Artists* (London, 1963); Raymond Klibansky, Erwin Panofsky, and Fritz Saxl, *Saturn and Melancholy: Studies in the History of Nature Philosophy Religion, and Art* (New York, 1964); Winfried Schleiner, *Melancholy Genius and Utopia in the Renaissance* (Wiesbaden, 1991).

45. Cf. the invocation of a multiplicity of deities in book 1 of Virgil's *Georgics*.

46. Cf. Milton's *Fifth Elegy*, similarly inspired by spring.

47. See Douglas Bush's account of Woodhouse's view that the two poems set forth "rival conceptions of a life of pleasure, the one active and social, the other contemplative and solitary." *Variorum Commentary*, vol. 2, part 1, 249.

48. *Comus*, lines 252–64.

Chapter 3

1 For background see Rosemary Freeman, *Edmund Spenser*, rev. ed. (London, 1962); Freeman, *"The Faerie Queene": A Companion for Readers* (London,

1970); Graham Hough, *A Preface to "The Faerie Queene"* (London, 1962); William Nelson, *The Poetry of Edmund Spenser: A Study* (New York, 1963); Nelson, *Fact or Fiction: The Dilemma of the Renaissance Storyteller* (Cambridge, Mass., 1973); Kathleen Williams, *Spenser's World of Glass: A Reading of "The Faerie Queene"* (Berkeley, 1966).

2. Gilbert, *Literary Criticism,* 277–88; see also Peter V. Marinelli, *Ariosto and Boiardo: The Origins of the "Orlando Furioso"* (Columbia, Mo., 1987).

3. Gilbert, *Literary Criticism,* 262–68.

4. Tasso, *Prose,* 397–98.

5. Tasso, "Allegoria del poema," in *Il Goffredo overo Gierusalemme liberata* (Roma, 1957).

6. J. B. Broadbent, *Some Graver Subject: An Essay on "Paradise Lost"* (London, 1960), 202–17.

7. Ibid., 202–71.

8. Gilbert Murray, *The Rise of the Greek Epic,* 3d ed., rev. and enl. (Oxford, 1924), 216, 298–99, 340–41. Diomedes took part in the Trojan war and in the second expedition against Thebes, which had been described in the lost *Epigonoi.* His father, Tydeus, had taken part in the first expedition against Thebes, recounted in the lost *Thebais,* once regarded as Homeric, and in Statius's *Thebaid.*

9. Gilbert, *Literary Criticism,* 132–33, 132n.

10. Ingram Bywater, ed. and trans., *Aristotle on the Art of Poetry* (Oxford, 1909), 70–73.

11. Else, *Aristotle's Poetics,* 569, 580.

12. Ibid., 569–86; cf. 301–8.

13. Gilbert, *Literary Criticism,* 132–33; Bywater, *Aristotle,* 72–73. Cf. Milton's *Second Defense; CP,* 838: "As the epic poet, who adheres at all to the rules of that species or composition, does not profess to describe the whole life of the hero whom he celebrates, but only some particular action of his life, as the resentment of Achilles at Troy, the return of Ulysses, and the coming of Aeneas, so it will be sufficient . . . that I have heroically celebrated at least one action of my countrymen. I pass by the rest, for who could recite the achievements of a whole people?" After touching on the prime cause of Adam's fall, briefly summarizing Satan's revolt and expulsion from heaven, *Paradise Lost* "hastes into the *midst of things, presenting* Satan and his Angels now fallen into Hell." The action of the poem begins at this point. *Paradise Regained* similarly begins in medias res, opening with the scene of Christ's baptism and alluding only briefly in the course of the narrative to earlier events in his life.

14. See Graham Hough on the beginning in medias res.

15. As Else observed (*Aristotle's Poetics,* 304–7), Aristotle's defense of poetry as more philosophical than history did not "take the crude form of identifying poetry with philosophy, and his 'universals' are not Plato's Ideas." Moreover, he spoke of tragedy "only as 'telling of' the universals: the word *mimesis* does not appear." The universals with which the poet was concerned pertained not to metaphysics, the science of Being, but to the practical sphere of human life and action, the subject matter associated with ethics and politics. Renaissance apologists for poetry and painting, on the other hand, often extolled the poet and artist as imitators of ideas as well as actions. Like the Platonic lover, the poet or artist fashions a purer, more perfect, more beautiful idea in his mind and copies that. See Erwin Panofsky, *Idea; a Concept in Art Theory,* trans. Joseph J. S. Pecke (Columbia, S.C., 1968).

16. With Ariosto's continuation of the narrative left by Boiardo's death, one may compare Chapman's continuation of Marlowe's *Hero and Leander* and Jean de Meung's continuation of Guillaume de Lorris's *Romance of the Rose.*

Chapter 4

1. Gilbert, *Literary Criticism,* 81.

2. Else, *Aristotle's Poetics.* See Bywater, *Aristotle,* 24–27.

3. Bywater, *Aristotle,* 6–7, 26–27. See Horace, *Épitres,* ed. François Villeneuve, 3d ed., rev. (Paris, 1955), book 1, Epistle 2, "quid virtus et quid sapientia possit, / utile proposuit nobis exemplar Vlixen." ("In Ulysses Homer has proposed to us a profitable example of what virtue and wisdom are able to accomplish.")

4. Cf. Aristotle, *Poetics,* chapter 24 (Bywater, *Aristotle,* 76–77): "Homer more than any other has taught the rest of us the art of framing lies in the right way." Horace subsequently praised Homer in similar terms. He "so employs fiction, so blends false with true, that beginning, middle, and end all strike the same note." Gilbert, *Literary Criticism,* 133. "atque ita mentitur, sic veris falsa remiscet." In commenting on Aristotle's theory, Butcher suggested that the "fiction here intended is . . . not simply that fiction which is blended with fact in every poetic narrative or real events," but rather "those tales of a strange and marvellous character which are admitted into epic more freely than into dramatic poetry." "By artistic treatment things incredible in real life wear an air of probability." Butcher, *Aristotle's Theory of Poetry and Fine Art,* 171–73; cf. 171n. on Horace.

5. Demaray, *Cosmos and Epic Representation.*

6. The average audience (whether classical or Renaissance) is often familiar with the place-names associated with historic or legendary battles without knowing much about the battles themselves or the actual sites where they occurred. The names and sites are remembered because the battles occurred there, or because the poets themselves had described them. Scamander and the warm and cold springs near Troy are remembered because Homer mentioned them. (The latter have sometimes been regarded as a poetic invention, and scholarship has questioned the applicability of his description of the former to the stream near Schliemann's Troy.) Although Kurukshetra is a real place, its fame depends almost entirely on the *Mahabharata.* An English poet might have greater license to invent and feign in describing the battles at Crécy and Agincourt than the battles of Hastings or Marston Moor.

The topographies of the romance, like those of classical and Renaissance epic, are sometimes developed in elaborate detail, as in Ariosto's account of the siege of Paris and the fortifications of the city.

7. On the relation of the Homeric epics to history, chronology, and geography, see Finley, *The World of Odysseus,* 17–45; Richmond Lattimore (trans.), *The Iliad of Homer* (Chicago and London, 1951; 1st Phoenix ed., 1961); and Lattimore (trans.), *The Odyssey of Homer* (New York, 1965; First Harper Colophon Edition, 1975). Citing Hesiod's *Works and Days* on the "godlike race of hero-men who are called demi-gods, the race before our own" who fought at Thebes and Troy, Finley observes that "few Greeks, early or late, ever doubted" that there had once been a time of heroes. Homer was "their most authoritative" but not their only source of information; but neither Homer nor Hesiod "had the slightest interest in history as we might understand the notion." As for the topography of Troy, the *Iliad* is "filled with details, for that is the stuff of heroic narrative," and they are indeed "so consistent that a serviceable map of the area can be drawn from the poet's specifications. See also G. S. Kirk, *The Songs of Homer* (Cambridge, 1962); Denys Page, *History and the Homeric Iliad* (Berkeley, 1959); Page, *The Homeric Odyssey* (Oxford, 1955); and Rhys Carpenter, *Folk Tale, Fiction and Saga in the Homeric Epics* (Berkeley, 1946).

8. It has been suggested that the reference to the Ethiopians involves a confusion between the peoples living on the east and west banks of the Nile and those dwelling on the eastern and western shores of the Red Sea and the Indian Ocean.

9. The image of the maze was itself ambiguous and multivalent. The labyrinth of love and the labyrinth of the philosophers were scarcely less common-

place than the metaphor of the world as labyrinth. See John M. Steadman, *Nature into Myth: Medieval and Renaissance Moral Symbols* (Pittsburgh, 1979), 158–68, 281–82; Steadman, *The Hill and the Labyrinth: Discourse and Certitude in Milton and His Near-Contemporaries* (Berkeley, 1984), 6–8, 12–13. Cf. Francis Quarles, *Emblems,* book 4, no. 2, "The world's a lab'rinth, whose anfractuous wayes / Are all compos'd of rubs and crook'd meanders." Francis Quarles, *Complete Works,* ed. Alexander B. Grosart (3 vols., Edinburgh, 1881), vol. 3, 79–80.

Chapter 5

1. Thomas M. Greene, "Antique World," in *The Spenser Encyclopedia,* ed. A. C. Hamilton et al. (Toronto, Buffalo and London, 1990), 42–46. In examining the "range of meanings" in Spenser's use of this term, Greene considers "the proems to the books of *The Faerie Queene.*" His study is concerned primarily with Spenser's relationship to the civilizations of Greece and Rome, as mediated through Renaissance humanism.

Andrew John Fichter, *Poets Historical: Dynastic Epic in the Renaissance* (New Haven and London, 1982), 1–2. The "common theme" of these dynastic epics is "the rise of *imperium,* the noble house, race, or nation to which the poet professes allegiance. To this subject the dynastic poem imports the narrative strategy established by Virgil in the *Aeneid* . . . : action is set in the period of the historical or quasi-historical past during which the struggle for the formation of *imperium,* the laying of geographical, genealogical, cultural, and moral foundations, takes place. . . . The 'Poet historical' speaks of the past as if it were a future—a future to which he and his heroics are granted access only in extraordinary moments of prophetic vision."

Michael O'Connell, *Mirror and Veil: The Historical Dimension of Spenser's "Faerie Queene"* (Chapel Hill, N.C., 1977). O'Connell calls attention to the views of Giraldi Cinthio and Giambattista Pigna in regard to historical elements in the *Aeneid,* stressing the importance of Servius's commentary.

For Tudor antiquarianism and historiography see Arthur B. Ferguson, *Clio Unbound: Perception of the Social and Cultural Past in Renaissance England* (Durham, N.C., 1979); F. J. Levy, *Tudor Historical Thought* (San Marino, Calif., 1967); Levy, "History" in *The Spenser Encyclopedia,* 371–72. See also Peter Burke, *The Renaissance Sense of the Past* (London, 1969); Roberto Weiss, *The Renaissance Discovery of Classical Antiquity* (Oxford, 1969); William Nelson, *Fact or Fiction: The Dilemma of the Renaissance Storyteller* (Cambridge,

Mass., 1973); Robert E. Burkhart, "History, the Epic and the *Faerie Queene,*" *English Studies* 46 (1975): 14–19. See also Achsah Guibbory, *The Map of Time: Seventeenth-Century English Literature and Ideas of Pattern in History* (Urbana and Chicago, 1986) and Judith H. Anderson, *Biographical Truth: The Representation of Historical Persons in Tudor-Stuart Writing* (New Haven and London, 1984); A. L. Rowse, *The Elizabethan Age* (3 vols. in 4; London, 1950–1972).

2. Hough, *Preface to "The Faerie Queene,"* 48–58.

3. Hough believes that although Tasso's discourses on the heroic poem could not have affected the beginnings of Spenser's romance, they nevertheless "affected the *Letter,* which adopts some similar points of view" (60).

4. See J. D. Spingarn, *A History of Literary Criticism in the Renaissance,* 2d ed. (New York, 1908; repr., 1949), 112–15. For Spenser's possible knowledge of Tasso's poetic theory, see Treip, *Allegorical Poetics and the Epic,* 267–74 and passim.

5. Hough, *Preface to "The Faerie Queene,"* 59–60, 161; 118–21.

6. Tasso, *Prose,* 458, 486–90. (*Discorsi del poema eroico.*) For allegory as "metaphora continuata" see Treip, *Allegorical Poetics and the Epic,* 23–27, 92–99, 255, 275, and passim.

7. See Mazzoni, *Della difesa della Comedia di Dante,* in Gilbert, *Literary Criticism,* 388.

8. See Gabriel Harvey's commendatory verses on *The Faerie Queene,* "To the learned Shepheard" (*PW,* 409).

9. For a detailed study of the poetics of Sidney and Spenser and the concept of imitation see Heninger, *Sidney and Spenser.* Heninger argues that "Aristotle's *Poetics . . .* provided the baseline for Sidney's theorizing about poetry, and the positive aspects of his program derive for the most part from it" (246). In his opinion Spenser "modified his expository technique" after "acquaintance with Sidney" and "sought to follow the new poetics of fictioneering, of 'representing, counterfeiting, or figuring forth to speak metaphorically.'" As "his career progressed, Spenser was groping toward an art of poetry based upon Aristotelian imitation," but "he never completely mastered the new poetics of mimesis" (394–95).

10. See *Elizabethan Critical Essays,* ed. G. Gregory Smith (Oxford and London, 1904; repr., 1937), vol. 2, 40–53.

11. See Bernard Weinberg, *A History of Literary Criticism in the Italian Renaissance,* 2 vols. (Chicago and Toronto, 1961), vol. 2, 991, 994, 1005–6, 1011–13, 1017, 1019, 1026–27, 1030–31, 1038.

12. Gilbert, *Literary Criticism,* 364n, 391, 305, 321, 389; Spingarn, *History of Literary Criticism,* 113–14, 120–21. As Spingarn notes, Castelvetro likewise distinguished these forms of heroic poetry. Mazzoni subsequently argued that "the poet will be able to set before himself for imitation several actions, provided one is principal and the others accessory." Cf. *Discorsi del poema eroico* in Tasso, *Prose,* 345–63.

13. Similar controversies occurred on a lesser scale in England. In *A Briefe Apologie of Poetrie,* prefixed to his translation of *Orlando Furioso,* Sir John Harington declared that poets "are allowed to faine what they list," quoting the line *"Mentiri astronomis pictoribus atque poetis"* ("Astronomers, Painters, and Poets may lye by authoritie"). In the same treatise Harington maintained that Ariosto meets the stipulation of Aristotle "and the best censurers of Poesie" that "the *Epopeia,* that is the heroicall Poem, should ground on some historie, and take some short time in the same to bewtifie with his Poetrie: so doth mine Author take the storie of k. *Charls* the great, and doth not exceed a yeare or therabout in his whole work"; *Elizabethan Critical Essays,* vol. 2, 200–201, 216. Harington referred also to Ariosto's conforming to the doctrine that "nothing should be fayned utterly incredible"; 216. Cf. Sidney's references to "the fayned *Cyrus* in *Xenophon*" and to "the fayned image of Poesie"; *Elizabethan Critical Essays,* vol. 1, 166.

14. On the glorification of Elizabeth see John N. King, *Spenser's Poetry and the Reformation Tradition* (Princeton, 1990), 7 and passim; Robin H. Wells, *Spenser's "Faerie Queene" and the Cult of Elizabeth* (London, 1983); Roy Strong, *The Cult of Elizabeth: Elizabethan Portraiture and Pageantry* (London, 1977); Rowse, *The Elizabethan Age.* See also Albert C. Labriola, "Milton's Eve and the Cult of Elizabeth I," forthcoming in *Journal of English and Germanic Philogy,* 1995.

15. See Fichter, *Poets Historical.*

16. King examines Spenser's "place in the Reformation literary tradition and his employment and redefinition of artistic practices, iconographical formulas, and royalist praise associated with Protestant poets and apologists," situating his work within "the context of English culture of the middle and latter parts of the sixteenth century." Spenser's "emulation of the archaic diction, style, and characterization of *The Canterbury Tales* and *The Plowman's Tale . . .* indicates his place within English Protestant tradition." King, *Spenser's Poetry and the Reformation Tradition,* 3–4.

17. See the discussion of Renaissance humanism by Thomas M. Greene in *The Spenser Encyclopedia.*

18. See the discussion of Spenser's cosmos by John G. Demaray in *Cosmos and Epic Representation: Dante, Spenser, Milton, and the Transformation of Renaissance Heroic Poetry* (Pittsburgh, 1991).

19. For sixteenth-century British views of Chaucer and for the use of the authority formula, see Alice S. Miskimin, *The Renaissance Chaucer* (New Haven and London, 1975). See also Richard Foster Jones, *The Triumph of the English Language: A Survey of Opinions Concerning the Vernacular from the Introduction of Printing to the Restoration* (Stanford, 1953).

20. Spenser's readers would doubtless have been as undisturbed by the lack of true fidelity to the manners of Celtic antiquity as were the audiences of Shakespeare's *King Lear* and Dryden's *King Arthur,* or the readers of romances concerning the exploits of Arthur's knights. Even if the author had possessed some real awareness of the customs of the times and societies he professed to be describing, the details would have seemed unfamiliar, pedantic, and (as Tasso suggested in regard to the customs of remote antiquity) even repellent to his readers.

21. See Tasso, *Prose,* 523–24.

22. See Steadman, *The Lamb and the Elephant,* 62, 64, 66.

23. For commentary on Spenser's typological or allegorical techniques, see O'Connell, *Mirror and Veil.* For Spenser's historical fiction as it relates to the monarchy, see Fichter, *Poets Historical.* For Spenser's conception of the hero and the heroic, see Maurice Evans, "Hero," in *The Spenser Encyclopedia,* 360–63, and Evans, *Spenser's Anatomy of Heroism: A Commentary on "The Faerie Queene"* (Cambridge, 1970). Evans observes that the "old heroes to whom Spenser so constantly alludes form a very curious collection: there are British kings such as Brutus and Malgo; 'famous founders' of 'puissant nations', of whom Inachus and Albion are examples; literary and mythical heroes like Orpheus, Odysseus, Hercules, Aeneas; and finally what Puttenham calls the gods of the gentiles, a category which includes Bacchus, Isis and Osiris" (6–7).

Chapter 6

1. In the light of Robert Ellrodt's study of Spenser's relation to the Neoplatonic tradition, one must recognize the limitations of the poet's firsthand knowledge of Plato's dialogues and of Neoplatonic philosophical works in comparison with the secondary or tertiary Platonism diffused through classical and Renaissance literature and through Christian theological tradition. See Robert Ellrodt, *Neoplatonism in the Poetry of Spenser* (Geneve, 1960).

2. See Hough, *Preface to "The Faerie Queene";* Kathleen Williams, *Spenser's World of Glass;* Freeman, *"The Faerie Queene": A Companion for Readers.*

3. Torquato Tasso, *Gerusalemme Liberata,* ed. Luigi Bonfigli (Bari, 1930), canto 1, stanza 1.

4. *Virgil,* trans. Fairclough, 240–41.

5. See Tasso, *Prose,* 370–74, 413.

6. Ibid., 362.

7. See John E. Parish, "Pre-Miltonic Representations of Adam as a Christian," *Rice Institute Pamphlet* 40, no. 3 (1953): 1–24; C. A. Patrides, "The Protevangelium in Renaissance Theology and *Paradise Lost," SEL* 3 (1963): 19–30; John M. Steadman, "Adam and the Prophesied Redeemer," *SP* 56 (1959): 214–25.

8. Cf. Hough, *Preface to "The Faerie Queene."*

9. Both Freeman and Hough emphasize the range of modalities in this "multiple allegory," from the "equation" of image and idea toward realistic detail at one extreme and abstraction at the other. Cf. Selincourt, "Introduction," in *PW,* liv-lvi.

10. See Hough, *Preface to "The Faerie Queene";* William Nelson, *The Poetry of Edmund Spenser.*

11. *Virgils Gnat,* "To . . . the Earle of Leicester, late deceased."

12. *Virgil,* trans. Fairclough, vol. 2, 370.

13. *Virgils Gnat,* stanza 1.

14. *Visions of the worlds vanitie,* stanza 12.

15. See Tasso, *Prose,* 472–74; John M. Steadman, *Redefining a Period Style: "Renaissance," "Mannerist," and "Baroque" in Literature* (Pittsburgh, 1990), 47–48, 181–82.

16. Cf. the seductive discourse of Spenser's arch-villains Despair and Archimago.

17. Even the Satan of the early books of *Paradise Lost,* for all his classical veneer, is far removed from both the Homeric and the Virgilian models of the hero, though he exhibits aspects of both. Milton skillfully adapts to Satan certain features of the Iliadic hero—Achilles' wrath and sense of injured merit and thirst for glory, and (to some extent) Hector's constancy in a doomed cause.

18. The kind of heroism represented by the Roland of the *Chanson de Roland* belongs largely to the old order. Although the older heroic ethos has been baptized into the faith, Roland's concern with his own honor, preferring to risk almost certain death—and the lives of his companions as well—rather

than call for help, links him with earlier generations of heroes. Nevertheless, he is simultaneously the *defensor fidei* and the martyr; this is a coherent image of "Christian heroism," however different it may be from that of Saint Paul or Spenser or Milton—or for that matter of Tasso. The ethos of any heroic society, as very different poets have portrayed it, bears a variable and sometimes indefinable relationship to that of the poet's own society, to an imaginary or quasi-historical antiquity, and to literary tradition (the last of these including both written and oral poetry). In the case of Teutonic poetry, moreover, there is often a substantial continuity between pagan and Christian societies in their images of heroic ethos. It would, however, be pointless, on the whole, to attempt to sort out Christian and pagan elements in a specific poem as though one were separating wheat kernels from barley.

19. For discussion of analogies between Tasso's and Spenser's conceptions of allegory, see Treip, *Allegorical Poetics and the Epic,* 95–105 and passim.

Chapter 7

1. See inter alia James Holly Hanford, "The Dramatic Element in *Paradise Lost*" in *John Milton, Poet and Humanist* (Cleveland, 1966), 224–43; John G. Demaray, "The Thrones Of Satan and God: Backgrounds to Divine Opposition in *Paradise Lost*," *Huntington Library Quarterly* 31 (1967): 21–33; Barbara Kiefer Lewalski, *"Paradise Lost" and the Rhetoric of Literary Forms.*

2. Gilbert, *Literary Criticism,* 479–83; 672–75. See also chapter 1, supra.

3. See Lily Bess Campbell, *Divine Poetry and Drama;* R. A. Sayce, *The French Biblical Epic in the Seventeenth Century* (Oxford, 1955); Burton O. Kurth, *Milton and Christian Heroism: Biblical Epic Themes and Forms in Seventeenth-Century England* (Berkeley and Los Angeles, 1959); Watson Kirkconnell, *The Celestial Cycle* (Toronto, 1952).

4. See Lawrence Babb, *The Moral Cosmos of "Paradise Lost"* (East Lansing, Mich., 1970).

5. See John Bunyan, *The Holy War, Made by Shaddai upon Diabolus; or, The Losing and Taking Again of the Town of Mansoul* (London, 1682).

6. *Complete Prose Works of John Milton,* vol. 8 (1982), 438.

7. See Babb, *Moral Cosmos.*

8. John D. Demaray, *Milton's Theatrical Epic: The Invention and Design of "Paradise Lost"* (Cambridge, Mass., and London, 1980), xvii, 38.

9. See Alice-Lyle Scoufos, "The Mysteries in Milton's Masque," *Milton Studies* 6 (1975): 113–42.

10. See Merritt Y. Hughes, "The Filiations of Milton's Celestial Dialogue (*Paradise Lost*, III, 80–343)," in *Ten Perspectives on Milton* (New Haven and London, 1955), 104–35.

11. On the Adam-Christ parallel in *Paradise Lost* see Steadman, *Milton and the Renaissance Hero*, 70–71, 81, 191; Steadman, *Milton's Epic Characters*, 33–36, 81, 87, 119, 124. See Rom. 5:12–20; 1 Cor. 15:21–22, 45–49. Cfs Col. 3:9–10 and Eph. 4:22–24. See also Norman Powell Williams, *The Ideas of the Fall and of Original Sin* (London, 1927).

12. See *Medieval Drama*, ed. David Bevington (Boston, 1975). Bevington calls attention to a *Pater Noster* play performed at Beverley, with a "mankind figure whose sins were being set forth in the work as a whole" (793). Quote in text is from Bevington, 911. See John M. Steadman, *The Wall of Paradise*, 59–60. Both Erasmus' *Enchiridion* and Thomas à Kempis's *Imitatio Christi* take this text as the basis of their conceptions of spiritual warfare. See also Gregory's *Moralia* on the alternative translations of this passage as *tentatio* and as *militia*.

13. Bevington, *Medieval Drama*, 804.

14. Ibid., 799; see also 800–803.

15. Ibid., 794, 796–97.

16. Ibid., 795.

17. Babb, *Moral Cosmos*, 12–13.

18. See John M. Steadman, "The 'Happy Garden': Felicity and End in Renaissance Epic and Ethics," in *Milton's Epic Characters*, 105–22, 109.

19. See Steadman, "The Christian Hercules: Moral Dialectic and the Pattern of Rejection," in *Milton's Epic Characters*, 123–36. For the scale of Satanic lures pertaining to the active and contemplative lives in *Paradise Regained*, see Howard Schultz, *Milton and Forbidden Knowledge* (New York, 1955), 225.

Epilogue

1. See John Dryden, Preface to *Fables Ancient and Modern* (1700), quoted in *Life Records of John Milton*, ed. J. Milton French, vol. 5 (New Brunswick, N.J., 1958), 47, "*Milton* was the Poetical Son of *Spencer*. . . . *Milton* has acknowledg'd to me, that *Spencer* was his Original."

Index

Adam-Christ parallel, 158–60
Addison, Joseph, 28
Agrippa of Nettesheim, Henry Cornelius, 175
Alabaster, William, 121
Alain de Lille, 136
Alamanni, Luigi, 152
Allegory, 127, 138
Amadis of Gaul, 76, 85
Antimachus, 12
Apocalypse, 6, 61
Archaism, linguistic, 119–20, 191
Arimaspeia, 60
Ariosto, Ludovico, 7, 33, 45, 58, 74–94,
    106–28, 130, 135–44, 180, 187, 191
Aristotle: neo-Aristotelian, 54, 74, 82–90,
    100, 103, 139, 147, 158, 163, 177–78,
    187
Arminius, Jacobus, 160
Augustine, Saint, bishop of Hippo, 6

Babb, Lawrence, 152, 160
Bacchus, 30, 56, 122
Bale, John, 6
Barber, A. D., 4
Baroque, 139
Bartas, Guillaume de Saluste, sieur du, 14–27,
    76, 89, 162, 165, 170
Bembo, Pietro, 12, 52
Beroaldus, Philippus, 175
Bevington, David, 160, 195
Blake, William, 6
Boccaccio, Giovanni, 119, 139
Boethius, 45
Boiardo, Matteo Maria, 74–86, 93, 102–9,
    111, 117, 126, 138–49, 187
Broadbent, John, 81
Bunyan, John, 152
Burton, Robert, 66, 184
Butcher, S. H., 187

Calliope, 2, 33, 43, 45, 49, 121
Camden, William, 109, 120
Camoëns, Luis de, 80–82, 92–96
Campbell, Lily Bess, 7
Carey, John, 5
Castelvetro, Lodovico, 11, 54, 107, 177, 191
Castiglione, Baldassare, 125
Castle of Perseverance, The, 128
Chanson de Roland, 138, 193–94
Chapman, George, 187
Chaucer, Geoffrey, 45, 62, 69, 93, 104, 107,
    119, 136–39, 182–83, 192
Cicero, 54, 60, 113, 128
Clio, 33, 108, 120–21, 164, 171
Cope, Jackson I., 4–5
Crashaw, Richard, 55, 65
Cyclic poets, 77

Daniel, Samuel, 121
Dante Alighieri, 12, 28, 44, 60–62, 81, 103,
    118–19, 169, 182
David, 15, 44
Davies, Stevie, 4
Della Casa, Giovanni, 12, 52
Demaray, John, 156–57
Demetrius, 13
Demodocus, 53
Diekhoff, John S., 44
"divine poem," 27–28, 48
Donne, John, 65, 124, 180
Dream of Rhonabwy, The, 95
Dryden, John, 162, 195
DuBellay, Joachim, 134, 170

Ecloga Theoduli, 153
E. K., 15, 102, 112, 133, 170–71, 177, 179
Elijah, 17, 24, 180
Elizabeth, Queen of England, 33, 81, 104–16,
    124, 162, 164
Ellrodt, Robert, 192